MAPPING ENVIRONMENTAL SUSTAINABILITY

Reflecting on systemic practices for participatory research

Edited by Sue Oreszczyn and Andy Lane

First published in Great Britain in 2017 by

Policy Press
University of Bristol
1-9 Old Park Hill
Bristol
BS2 8BB
UK
t: +44 (0)117 954 5940
pp-info@bristol.ac.uk
www.policypress.co.uk

North America office:
Policy Press
c/o The University of Chicago Press
1427 East 60th Street
Chicago, IL 60637, USA
t: +1 773 702 7700
f: +1 773-702-9756
sales@press.uchicago.edu
www.press.uchicago.edu

British Library Cataloguing in Publication Data
A catalogue record for this book is available from the British Library

Library of Congress Cataloging-in-Publication Data
A catalog record for this book has been requested

ISBN 978-1-4473-3157-5 hardcover
ISBN 978-1-4473-3531-3 ePub
ISBN 978-1-4473-3532-0 Mobi
ISBN 978-1-4473-3158-2 ePdf

Cover design by Hayes Design
Front cover image: Getty
Printed and bound in Great Britain by TJ International, Padstow
Policy Press uses environmentally responsible print partners

We dedicate this book to the many people involved in all the projects featured in this book. Our research participants, partners and colleagues. It was their enthusiasm and generosity with their time that made our research possible.

Contents

List of figures, tables and boxes

List of figures

List of tables

List of boxes

List of acronyms

AMP6	Asset Management Programme 6
BATWOVE	Beneficiaries, Actors, Transformation, Worldview, Owners, Victims, Environmental constraints.
BoE	Band of Equilibrium
CaBA	Catchment Based Approach
CADWAGO	Climate Change Adaptation and Water Governance
CAMP	Costal Area Management Programme
CAP	Common Agricultural Policy
CoP	Community of Practice
CSH	Critical Systems Heuristics
CSO	civil society organisation
CREPE	Cooperative Research on Environmental Problems in Europe
DECC	Department of Energy and Climate Change
Defra	Department for Environment, Food and Rural Affairs (UK)
DWI	Drinking Water Inspectorate
EU	European Union
ECOSENSUS	Ecological/Electronic Collaborative Sense Making Support system
ESRC	Economic and Social Research Council (UK)
FSEs	Farm Scale Evaluations
GIS	Geographical Information System
GM	genetically modified
GST	General Systems Theory
HSE	Health and Safety Executive
ICT	information and communication technology
ICZM	Integrated Coastal Zone Management
IFSA	International Farming Systems Association
ISSS	International Systems Sciences Society
IWC	International Water Centre
LFA	Logical Framework Approach
MDGs	Millennium Development Goals
NFU	National Farmers Union (UK)
NGO	non-governmental organisation
OFWAT	Office of Water Services
OR	operational research

PAPRAC	Priority Action Programme Regional Activity Centre
PEG	Precautionary Expertise for GM Crops
PITA	Policy Influences in Technology for Agriculture
PP	participatory photography
PV	participatory video
RAC	Regional Activity Centre
RBMP	River Basin Management Plan
RDPE	Rural Development Programme for England
SCIMAC	Supply Chain Initiative on Modified Agricultural Crops
SDGs	Sustainable Development Goals
SPSA	Systemic Prospective Systemic Sustainability Analysis (an evolution of SSA)
SSA	Systemic Sustainability Analysis
SSM	Soft Systems Methodology
UDIG	User-friendly Desktop Internet GIS
WTO	World Trade Organisation

Notes on contributors

Andrea Berardi and Jay Mistry are academics working in British institutions. They have more than 22 years' experience in teaching, researching and building capacity for natural resource management with local communities. After having met while undertaking their undergraduate studies, they went on to complete a number of postgraduate degrees in environmental management and biodiversity conservation. Andrea is currently a senior lecturer at The Open University while Jay is a professor at Royal Holloway, University of London. Their particular interests include supporting local livelihoods and biodiversity conservation, local environmental governance, action research using participatory video and capacity building for natural resource management. Andrea and Jay have been involved in research in the North Rupununi since 1999 and have led all the research projects discussed in Chapter Five. The other contributors to Chapter Five are Elisa Bignante, Grace Albert, Rebecca Xavier, Ryan Benjamin, Lakeram Haynes, Deirdre Jafferally, and Géraud de Ville, whose biographies you will find below.

Grace Albert, Rebecca Xavier and Ryan Benjamin are all Indigenous community members based in the North Rupununi. Fluent in Makushi, the indigenous language of the North Rupununi, they have strong skills in community facilitation and engagement, visual methods, and their local Indigenous traditions. Grace and Rebecca have studied wildlife and natural resource management, agriculture, information technology, filming, leadership and culture, and have both worked for the North Rupununi District Development Board (NRDDB) in several roles including community radio broadcasters, community film makers and, most recently, as community researchers, including working on projects with Andrea Berardi and Jay Mistry since 2008. Ryan has experienced a number of challenges typical of a young male Indigenous community member, forced to seek employment in informal gold mines, although in the last decade he has dedicated himself to his community by, for example, being elected as one of its councillors. These experiences were invaluable in his more recent work as community researcher which began with Project Cobra in 2011.

Simon Bell is Professor of Innovation and Methodology in the Department of Engineering and Innovation at the Open University.

He has been writing on sustainability for 30 years and has written over 100 publications, including five books, with more commissioned. Simon has developed and applied a number of methodologies including: Multiview for information systems, Triple Task for group work and, most importantly, Imagine. This last approach has been applied all over the world and in all kinds of contexts from internet 2 to community conflict; from London Olympic Legacy to the future of the UK Health Service. He is currently engaged with a systemic study of climate change fear.

Elisa Bignante has more than 15 years' experience in researching and teaching in the field of development geography and in the use of participatory research methods with local communities in the global South. After achieving a BSc in Economics and PhD in Local Development and Territorial Planning, she focused on Development Geography working extensively in international aid projects in Africa and Latin America. She is currently senior lecturer at the Department of Cultures, Politics and Society, University of Torino, Italy. Elisa began her research experience in the North Rupununi in 2011 with Project Cobra after having met Andrea and Jay while undertaking a visiting lectureship at Royal Holloway in 2008.

Chris Blackmore is a senior lecturer in Environmental and Development Systems at The Open University. She has played a key role in developing Masters level programmes in Environmental Decision Making and Systems Thinking in Practice, chairing a range of modules and writing open learning materials. Her main research area is in learning systems and communities of practice for environmental decision making, including issues of social learning, systems thinking, managing systemic change, sustainability and responsibility. She has produced an extensive range of publications since joining The Open University in 1986. She developed her research initially through taking an active role in national and international multi-stakeholder processes around Agenda 21 in the 1990s, subsequently through various international research projects, including: SLIM (Social Learning for integrated management and sustainable use of water at catchment scale), LEARNing (Learning in European Agriculture and Rural Networks: institutions, networks and governance) and CADWAGO (Climate Adaptation and Water Governance).

Kevin Collins is a senior lecturer in Systems and Environment at The Open University. His interdisciplinary research and scholarship focuses on managing socio-ecological systems using social learning and systems concepts and practices. He has produced a wide range of related publications. Since 2000, he has worked on a range of individual and collaborative research projects (SLIM; CADWAGO) centred on water resources and water policy in the UK, EU and internationally. Current projects include designing social learning systems for improving drought responses as part of the international DRIVER project. He develops, teaches and chairs undergraduate and postgraduate modules relating to systems, environmental management and research skills.

Géraud de Ville's expertise lies in the use of communication to draw bridges between research and policy, in order to facilitate cooperative and multi-disciplinary work and generate creative solutions. After achieving a number of degrees in International Development and Law, he worked for an environmental NGO in Belgium which was a partner on Project Cobra, and in 2012 enrolled at The Open University to undertake a PhD investigating how information and communication technologies affect the wellbeing of Indigenous communities in the North Rupununi, Guyana. Andrea acted as Géraud's PhD supervisor.

Natalie Foster is a research associate at The Open University. Her PhD, from Southampton University, was in environmental decision making in the context of conservation and sustainable use of intertidal mudflats and saltmarshes in the UK. She is a skilled presenter and facilitator and has considerable experience of using systems tools and techniques, including diagramming, to enable learning in a range of multi-stakeholder situations. She has worked on international and national research projects, including CADWAGO (Climate Adaptation and Water Governance) and CAPE (Community Action Platform for Energy).

Lakeram Haynes is an Indigenous researcher and community leader from the North Rupununi, with key skills in community facilitation and engagement, visual methods, environmental monitoring, and sustainable Indigenous resource management. He has had senior management and researcher roles in several projects, and first worked with Andrea Berardi and Jay Mistry in 2003. His work experience and traditional foundation provide a strong base for continued leadership and commitment in the area of community-based natural resource management in the North Rupununi. Lakeram is currently a senior councillor for Kwatamang Village and on the management team of the NRDDB, a local Indigenous community-based organisation.

Ray Ison has been Professor of Systems at The Open University since 1994. His research and scholarship spans the biophysical and social and is primarily interdisciplinary and collaborative. He is involved in: (i) managing and presenting the postgraduate program in Systems Thinking in Practice (STiP) and undertaking associated Systems scholarship; (ii) contributing to the activities of the Applied Systems Thinking in Practice Group and (iii) undertaking international research. In 2014–15 he was President of the ISSS (International Society for the Systems Sciences); he is also a Director of the World Organisation of Systems and Cybernetics (WOSC) and Chair of Trustees of the American Society of Cybernetics. From 2008–15, having moved from a full-time to a fractional appointment at The Open University, he established and led, as Professor, Systems for Sustainability, the Systemic Governance Research Program within Monash Sustainability Institute (MSI), Monash University, Melbourne. He is the (co) author or (co) editor of five books, 35 book chapters, over 100 refereed papers, numerous other publications, five journal special editions and has delivered many invited keynotes and workshops.

Deirdre Jafferally has 17 years' experience working in community-based wildlife management and conservation. Deirdre first started working at the Iwokrama International Centre for Rainforest Conservation and Development, Guyana, in the area of environmental monitoring. This developed into a broader interest in community-based natural resource management. She was able to explore this interest during her extensive engagement with communities of the North Rupununi in managing and conserving their resources especially in the area of fisheries management. Recently, Deirdre has focused on the pursuit of a PhD exploring the implications of socio-ecological changes on Indigenous knowledge and practices, and its impact on forest conservation. Jay Mistry acted as Deirdre's PhD supervisor.

Andy Lane is Professor of Environmental Systems at The Open University. He is a Member of the Chartered Institute for Ecology and Environmental Management; a Chartered Environmentalist and a Principal Fellow of the Higher Education Academy. His research and scholarship covers (i) the management of complex environmental situations and (ii) systems of open education. He uses systems approaches to frame the research and scholarship in both domains coupled with an action research philosophy; both use visual methods (normally diagramming) as a means to engage participants and to elicit and sometimes analyse data and evidence provided by the participants; and both use innovation and social learning as key theoretical concepts for explaining the outcomes of the research and scholarship. The work on the management of complex environmental situations looks in particular at attitudes, intentions and behaviours of the main participants in these rural or urban situations ranging from famers use of new technologies such as GM crops to organic waste recycling.

Les Levidow is a senior research fellow at The Open University, where he has been studying agri-food-environmental issues since the late 1980s. His research topics have included the following: sustainable development, agri-food-energy innovation, agricultural research priorities, governance, European integration, regulatory expertise, scientific uncertainty, and the precautionary principle. He is co-author of two books: *Governing the Transatlantic Conflict over Agricultural Biotechnology: Contending Coalitions, Trade Liberalisation and Standard Setting* (Routledge, 2006); and *GM Food on Trial: Testing European Democracy* (Routledge, 2010). He is also editor of the journal *Science as Culture*.

Sue Oreszczyn is a research fellow at The Open University. Sue runs the Open University's first year doctoral training workshops programme and is a postgraduate tutor for the School of Engineering and Innovation. She has been involved in research projects concerned with understanding the views and issues associated with agricultural environments that concern all stakeholders, from those at the policy level, such as senior policymakers, environmental NGOs and consumer groups, through to the public and the farmers working at the ground level. Sue is a Fellow of the Royal Society of Arts (RSA) and her research interests include linking policy research and practice; cooperative and participatory research; knowledge exchange; communities of practice; attitudes, values and learning concerning new technologies; systems approaches to landscape management and evaluation and agri-environmental issues; environmental perceptions and decision making. She has a particular interest in participatory methodologies and the use of visual techniques in research, such as scenario mapping, influence mapping and cognitive mapping.

Martin Reynolds is a senior lecturer in Systems Thinking at The Open University. Martin was lead editor of both *The Environmental Responsibility Reader* (2009) and *Systems Approaches to Managing Change: A Practical Guide* (2010). He has taken an active role in developing the STiP postgraduate programme at The Open University and contributes scholarship and research associated with the Applied Systems Thinking in Practice (ASTiP) Group. Martin specialises in applying critical systems thinking in practice with different areas of professional development and intervention including international development, public sector management, business development, education, health, environmental management and evaluation.

Rachel Slater is a lecturer in Sustainable Resource Management at The Open University. She has over 20 years' experience of working, researching and teaching related to sustainability. Since taking up her post at The Open University in 2002, her research has focused on social and policy aspects of waste and resource management, particularly recycling and composting. Rachel's research is collaborative and transdisciplinary using participatory and stakeholder engagement methods; she has researched with policymakers and practitioners in the public, private and community sectors.

David Wield is Professor of Innovation and Development at the Open University and a co-director of the Innogen Institute based at The Open University and the University of Edinburgh. From 2007 to 2014 he directed the ESRC Centre for Social and Economic Research on Innovation in Genomics (Innogen), University of Edinburgh and Open University. Previously, he worked at Imperial College, University of Dar Es Salaam, Tanzania, Eduardo Mondlane University, Mozambique and Aston University. He has also been a Senior Fulbright Fellow at Stanford University/University of California, Berkeley. His research focuses on the policy and management of technology; development policy and practice with emphasis on industrialisation and technologies; innovation, knowledge and learning in organisations; and technology capabilities in East and Southern Africa. He has published ten books and over 100 journal articles.

ONE

Introduction

Sue Oreszczyn and Andy Lane

This book is based on the collective work of academics from The Open University in the United Kingdom who have been teaching about and researching complex environmental situations using systems concepts, techniques and theories for over 30 years. These techniques have particularly included the use of mapping or diagramming to visually explore, create, enquire, and communicate people's thinking and perceptions (throughout the book we use the words mapping and diagramming interchangeably to describe the visualisation practices discussed further in Chapter Two). From our experience of using mapping extensively within our research and teaching practice, and of supervising and examining many research students, we observed that there is a distinct lack of publications that provide practical examples and reflections on *actual* research projects and what happens in the practice of conducting research generally, and in particular when and how they use diagrams. Further, we found the majority of research publications, book chapters and journal articles dealing with complex environmental situations involving many stakeholders provide straightforward accounts of the methods used. They ignore the 'messiness' of the processes used, and the specific practices of the researchers are rarely analysed or explained in sufficient detail to be of more practical use to other researchers. They also do not provide an account of how such diagramming practices evolve over time, either within specific projects or within the working lives of the researcher themselves. These trajectories provide additional insights into how, as researchers, we intertwine theory and practice in understanding about, and acting in, complex environmental situations.

Diagramming in research not only represents and helps to explore the messiness, but also enables the researcher(s) to draw out and build on multiple perspectives on an issue. Involving users and non-researchers in research processes is increasingly widely accepted and is often required by research funders (see Lyall et al, 2015), particularly within the field of environmental sustainability where people need to interact to bring about desirable changes. Yet again, there is little critique on the realities and messiness of engaging people in this type of participatory, or action-orientated, research where researchers research *with* people rather than on people. Recently environmental researchers engaged in this type of research have begun to reflect more critically on their practices. In 2014 the annual Royal Geographical Society/ IBG conference – The Geographies of co-production (London, 26–29 August 2014) – provided an opportunity for researchers from a variety of different disciplines to reflect on their particular participatory research methods. The need for development in the area of co-production of knowledge, and particularly participatory mapping techniques, and the need to describe these methodologies more precisely, has also been highlighted recently in a research call from the UK Economic and Social Research Council (ESRC, NCRM, 2015). Although visual methods in research have been developed and tested more widely, as partly evidenced by the Fourth International Visual Methods Conference held in Brighton, UK in September 2015, these methods cover a wide and diverse set of subjects and purposes that are based on an equally wide set of concepts and theories. In this book we focus on diagrams based on systems concepts in situations dealing with environmental sustainability.

Thus we have sought to produce a book that pulls together some of the lessons we have learned, individually and collectively, as researchers using mapping techniques and diagrams over the course of our research careers. Our work has been largely informed by systems thinking and practice, and includes a range of different environmental projects where participation by others was central. This is not, however, a manual on how to use a particular diagramming or mapping tool, but an account of how and why we have used such tools in our research practice. We particularly wished to reflect on our use of participatory mapping techniques for working with the many different types of stakeholders and research partners we have been involved with. We have, for example, worked with farmers, civil society organisations, government agencies, non-governmental organisations, policymakers, companies and community groups around the world on a wide range of complex and/or controversial environmental and agri-environmental issues (those involving agriculture). We wished to draw out the lessons we have collectively learned through the use of these mapping tools and techniques, first for those researching environmental sustainability, but also for practitioners involved in managing complex environmental situations (and possibly participants who are living within those environmental situations). It is our hope that other environmental researchers and practitioners will find our experiences and uses of mapping useful for their own practices.

Our experience of research in practice is that things often do not go according to plan. So, this book provides academic and non-academic researchers, and those involved in working with stakeholders on environmental sustainability, with a very practical insight into systems-based mapping tools and techniques (tools and techniques facilitating learning by all those involved in the research, rather than simply the researchers). It also enables others to develop their own praxis based on the learning they take from our practical, often 'messy' experiences. This book therefore aims to provide more detail on research processes that involve complex environmental situations than you would normally find in publications where researchers write about their work. Moreover, we also wanted to draw on our experiences over time to provide insights into how our methodologies and methods have evolved and developed over the years.

Interweaving themes

This book has four interweaving themes. These are set out in its full title: (1) Mapping (2) environmental sustainability: (3) reflecting on systemic practices for (4) participatory research. Here we explain what we mean by each of these themes and how they fit together. In Chapter Ten, the conclusions to the book, we return to these themes.

What do we mean by mapping?

Mapping or diagramming is one form of visual method for representing the world as we see it. This is explained further in Chapter Two. Such visual methods are not restricted to research but are increasingly used in businesses and by professional practitioners in many different sectors of the economy. Some of the same methods or techniques are used in both research and business, but often with different purposes, so there is a need to be careful in employing them. However, it is also important to recognise that, for some types of research and particularly participatory research, this can mean important synergies in making the research have more impact.

Visual methods in research cover a wide spectrum of approaches as well as being used in different fields of study (Spencer, 2011; Margolis and Pauwels, 2011; Banks and Zeitlyn, 2015). These approaches include, for example, the study of 'found' iconographic, photographic and televisual images; the use of participatory or community video and of diagrams to facilitate, explore and capture different understandings in different situations; and the use of computer based graphical packages to visualise large data sets. This by no means exhaustive list means that there is a diverse set of theoretical and methodological considerations feeding into these approaches, some common to all, some to only one or two. It is therefore important for us to be clear on where our work fits into this wide spectrum.

A distinctive aspect of this book is that it examines the specific mapping or diagramming techniques we have used within the particular systemic approaches we take. Thus the theory and practice of using mapping techniques based on systems concepts and theories as tools for researching environmental sustainability are explained, rather than mapping techniques in general. These theoretical ideas mean that we employ visual methods that facilitate, explore, and capture different people's understandings of the relationships, perspectives and boundaries within situations involving environmental sustainability. These theories help us to obtain a more complete picture of the situation and how to act within it. They emphasise the importance of taking a more holistic approach to environmental sustainability research and embrace the complexities involved, rather than attempting to reduce them. The focus is on finding ways to include different individual or group perspectives, and on relationships and boundaries, to enable action to be taken or decisions made; hence the book also focuses on participation and the roles of different practitioners within the situations being investigated.

Visual techniques, particularly when used as part of a wider research design based on a conceptual framework that places emphasis on working with people rather than doing research on them, can significantly enrich the analysis. Rather than simply considering the outcomes of what people do, these tools can be used to capture the complexity of the processes and interactions involved. They may also be used to explore strategies, different pathways for the future and solutions that people may have to current problems.

What is environmental sustainability and how can mapping techniques help?

This book is concerned with mapping techniques that have been used more specifically to consider issues relating to environmental sustainability. Like most concepts, environmental sustainability means different things to different people and also different academic disciplines. A quick online search for recent (at the time of writing) journal articles and books that include 'environmental sustainability' in their title, came up with the following: Green logistics: Improving the environmental sustainability of logistics; Multi-objective decision support to enhance environmental sustainability in maritime shipping: a review and future directions; Planetary Praxis & Pedagogy: Transdisciplinary Approaches to Environmental Sustainability; The Power of One: How CEO Power Affects Corporate Environmental Sustainability; and Mapping future changes in livelihood security and environmental sustainability based on perceptions of small farmers in the Brazilian Amazon. This small selection indicates this diversity of possible meanings and how it probably encompasses the full range of scientific and social-scientific disciplines that touch upon environmental matters.

Yet defining environmental sustainability is not straightforward. For example, some definitions of sustainability take a more anthropocentric view, whereas others take a more holistic view. Many, however, are relational and build on the Brundtland definition of sustainable development (Brundtland, 1987), such as Morelli (2011). In his article on finding a useful definition of environmental sustainability for professionals, Morelli first notes the difficulties with finding a useful working definition of sustainability, and then suggests that the addition of environment helps it to connect more clearly to the ecological concept of interdependence. He goes on to define environmental sustainability:

> as meeting the resource and services needs of current and future generations without compromising the health of the ecosystems that provide them, and more specifically, as a condition of balance, resilience, and interconnectedness that allows human society to satisfy its needs while neither exceeding the capacity of its supporting ecosystems to continue to regenerate the services necessary to meet those needs nor by our actions diminishing biological diversity.

Morelli then sets out 15 specific guiding principles to assist environmental professionals to operationalise the concept.

While Morelli's definition is a reasonable starting point for this book, the authors all come from different disciplinary backgrounds with different ways of viewing environmental sustainability and we could spend a lot of time teasing out and debating them as we do in the courses we teach. However, we all draw on systems thinking (as noted earlier and more fully explained below and in Chapter Two) as a theoretical and practical framing for our work and so view environmental sustainability not as something that is a set, real and tangible goal, but rather as something that has a negotiated meaning that may change according to the context. Environmental issues can be framed in many different ways according to the different perspectives of those involved and so there can be many different answers or solutions. So each person involved in attempting to achieve environmental sustainability in a given context will have a particular view on what it is, how it affects them and others, and how it may be achieved. More than this, we recognise that it cannot be assumed that individuals or groups will necessarily be able to readily see it the way that others see it, as there are many different worldviews (that is the social, psychological and cultural 'lens' or 'window' through which we view our world).

Thus the challenges of moving towards more sustainable environmental management, in the face of both policy changes and natural environmental change, are complex, involve many actors or stakeholders, a diversity of knowledge and types of expertise and ways of seeing the world. Nearly all environmental situations or issues generally involve a number of stakeholders, whether as active or passive participants. The complexity of relationships, and the partial understanding that each stakeholder has of the whole situation, provides challenges for researching their separate views and providing ways for them to individually and collectively gain a better understanding of that situation. Such systemic understanding is required to decide upon the separate but collective actions needed to resolve the issues and/or improve innovations, practices and knowledge exchange.

What are systemic practices and why do they matter?

We have already talked about systems thinking. As explained more fully in Chapter Two, systems thinking is a different way of thinking about the world we observe and experience. Scientific thinking is based on identifying patterns and reasons for why things are as they are. It does so by breaking down the identified 'problem' into simpler parts to reduce the complexity in order to understand causes and effects or provide a 'solution' through repeatable testing. Systems thinking, on the other hand, acknowledges the complexity in many situations. It enables the researcher to identify a system of interest that contains and is contextualised by that complexity, in order to surface and explore the intended and unintended properties emerging from the system of interest. So systems thinking seeks to support people, the stakeholders, in that system of interest, explore their collective understanding of the system, consider the power relations involved and how things might be improved. More often than not this is done through using mapping techniques that are part of the systems thinking canon. Systems thinking is not only used to investigate why things are as they are and could be, but also what should be to the satisfaction of the participants.

So it is the practices that flow from thinking systemically, in particular systems-based diagramming techniques that we find crucial to our teaching and research work. We do not see systems thinking as an alternative approach to scientific thinking and practice but as a complementary approach, given that systems thinking is all about recognising and valuing different perspectives and methods. Indeed systems thinking itself can be used in scientific studies, for example, in operational research and mathematical modelling. However, this book focuses on our work on complex environmental situations involving stakeholders or others who are both part of that situation and very often being affected by it now and in the future. Thus it involves investigating human activity systems more than natural or physical systems, although as we are looking at environmental sustainability, an understanding of the natural and physical processes and patterns is not ignored.

Participatory research: why engage users?

There are different ways of doing research – see Figure 1.1. While some researchers act more as critical observers – analysing and passing commentary on what they see happening before them – others are concerned more directly with influencing the situations they see before them.

The latter is where participatory and more action-orientated research sits. This type of research seeks to address the way that most forms of research tend to be 'expert' led and give more weight to expert opinion than that of the stakeholders, actors or participants in the system of interest. Non-researchers tend to be involved in the research as subjects rather than as equal participants (Phillipson et al, 2016). Such research further seeks to address the way that research dissemination tends to pay little attention to how much is actually assimilated by the users of the research, and to what extent the users consider it to be relevant. Introducing stakeholder and user engagement within the research process itself in a participatory way offers a means of ensuring that research is both relevant and useful to those who may make use of it.

Participatory research involves working in a more equal way, often with different academic disciplines, practitioners and users of

Figure 1.1: The relationship between the researcher and the system of interest

A. Researching on people. The researcher places themselves outside the system of interest. The researcher learns.

B. The researcher places themselves within the system for a short while and then leaves. The researcher learns but the participants only do so while the researcher is present.

C. The researcher as co-researcher (the action research model). The researcher places themselves within the system and works with the people. In this case learning is assumed to continue once the researcher leaves the system

Note: Although three discrete models are depicted here, in practice it is more a continuum.
Source: Oreszczyn, 1999

the research (or those affected by it) working together. It recognises the value of the many different types of knowledge or expertise involved. Emphasis is placed on the inclusion of a range of different stakeholders to ensure research is relevant, useful and also grounded in the 'real' world. Not only are attempts made to draw in those who may previously have been excluded from research processes, but also for researchers to work *with* people, so placing emphasis on the importance of learning by both the researcher and those involved in the research.

The development of these more participatory models has often drawn on systems theories (see, for example, Leeuwis and Pyburn, 2002; Cerf et al 2000; Roling and Wagemakers, 2000). Such models place an emphasis on how environmental knowledge may be co-constructed or co-created. Social learning has also developed as a significant theme in the literature on environmental management. Social learning refers to the process of iterative reflection that occurs when we share our experiences, ideas and environments with others (Keen et al, 2005). These theories share many ideas with the field of Action Research and Participatory Action Research. As Bradbury

(2010) notes, 'action researchers seek to take knowledge production beyond the gate-keeping of professional knowledge makers' (Bradbury, 2010: 93). People working together in partnership helps to address the complexity of economic, environmental, social and technological problems the world faces. Through such partnerships, research institutions and organisations go beyond simply working with one another and expand their networks, and ways of doing things, to include and involve others, such as public, private and civil society organisations (CSOs) or non-governmental organisations (NGOs), policymakers and members of the public.

So today, transdisciplinary research (see for example, Lang et al, 2012; Lawrence, 2015; Bracken et al, 2015; Bernstein, 2015; Lyall et al, 2015), participatory research and action research (see Bradbury, 2015; Allen, 2016) are all significant themes in the academic literature and are evolving research practices. All recognise the way that not all knowledge comes from formal or conventional research processes. They seek to formalise the informal knowledge through greater engagement with, and interactions between, formal researchers and those who may have in the past been viewed simply as those to be researched on. As you will see in this book, in this type of research, co-building knowledge and mutual learning between researchers and non-researchers becomes important and processes such as self-reflection and joint reflection form necessary elements of these kinds of research projects. However, while reflection on the outcomes or impacts of research are becoming increasingly important in the current research environment (see Lyall et al, 2015), reflections on the processes involved are equally important. Indeed, it is the processes themselves that may end up having the most important impacts. This is something we will return to in the final chapters of this book.

Putting it all together

A key feature of this book is the way we reflect on not just one particular research project, but on our collective research on many different projects over a lengthy period of time. This has enabled us to draw out the way that, as a necessary aspect of our research, our research projects, in their individual ways, have become increasingly more participatory over time. This mirrors the academic move towards finding ways to better engage with research participants as noted earlier. Our personal reflections on our work and the transitions in methodology and method that we have made offer an insight into why this change has transpired and how the challenges it creates may be addressed.

The mapping techniques and diagrams that the authors in this book use are not used in either a simple way or a single way. While for some authors diagramming was used as only a small part of the research project, for others it formed part of the overall framing and was central to all stages of the research. As noted earlier, the authors are all committed to researching sustainable environments *with* people. These visual techniques help us to foster conversations between people, to express our research processes and aid our methods. There are many different ways to involve stakeholders (that is, people with a stake or interest) in your research (see Bracken et al, 2015) and the authors in this book have engaged with people in a variety of different ways, and at different levels; that is, from those working in the policy environment to those working in practice on the ground. However, a key aspect is that they have sought ways that enable relevant participants in their research studies to research and, crucially, to learn together and so better connect on the ground practice with environmental management and policy. Another feature of the authors' research as it has developed is that, where possible, it has been concerned with going beyond participatory research that simply engages with people to that which involves them more fully, for example, from the initial conception of the project. Greater ownership of the project, or outcomes, offers greater opportunity for any benefits to last beyond the life of the initial research project funding. However, as earlier noted, researching with people is not straightforward. The multifaceted nature of environmental projects and the complex sets of practices and ways of seeing environmental issues combine with a variety of roles and identities, relationships and social interactions, benefits and issues that the researcher has to contend with.

The case studies in this book explain how mapping techniques have helped us deal with these issues (or not) in real research projects around different aspects of environmental sustainability. Chapter authors critically reflect on their experiences and examine the ways in which systems-based mapping techniques may or may not contribute to improving understandings and actions for environmental sustainability. Where possible, perspectives from those we have worked with are also included.

Structure of the book

In **Chapter Two** you will find an overview of systems thinking and practice – notably diagramming – including descriptions of the most common types of systems diagrams used by the various authors in this book and how these diagrams may be used for working with others. The authors of this chapter – Andy Lane and Martin Reynolds – first introduce the particular systems approach to research and mapping taken by the authors in the book. As noted earlier, systems thinking in practice is a particular way of approaching the understanding of messy situations such as those associated with environmental sustainability. The authors explain the core concepts of systems theories and how they may be used for sharing multiple perspectives on complex situations. They comment on the importance of systems-based mapping techniques and demonstrate how these systems ideas and techniques may be used in practice. The chapter gives a flavour of a range of different types of mapping you could use in your research and practice. Where necessary the authors point you in the direction of further sources of information on how to use them.

Chapters Three to Nine then provide examples of how mapping has been used in our research from different case studies.

In **Chapter Three** Sue Oreszczyn, Les Levidow and Dave Wield draw on 13 years of research involving three large and increasingly more participatory European Commission funded projects. In their first project they describe how participants were necessarily treated more as informants than project partners. Cognitive maps were used to focus on technology strategies and trajectories of 14 major agro-chemicals and seeds companies. The maps highlighted the thinking of key actors in decision making about new technologies and were used as an essential form of analysis in the project. Their techniques evolved with the use of a more participatory approach in a second project in an attempt to better link policy, research and practice. In this case a scenario mapping technique was used with senior policy actors, to explore potential futures for genetically modified (GM) crops in the UK. A third and final project they describe, while not an exemplar of mapping techniques, is included as it is a unique example of participatory or partnership research. The unusual funding arrangement, whereby all project partners (academics and CSOs) received equal funding, meant that rather than the academic partners taking the lead on the research, researchers and non-researchers worked together in a more equal way and had more equal stakes in the research. CSO researchers and academic researchers all devised the project at the outset and developed the processes within it as it progressed.

In **Chapter Four** Sue Oreszczyn and Andy Lane also consider the increasingly more participatory approach to their research over time, through one big project and two follow-on opportunities.

Three mapping techniques – cognitive mapping, influence mapping and scenario mapping – were used at different points within a single three year project as it became increasingly more participatory. The project considered farmers' understandings of GM crops and new innovations more generally and, like Chapter Three, highlights the advantages of using mapping techniques when exploring different perspectives on controversial environmental issues. The authors also reflect on the subsequent work this project led to regarding knowledge flows. They provide insights from their work with various stakeholders to consider complex interactions among knowledge brokers in a number of different contexts – agriculture, health, food, international development and hedgerow management systems. This chapter also provides examples whereby diagrams, and processes for their use, were necessarily specifically devised for the circumstances of the research project – rather than the researchers using something 'off-the-peg'.

Chapter Five portrays the development of a research programme involving a number of phases and funded projects over the longer term. Andrea Berardi, Jay Mistry, Lakeram Haynes, Deirdre Jafferally, Elisa Bignante, Grace Albert, Rebecca Xavier, Ryan Benjamin and Géraud de Ville depict a lay expertise model of development where local people promote their own solutions to environmental problems. The authors comment on the way their methodological approach changed over the 15 years of researching with indigenous forest communities in Guyana to find solutions to their complex environmental issues. Their initial expert led approach, using quantitative methods, became increasingly participatory as more appropriate qualitative and visual methods were employed. The chapter provides an example of how such techniques can be used to overcome communication barriers, such as different languages or cultures and how they can aid the interactions between academic researchers and non-academic researchers and between local people and policymakers. Importantly, this chapter also provides an example of how research and visual techniques may be used not simply to empower local communities to take action themselves but also to take ownership, offering the potential for longer term outcomes.

In contrast **Chapter Six** portrays two research projects that were more constrained as a result of the nature of their funding. Andy Lane, Rachel Slater and Sue Oreszczyn draw on their experiences of two UK government department funded environmental projects of contrasting scale concerned with issues around managing organic waste within a much bigger government research programme on waste in general. The broad scope and purpose of both projects were specified by the funder, which placed constraints on the approaches to be used, as did the need to report regularly to the funder. In both projects the use of visual mapping techniques was central to the research process and the research outcomes. In the first project, a study of attitudes and perceptions towards the spreading of organic waste-derived resources on land, they brought together for the first time attitudes of stakeholders from all parts of the organic resources use cycle in an interactive and iterative research process. The second project explored the potential of community composting in contributing to government waste targets and wider social objectives. The authors of this chapter comment on the way that stakeholder perspectives were drawn in at each stage of the projects as the project evolved. The projects worked closely with the funders and were intended to directly inform further research and/or current policy decisions and so the authors specifically reflect on the impacts on both policymakers and practitioners.

In **Chapter Seven** Chris Blackmore, Natalie Foster, Kevin Collins, and Ray Ison draw on their experiences over many years of research into social learning systems. The authors particularly focus on their work on communities of practice as social learning systems and reflect on their experiences of using diagramming to map and share understandings and develop knowledge, in the context of water governance and climate change. As with the other authors in this book, they build on a range of systemic and participatory traditions to design their research processes. Some of the authors have also taught these techniques and have developed an understanding of how skills in diagramming can be developed both for exploration and for communication. The authors therefore reflect on the effectiveness of diagramming processes for different purposes, reviewing a range of the techniques' strengths and limitations from their use in different contexts.

In **Chapter Eight** we turn to the development of a research method – Imagine – to address a particular issue influenced by systems thinking and diagramming over a number of years. In this case Simon Bell tells the story of the development of sustainability indicators that aimed to include the needs of the variety of different stakeholders, rather than just policymakers and scientists. Such indicators tell us how much oil we have left, how our GDP is growing or shrinking, how our planet is warming, how much pesticide our crops are using, how much our health is costing, for example. The chapter describes the way he and colleagues got people in communities to think about sustainability by using indicators and metrics. The evolving project that he describes provided a generic means to allow communities to engage in the discussion with these metrics that can be used by non-specialists. Two particular types of participatory mapping techniques were involved in the projects development – rich pictures and an Amoeba diagram. Both techniques were used to assess which aspects of sustainability the various stakeholders thought was most important at a particular time, but also historically and in the future. This chapter also describes and reflects on how the approach described has been taken up and applied in a range of different European countries in the context of managing coastal environments, with the process evolving as the projects moved from location to location.

Martin Reynolds in **Chapter Nine** takes a rather different approach. In this chapter he addresses failures with interventions addressing complex issues of sustainability and the need, at all levels, for evaluation of interventions. He notes the lack of adoption of new ideas in this area and the way that stakeholders are often talking past each other. He considers how diagramming can address this by making space for conversations (between thinking and practice) in disciplinary, interdisciplinary and transdisciplinary research practice. Drawing on the ideas introduced in Chapter Two this chapter explains the use of a particular systems-based influence diagram Martin has developed and adapted over the past 15 years and discusses diagramming as both a means of praxis (the braiding of thinking and practice) generally, and more specifically, as a means for evaluating environmental sustainability as praxis.

Finally, **Chapter Ten** draws the themes of the book together once again and in particular reflects on the use of the mapping techniques used by the various authors in the book in helping the research process. It highlights key aspects and outcomes from the case studies and considers the lessons that may be learned for researching environmental sustainability.

References

Allen, W. (2016) 'Learning for sustainability' website, http://learningforsustainability.net/action-research

Banks, M. and Zeitlyn, D. (2015) *Visual Methods in Social Research*, London: Sage.

Bernstein, J.H. (2015) 'Transdisciplinarity: A Review of Its Origins, Development, and Current Issues', *Journal of Research Practice*, 11(1), Article R1, http://jrp.icaap.org/index.php/jrp/article/view/510/412

Bracken, L.J., Bulkeley, H.A. and Whitman, G. (2015) 'Transdisciplinary research: understanding the stakeholder perspective', *Journal of Environmental Planning and Management*, 58(7): 1291–308.

Bradbury, H. (2015) *The SAGE Handbook of Action Research*, 3rd edition, London: Sage.

Bradbury, H. (2010) 'What is good action research? Why the resurgent interest?', *Action Research* 8(1): 93–109.

Brundtland, G.H. (1987) *Report of the World commission on environment and Development: Our Common Future*, www.cfr.org/economic-development/report-world-commission-environment-development-our-common-future-brundtland-report/p26349

Cerf, M., Gibbon, D., Hubert, B., Ison, R., Jiggins, J., Paine, M., Proost, J. and Roling, N. (eds) (2000) *Cow up a Tree: Knowing and Learning for Change in Agriculture*, Paris: INRA.

ESRC, NRCM (2015) *National Centre for Research Methods call for Methodological Research Projects*, call specification, www.esrc.ac.uk/files/funding/funding-opportunities/ncrm/ncrm-methodological-research-projects-call-specification-pdf

Keen, M., Brown, V.A. and Dyball, R. (2005) 'Social Learning: A new approach to environmental management', in M. Keen, V.A. Brown, and R. Dyall (eds), *Social Learning in Environmental Management: Towards a sustainable future*, London: Earthscan, pp 3–21.

Lang, D., Wiek, A., Bergmann, M., Stauffacher, M., Martens, P., Mool, P., Swilling, M. and Thomas C.J. (2012) 'Transdisciplinary research in sustainability science: practice, principles, and challenges', *Sustainability Science*, 7 (Supplement 1): 25–43

Lawrence, R.J. (ed) (2015) 'Advances in transdisciplinarity 2004–2014', *Futures*, 65: 1–216.

Leeuwis, C. and Pyburn, R. (eds) (2002). *Wheelbarrow full of frogs: social learning in rural resource management*, The Netherlands: Koninklijke Van Gorcum BV.

Lyall, C., Meagher, L. and Bruce, A. (2015) 'A rose by any other name? Transdisciplinarity in the context of UK research policy', *Futures* 65: 150–62.

Margolis, E. and Pauwels, L. (eds) (2011) *The SAGE Handbook of Visual Research Methods*, London: Sage.

Morelli, J. (2011) 'Environmental Sustainability: A Definition for Environmental Professionals', *Journal of Environmental Sustainability*, 1(1), Article 2, http://scholarworks.rit.edu/jes/vol1/iss1/

Oreszczyn, Sue (1999) 'Participative approaches to hedgerow conservations', PhD thesis, The Open University, http://oro.open.ac.uk/30150/

Phillipson, J., Proctor, A., Emery S.B. and Lowe, P. (2016) 'Performing inter-professional expertise in rural advisory networks', *Land Use Policy*, 54: 321–30.

Roling, N. and Wagemakers, M.A.E. (eds) (2000) *Facilitating sustainable agriculture: Participatory learning and adaptive management in times of environmental uncertainty*, Cambridge: Cambridge University Press.

Spencer, S. (2011) *Visual Research Methods in the Social Sciences: Awakening Visions*, Oxford: Routledge.

TWO

Systems thinking in practice: mapping complexity

Andy Lane and Martin Reynolds

Editors' introduction

In this chapter the authors provide an overview of systems thinking in practice, the key concepts involved in it and in particular the role of mapping in addressing complex situations. While the chapter touches on all four themes of the book it focuses mainly on the systems thinking philosophy that underpins the work of nearly all the authors in this book; how that philosophy relates to the use of diagramming to capture systemic thinking; and how to engage research participants in trying to think more systemically. It finishes with some more practical advice on the use of diagrams in general and within participatory and action-oriented modes of research in particular.

Introduction

Complexity and uncertainty can be features of any human activity system but this is more so when considering environmental situations and environmental sustainability (Ison, 2010). The number of facts and factors involved, the number of people with different perspectives and disciplinary expertise, all grow larger and seemingly more intractable. To be able to represent a complex messy situation by showing most of the components and how they are thought to fit and work together is therefore very helpful when understanding, researching, designing and implementing systemic changes that draw upon and integrate the thinking from many disciplines.

Systems thinking in practice is a particular way of approaching the understanding of messy situations for some purpose, usually to effect some changes. It is very suited to participatory, action-oriented research and environmental sustainability and is a philosophy that underpins both the teaching and research praxis of the many authors in this book. By praxis we mean the process by which a theory is enacted, embodied, or realised. Drawing on some basic features of systems thinking (see Chapman, 2004; Midgley, 2007), we can identify three generic imperatives as underpinning systems thinking in practice (Reynolds, 2011; 2013; 2014; Reynolds and Holwell, 2010):

- understanding inter-relationships ('thinking' about the bigger picture)
- engaging with multiple perspectives (the 'practice' of joined-up thinking)
- reflecting on boundary judgements (the praxis of thinking *in* practice).

A key feature is that one part of the praxis around systems thinking is finding ways of representing a chosen 'system of interest', and that is often best done through diagrams, maps or other visual techniques. We believe that representing 'systems of interest' using visual techniques is therefore an essential part of any participatory and action-oriented researcher's personal toolkit (Armson, 2011). Some might argue that it is not essential to adopt systems thinking to be able to use diagrams to understand, research and design interventions into complex messy situations; but we feel it is essential you understand how diagramming and its relationship to systems thinking influences our teaching and researching praxis in order to better appreciate its potential value for your own praxis. This is because the choice of communication modes and tools we use, along with the language used to represent how we see and think about the world, affects the way we engage our cognitive abilities. This will have significant consequences on how we organise ourselves socially through, for example, organisations and communities.

The use of written communication to represent our thoughts and perceptions, as is mainly the case in this book (although ironically it is about mapping), favours a specific subset of mental conceptualisations: those requiring a logical and linear interpretation. Written mass culture, made possible by the invention in the 15th century of mass produced text through the Gutenberg press, brought about the cultural predominance of written communication over oral and visual communication. Written text has many advantages in that it follows a relatively clear set of rules or grammars that allows the writer and the reader to fully understand the messages and thoughts being conveyed, particularly a set of arguments or statements. However, written text has major limitations in representing relationships between things when they do not follow the linear structure of the text. While speech based communication in the form of broadcasting added another dominant cultural form in the 20th century, much of this still works round a linear narrative. Relationships, however, can be extremely complex, even circular. In particular, the linear sequence of text, or even a documentary film, is not able to clearly show context, elements, structure, processes and functions of systems without extensive explanation and without resorting to visual representations. The nested nature of systems within systems is also very difficult to show. In many ways, writing favours an analytical approach, since you can go into an increasing level of detail as you move down the page. A visual approach to communication can take a radical departure from the linear logic of written communication. Maps, diagrams, photographs, and even physical models are all forms of visual communication. The strength of these techniques is that they can focus on relational logic and also break the dominance of words through using images as part of the representation.

All representations of the perceived world are sense making models of situations that are themselves attempts to simplify messiness and complexity. Diagrams, maps or other visual models are pictorial representations of our individual and/or collective views, and can include both rational thoughts and emotional feelings. They can help by attempting to capture as much of a situation as possible, on paper or computer screens, showing both components and connections in different ways (Carter et al, 1984; Lane, 2002). They can be used for influencing personal actions and personal learning (Lane, 2013) or for collective action and social learning (Blackmore, 2010) where many participants contribute to their construction and interpretation and so share their thinking about a situation. As noted in Chapter One, they are also very important tools to use in participatory modes of research, where the participants are seen as co-researchers who have some stake in the conception, design, implementation and/or reporting of the research and some stake in implementing any outcomes or recommendations that arise from that research (Oreszczyn and Lane, 2012). Finally, they can offer important sources of insight and support for policymakers (Chapman, 2004).

As diagrams are used to test out our thinking they are particular to the situation and the people involved. So while we, the authors of this book, have described some of the diagrams, maps or visual methods that we have used in our own teaching and research into environmental situations in our many teaching and research publications, we have more rarely described the full flavour of activities and changes in thinking and actions that occurred during those projects within the confines and culture of the traditional academic literature. Even when the use of diagrams in systems studies is included in the literature, how they were developed and used are not often reported – only the outcomes or the final version used for public consumption (Lane and Morris, 2001). So our aim in this book is to do just that – to show and reflect upon how we used visual techniques within our own teaching and research practices. What we will not be showing you specifically is the full mechanics and protocols of how to draw particular types of diagrams, as we can point you to other sources that do this in much more detail than we could possibly do in this book. Also while there is a canon of commonly used diagram types with guidelines for their use, the exact purpose and value of any diagram has to fit with the research project and the people involved in that study. What we will do is explain some of the more common forms of diagram we have collectively used in many different situations as well as some particular styles of diagram used for very particular projects and situations.

To summarise our views and experiences, diagramming is:

- able to clearly represent relational information, something that text struggles with;
- a great way of quickly summarising an individual's or a group's understanding
- accessible (you do not need high levels of literacy);
- recordable, adaptable and reproducible for asynchronous working over time and space, and dissemination/engagement with wider stakeholders;
- fun and engaging (compared to collaboratively writing pieces of text in a meeting); and
- sophisticated (different diagramming techniques can reveal in-depth insights of different aspects of a situation).

However, as system thinking underpins much of our teaching and research activities it is important and necessary to briefly outline some of its key principles and practices (such as diagramming) for you to make sense of the many case studies that follow in later chapters and for the examples used in this chapter.

Systems principles and diagramming

Understanding systems of interest

The tradition of systems thinking is both broad and deep. It has arisen out of a number of other disciplines (for example, biology, cosmology, psychology, cybernetics, operational research, management science) and some aspects of its central tenets have equally been applied to many other disciplines (Checkland and Haynes, 1994; Capra, 1997; Checkland, 1999; Ramage and Shipp, 2009; Armson, 2011). It is axiomatic of nearly all academic inquiry in the past century or more that it is organised into disciplines. It is likely that this splitting up of the whole field of human endeavour is due to the prevailing and predominant Cartesian approach to research whereby analysis involves breaking the situation under examination into smaller and smaller components, identifying testable and repeatable relationships between those components, or providing other evidence which can be assessed (Capra, 1997). The degree of testability, repeatability or evidence required differs greatly between disciplines (particularly science-based disciplines like physics and humanities-based disciplines like history), but it is usually possible at the broadest levels to identify an agreed canon of knowledge, understanding and techniques that paradigmatically defines that particular discipline.

This situation has been complicated through the continued expansion of academic research as a professional activity and professions that rely heavily on academic research, so that more and more disciplines (professions) or sub-disciplines (sub-professions) are named or promoted by individuals or groups of like-minded people. This may be through the close relevance of two disciplines or professions, for example agriculture and forestry combining as agroforestry, or where research techniques allow largely unexplored areas to become prominent fields of enquiry, such as cell biology, genetics and organic chemistry all being dominated by molecular biology.

There are many strengths to such reductionist approaches and they underpin much of our scientific and technological development, but there are limits to the power of reductionist approaches to resolve complex real world problems (and often, they even make the situation worse). So, although there has been a reductionist tendency to specialise into more and more 'recognised' disciplines or professions there have been two other opposing forces. One is systems or holistic thinking, where the aim is to look at the behaviour of 'wholes' rather than 'parts' – 'getting the bigger picture' (Checkland, 1999; Armson, 2011), and the other is the promotion of multidisciplinary, interdisciplinary or transdisciplinary activity (Lyall et al, 2015), moving towards more 'joined-up thinking'. These two forces have not necessarily worked in concert, which may be due in part to the fact that there is no shared or agreed view on what multi/inter/transdisciplinary activity actually involves in practice (the widespread use of three separate terms as buzzwords for suggesting more joined-up thinking, and/or frequent invoking of 'holistic' approaches, is a telling fact). But also in part, we believe there is a lack of rigorous application of systems-based thinking to this issue of reductionist professionalisation of practices. In particular, each discipline or profession creates and sustains a certain way of viewing the world that may exclude other views, including those of 'lay' people who may be either the object of, or subject to, the consequences of research findings. A key feature of systems thinking in practice is to try and expose those multiple views to the people involved in a situation to provide a fuller description of the system of interest and possibly a better prescription of what to do next in terms of (policy and practice) action, research or action-oriented research.

It is generally helpful to appreciate three broad areas in which 'systems' are generally understood and used (see Chapman, 2004):

- *Natural systems* – individual living organisms (individual plants, animals, bacteria, and so on) or wider biophysical entities like ecosystems, the planet Earth or the solar system
- *Engineered (purposive) systems* – mechanical equipment (laboratory tools) clocks, vehicles, computers, heating or irrigation systems
- *Human (purposeful) systems* – organisations (environmental impact agencies, NGOs, government departments, community services, and so on), the economy, education, environmental management systems, policies, programmes, projects, and others.

The concern for environmental management practice is clearly one of focusing on purposeful systems where, because of the human factor, the purposes and the activities involved are varied and changing, as distinct from having just one attributed purpose or set of activities as with a mechanical or engineered system. But systems thinking, as used for understanding and designing human purposeful systems associated with environmental sustainability practice, can variously and helpfully apply the use of systems ideas from natural systems and mechanical systems.

The core systems concept, for example, has been that borrowed from natural systems; an adaptive whole (a 'system of interest') with irreducible properties that is able to create and maintain itself in response to its changing environment (Checkland, 1999). Such wholes are regarded as complex adaptive systems. The underlying philosophy of purposeful systems thinking is to be holistic, to look for wholes at the highest appropriate level, rather than to reduce things to ever smaller components. This concept is both simple to state and yet complex to enact because of differing philosophical and practical approaches to the concept of a system.

A definition developed by Open University systems academics suggests that a system is a collection of entities that are seen by someone as interacting together to do something (Morris, 2009).

A much fuller description of a (purposeful) system of interest at a finer level of granularity was provided by Bronte-Stewart (1997):

- a purpose – it does, or can be perceived to do, something
- an environment that affects it
- a namer – someone who is interested in it
- a boundary distinguishing it from the environment and identified by the system namer
- inputs and outputs
- transformational processes that convert inputs to outputs
- parts (subsystems) that interact, a pattern of relationships
- hierarchy – each part is itself a system and can be treated as such
- dependency – addition, alteration or removal of a part changes both the part and the system
- communication and feedback among the systems
- control, both within the system and through the hierarchy
- emergence – the whole system exhibits properties and outcomes, sometimes unpredictable, which derive from its parts and structure but cannot be reduced to them
- dynamism – it is subject to change including growth, adaptation and decay.

There are three features in this list that are particularly important to this book. The first is that a system is a notional concept. There are frequent arguments in the systems movement over whether systems really exist or are constructs of the namer(s) (Checkland, 1999; Armson, 2011). Along with Checkland and Armson, our own view is that systems do not exist as such since the boundary of the system of interest is defined and redefined by people; this being particularly the case where the complex adaptive system is a human activity system involving people rather than just natural or physical phenomena. However, there is inevitably a range of systems that can be investigated, from those that it is reasonable to view for the purposes of the namer 'as if they do exist' (such as the solar system, a cell as a system, a particular organisation as a system), to those systems that are more abstract and which would appear incongruous to claim as if they exist as a specific entity but which may be identified as worthy of inquiry (an ethical investment system, an environmental management system).

The second important feature is that any system has components or subsystems that may exhibit an hierarchical set of relationships. The best way to explain this is by using a diagram known as a systems map applied to two examples: a human body and the systems movement itself (Figure 2.1). In the case of the human body the simplistic view is taken here that this organism comprises a set of defined subsystems within the system of the human body but that these are not necessarily clustered or nested. In contrast the map of the systems movement looks as though it has a nested set of discrete subsystems with certain relationships between some of the components. This, in part, reflects the more abstract nature of the subject and the importance of the perspective of the system namer. For the systems movement map, for example, we have distilled four interrelated and roughly parallel traditions of practice since the mid-20th century, which we regard as having provided rich pickings for contemporary support in dealing with complex issues of environmental sustainability – general systems theory (GST), cybernetics, complexity sciences, and operations/operational research (OR). While GST evolved from 'natural' systems, cybernetics evolved principally from 'engineered' systems. Complexity sciences evolved more as a hybrid from natural and engineered systems, and OR was more directly linked with human purposeful systems.

A further difference between the two diagrams is that with the human body as an organism, this model might be widely viewed as appropriate by nearly all working in medicine, whereas with the systems movement, there may be several different models put forward reflecting the perspectives of their proponents because both the parts and their relationships are less clear cut. This distinction is encapsulated in systems thinking by the terms difficulty and mess. A difficulty applies to a situation where the problem or issue under investigation is well bounded and the purpose of investigating it is fairly clear. A mess covers less well defined, unbounded situations where the ultimate purpose of the investigation may not even be known (Checkland, 1999; Armson, 2011).

A third important feature of systems thinking in practice is the dynamic and malleable nature of systems (notably environmental systems). This allows for adaptation in circumstances of change and uncertainty including the fact that different practitioners will interpret the boundaries in different ways. Such dynamism can itself be manifest in the growth of the systems movement; a feature not captured in a bounded systems map. Ison (2010) has captured some essence of the fluidity of the systems movement through an influence diagram

Figure 2.1: A systems map of (a) the human body and (b) the systems movement

(a)

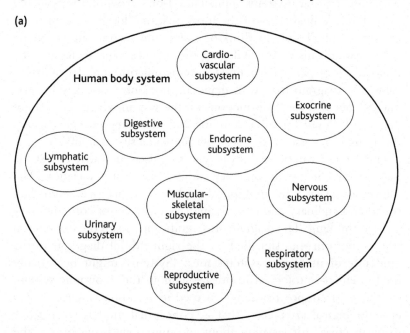

(b)

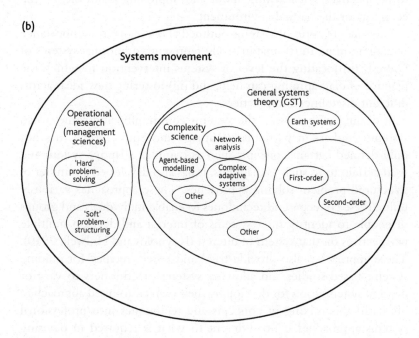

(Figure 2.2) that outlines the main influences and lineages associated with contemporary systems approaches. Ison's viewpoint is explicitly 'partial' in the dual sense of the term: first, he does not claim to be exhaustive of all systems thinking ideas; and second, he is openly biased towards his own privileging of particular trajectories and the importance of particular named systems practitioners. Its heuristic value as a diagram here is in depicting not only some key historic lineages but also some distinctions on the way in which the systems idea can be used for understanding and managing complex issues; including issues associated with environmental sustainability.

The diagram can be read (from left to right) as indicative of historic 'sets' of influences with some key authors/players in association. The influences come from multiple disciplines and practices, signalling the interdisciplinary and transdisciplinary character of contemporary systems thinking. The diagram also significantly maps the orientation (top to bottom – as signalled on the right side of diagram) in the tendency of using the systems idea. 'Systems' might be broadly used as either ontological realities – such as 'the' economic system, or 'the' waste disposal system – as used in common language, or as epistemological artefacts – that is, conceptual models (as a proxy to perspectives) for learning about and improving issues of, say, the economy or the natural environment.

The three features of systems outlined above signal the importance of diagramming in (i) imaginatively representing notional systems of interest, (ii) locating the level of systems intervention to which the practice of diagramming can help, and (iii) fostering new ideas across different disciplines and practices.

In dealing with messes, the systems community, and some noted systems thinkers in particular (Ramage and Shipp, 2009), has not only defined certain concepts such as complex adaptive system and used certain tools such as diagrams, it has also developed a number of structured problem solving approaches. These approaches variously utilise these concepts and techniques to enable individuals and groups of people to identify their systems of interest and develop multiple perspectives on that system of interest (Reynolds and Holwell, 2010). These approaches also provide tried and tested 'recipes' for guiding systems-based studies and allowing systems practitioners to vary or develop systems tools for developing their own customised approaches. Similarly, this mixing of concepts and techniques into professional systems approaches is no different to what is required in devising action-oriented research methods. This book provides details of some approaches we have used, the key concepts involved and diagram types

Figure 2.2: Influences that have shaped contemporary systems approaches and the lineages from which they have emerged

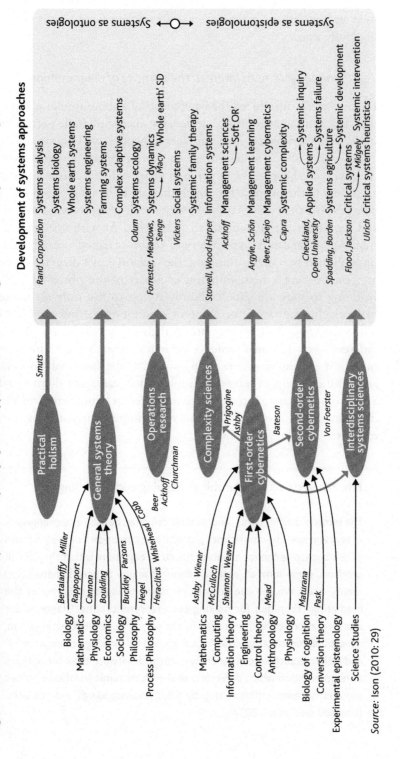

Source: Ison (2010: 29)

used and how these were woven together, and from which you can hopefully learn.

Representing systems of interest: the purpose of diagramming

Having briefly introduced the basic tenets of systems thinking and our view that systems are notional devices for sharing multiple perspectives on a complex situation involving lots of people, we now want to say a little more about representing, or more properly engaging with, them visually. Diagrams can come in many different forms and types according to the purpose for which they are to be used (see Box 2.1). The purpose then relates to both what the diagram is trying to depict and the wider activity to which it informs. As with systems-based studies in general and participatory or action-oriented research studies underpinned by systems thinking, the creator(s) of a diagram or map are constructing a representation of a part of the observed world. In doing so they are simultaneously trying to not only distinguish between different levels or scope of description to find the level or scope they feel most appropriate to their study but to also see how different levels or scopes relate to and influence each other (this comes out most strikingly when trying to place the notional boundary around the system of interest). Similarly, this can force them to take an interdisciplinary approach, drawing in factors from across different discipline areas, as well as help to make implicit assumptions more explicit.

Box 2.1: Systems diagramming: mapping and modelling

The terms 'systems', 'maps', and 'models' can often be used interchangeably in text and speech – sometimes giving rise to confusion. For the purposes of this book, one common feature shared by each term is that they are all artefacts; some form of 'representation' of reality as against naturalised reality itself. We see the activity of diagramming or mapping as the mediating technique for making such representations. Diagrams are representations of reality as seen by the person or people creating them, conceptual constructs given a physical form to aid thinking, communication and action. As such we can generally distinguish between three broad types of representation which differently deal with 'systemic (relational, joined up) and systematic (linear, step by step) understandings and practices' (Ison and Blackmore, 2014):

- *Analogue representations*, where the diagram looks similar to the object or objects it portrays. At their simplest they are line drawings of real objects and at their most complicated they are colourful, fully labelled drawings of the inner workings of organisms or machines. While they can aid understanding such diagrams play little part in most systems-based or action-oriented research studies but are widely used in scientific and technological work and can be used to inform other representations.

- *Schematic representations*, such as geographical maps or plans, where the map or plan represents the essence of 'real world' objects or phenomena but do not look similar to them. They essentially show the relationships between 'things' in either a systemic or systematic manner. Diagrams like these are often used in systems-based or action-oriented research studies and can be extremely valuable, for example, where they are used for debating and negotiating large scale land use and planning issues or for presenting the outcomes of a project. In effect the map or plan becomes a focus for structuring discussion between different stakeholders where the (often geographically based) inter-relationships between the activities of one party and another can be seen and future actions can be mediated and negotiated.

- *Conceptual representations*. These maps or diagrams largely try to describe inter-relationships between people, ideas or processes that are not so readily observed or depicted as 'things' but are put forward as a model for acceptance by others. They are mostly used to represent non-visual features where the emphasis can be as much on emotional or abstract relationships as with rational and real relationships. These interpretations may not be shared by others but are essential elements of the diagram creator's personal view of the world as they perceive it. Conceptual maps and diagrams feature most strongly in systems-based or action-oriented research work, even where the components or 'things' are seen as fairly real to those involved. (Conceptual diagrams can feature strongly in other types of study as well but we are focusing on the value of these approaches specifically to systems-based and action-oriented research studies rather than their generic value as thinking tools).

While 'maps' (the artefact) are diagrams associated with depicting the inter-relationships between parts of a system (schematic representations), 'models' can be used either as analogue representations (physical town planning model), or through diagramming or mapping (the activity) as

> conceptual representations – depicting either mental models of the way
> in which someone is thinking, or conceptual models associated with plans
> of action.

From the typology in Box 2.1 it is possible to derive another distinction – whether the diagram is portraying mainly elements of *structure* in a situation or the networks and patterns of *processes* thought to be occurring or both. Structure-based diagrams tend to represent largely *static* relationships – this is how a set of things or activities are organised or configured. Process-based diagrams tend to represent situations *over a period of time* – that is how one activity, idea of event leads on to another and another and so in a chain of processes (as has been attempted in the influence diagram in Figure 2.2). Though some, like the influence diagram, may appear to contain both structure and process, the emphasis tends to be on the static relationships, not the temporal processes, in the situation. Rich pictures (discussed below and which you will encounter in Chapters Three, Seven and Eight) are different in that they capture as many different features as possible – such as structure, process, relationships, the emotional states of participants, among others.

So diagrams for use in understanding and influencing environmental sustainability are implicit conceptual models made explicit as a pictorial representation that mostly captures qualitative or conceptual relationships. But the choice of which diagram to use when is determined as much by the purpose of the study or investigation and by the nature of the participants involved in the study as by the purpose of the particular type of diagram.

Some diagrams are specifically used to represent a system of interest from the start while many others are able to capture components of a messy situation from which it may be possible to define a system of interest. The distinction here is between diagrams which more explicitly define the boundaries between subsystems and a system of interest and between a system of interest and its environment or context and those that are used to explore a situation and from which it is then possible to determine implicit boundaries to the system and subsystems. The significance of this distinction is that diagrams where the components, relationships and boundaries are more explicit and rigorously agreed are better suited for developing a specification for a quantitative model if that is likely to be part of the study or research, so that the diagram may simply be a stage in a longer process of inquiry and evaluation. For other diagrams the diagram itself is the definitive stage and the subject of deliberation, debate and/or discussion in order to elicit information about a system of interest or messy situation from different people, to share understandings between participants or for prescribing an agenda for change. This is much more relevant to participatory or action–oriented research than a practitioner investigation as a key element is using the process to directly elicit and analyse 'data' (information, evidence, facts, opinions) in order to primarily answer research questions rather than looking for improvements in a complex situation.

Diagrams can be used at different times and in different ways within the same investigation, and many investigative methods involve these different phases:

- understanding a situation through eliciting or gathering 'data';
- analysing a situation through structuring and interpreting that 'data';
- communicating with others about that analysis by presenting that 'data';
- planning to deal with a situation, both logically and creatively, by acting on the collective evaluation of the 'data' analysis; and
- implementing, monitoring and evaluating those plans through further 'data' collection and analysis.

Common types of 'systems' diagrams

In the following paragraphs we mention some well used and well known diagram types for systems studies. This list is by no means exhaustive but is here to highlight the ways in which they can be used (see also Box 2.2 for pointers to additional information). As you read this book you will find that the authors have used these diagrams as described here, adapted them for their particular projects and also invented their own types when necessary. This highlights the fact that diagrams, as with text, can take many forms as long as the structure and 'grammar' of them aids rather than obscures the meaning(s) captured and contained within them.

Most diagrams begin at the centre of the sheet of paper and work outwards. Tony Buzan's (1974) *spray diagram* (an example is shown in Figure 2.3 and also Chapter Five) is built up from an initial idea with its branches; these branches have their own branches and so on until you reach the detail at the end of each twig. This technique is particularly useful for systematically capturing a complex array of 'data' for seeing how comprehensive, balanced or disjointed the 'data' might be and for thinking about further analysis.

Figure 2.3: Example of a spray diagram

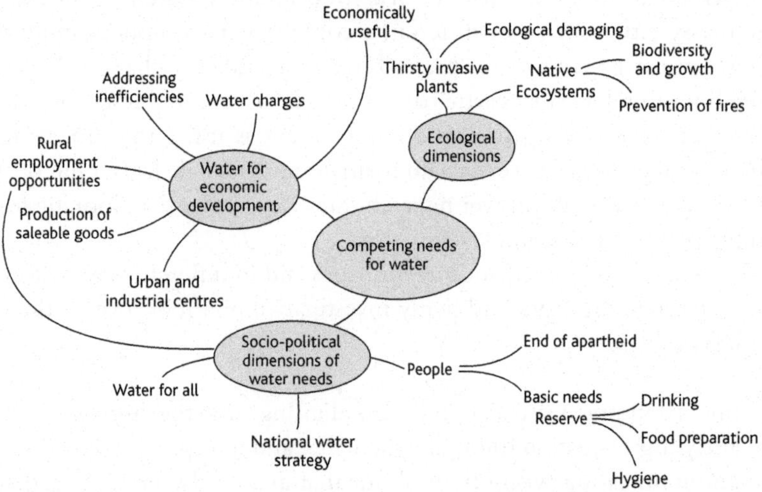

Source: Taken from an Open University Development Management free course on OpenLearn (www.open.edu/openlearn/science-maths-technology/computing-and-ict/systems-computer/diagramming-development-1-bounding-realities/content-section-0)

However, spray diagrams rely on there being logical connections between the elements and relatively linear relationships between the core idea and the detail at the periphery. So they tend to be more useful when you want a relatively straightforward 'understanding' of the 'data' and/or situation and not when you want to develop a more creative understanding.

When Peter Checkland (1999) began to analyse human activity systems, he and his colleagues developed a technique that he called the *rich picture* (a diagram used widely in systems work as exemplified by the examples within Chapters Three, Seven and Eight) because it contains more than should be necessary to understand the situation. Rich pictures need a lot of space and you do not have to be an art expert – indeed, artistic flair can sometimes be a diversion from the goal of drawing useful rich pictures.

Rich pictures require you to make pictorial representations of each of the elements in a situation and annotate any interactions and relationships between the elements in the situation. These are not normally linear and the precise nature of the relationships between certain elements may be unclear. The aim is not to try and impose order on a rich picture; it is intended to assist in understanding a complex situation and trying to impose order denies the very complexity of the situation. For example, if you identify 'problems' in a rich picture, you will have prejudged the situation and thus also what might be 'solutions'.

Having said that, a rich picture may suggest interactions and relationships of which you had been unaware and you may wish to 'redraw' the picture to highlight these interactions and relationships. This is perfectly OK as long as you keep the original picture to remind you what it looked like and remember that 'redrawing' a rich picture is the equivalent of moving from the creativity to the connectivity phase and imposing your version of a more ordered reality on the complex situation. Furthermore, rich pictures are the product of a creative process and while they capture certain 'data' themselves, for action-oriented research this may be harder to interpret unless notes or a record of the conversations that happened during its creation are made. Indeed it is good practice when using diagrams to elicit 'data' to not just rely on the finished diagram as the only source of 'data'.

Systems maps (as exemplified by Figure 2.1 and in Chapter Seven) are another way of developing your understanding of a situation. Systems maps are essentially 'structure' diagrams. Each element or subsystem is contained in a circle or oval and a line is drawn round a group of elements or subsystems to show that the things outside the line are part of the environment while those inside the line are part of the system. There are NO lines connecting elements, subsystems or systems in a systems map; it is purely a statement of the structure as seen by its creators.

Influence diagrams (as exemplified by Figure 2.4) can be developed from systems maps and indicate where one element in the situation has some influence over another. Arrows indicate the direction of the influence and the lines between elements may be of different thickness, shading or colour in order to distinguish strong and weak influence. Strictly speaking, influence should only be shown from elements at a higher or at the same level in the system; that is to say, subsystems cannot influence systems and subsystems and systems cannot influence the environment – but some people do not follow this convention.

Where a clear pattern of cause and effect can be discerned in a situation, then *causal loop* and *multiple cause diagrams* (as shown in Figure 2.5) may be useful in describing the interactions between different elements in a situation. By convention, multiple cause diagrams have the elements (events, activities, and so on) laid out, without ovals or any other sort of enclosure, in whatever way assists in clarifying the processes. Elements are joined by arrows indicating where there is a causal relationship between the elements. Where there is cause

Figure 2.4: Example of an influence diagram

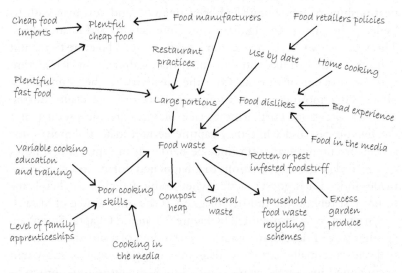

Influence diagram of household food waste

Source: Taken from a free interactive media guide to diagrams from The Open University, on OpenLearn (www.open.edu/openlearn/money-management/management/guide-diagrams)

Figure 2.5: Example of a causal loop diagram

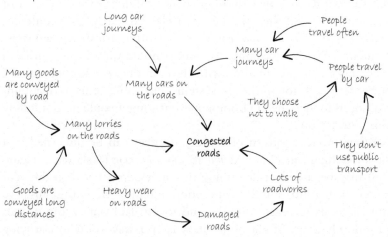

Multiple cause diagram exploring some of the causes of road congestion

Source: Taken from an animated tutorial from the Systems Group at The Open University (http://systems.open.ac.uk/materials/t552/index.htm)

and effect in both directions between two elements, separate arrows indicate this. These types of diagrams have featured very strongly in the work of Peter Senge (1990) and colleagues in the United States of America (for example Anderson and Johnson, 1997) and the systems dynamics movement started by Jay Forrester (see Meadows, 2008) and have been useful for establishing the variables and relationships needed for a quantitative mathematical model.

'Systems' diagramming in practice

Individual, collective and concerted practice and action research

We have already alluded to the distinctions that can be made between using systems thinking and systems diagrams as the basis for investigating your personal and collective understanding of, and behaviours in, a complex (environmental) situation where you take the role of either a practitioner helping with systemic inquiries or as a researcher. In the former role you may be an environmental professional who has to undertake consultations with stakeholders on a planned road development, in the latter role you may be researching the motivating factors for farmers' adopting particular environmental practices. However, there can also be a merging of these roles within a participatory and action-oriented research approach where you are not only researching a situation to better understand it within certain theoretical frameworks, but are also expecting that the participants learn from the process so as to change their behaviours that then improve that situation for those participants (and others). This then throws up questions about the relationship between you as either a practitioner or a researcher with the system of interest you are inquiring or researching into.

As noted in Chapter One, in most of our research projects, including those discussed in this book, we have been interested in going beyond participatory research that simply involves people to that which researches *with* people and involves them at the conception of the project (see Figure 1.1 in Chapter One). This is not to say that researching on people is wrong or cannot provide interesting research findings. It is more that the systemic philosophy we place at the heart of all our practices encourages us to develop reflexive learning systems – systems that take count of the practitioner influence on the area of practice as part of the practical process – whether that be in our teaching (Ison and Blackmore, 2014) or our researching as described in this book.

It is within this philosophy that we chose which diagram types we use for which purpose at which stage of an inquiry or investigation. In this sense the diagram is another tool or device to help elicit primary 'data' from others in the same way that a questionnaire, an interview or observation does. However, diagrams can also be used as tools for analysis, synthesis and communication as well as data collection so it is important to be explicit about why they are used and how they are used within a research approach, whether participatory and action-oriented or not.

Diagrams and data elicitation

One significant use of diagramming is for data elicitation or gathering of 'evidence' from research participants (Hughes, 2012). In other words, a particular type of diagram is used to get one or more research participants to structure and (hopefully) capture their thinking about a given topic and that expression of their thinking alongside observations and notes becomes primary data to be analysed. We have found over the course of our research that the choice of diagram used to elicit data, as well as the specific topic or theme used to initiate the discussion and mapping process, needs to fit with the purpose and objectives of the investigation. This does not mean that if we had used a different diagram with our participants we might not have elicited a similar data set for analysis. Equally a different set of participants using the same diagram might not necessarily lead to different data sets, but as with interviews the data represents the thinking of these particular participants at that particular time. It does mean that as a researcher you need to understand and acknowledge the limitations and constraints that a particular diagram brings to your study (as you would with other research tools such as questionnaires and telephone interviews) and to build in processes that ensure a reasonable degree of robustness to the data and how it is analysed and reported. An example, if possible, is to have more than one group do the same exercise so that you have multiple data sets to compare and contrast. A key feature throughout the book is that mapping is very useful at eliciting individual and collective perspectives on a human activity system where understanding those multiple perspectives is a necessary feature of the research.

Working alone

While working with others may be key to your research or practice you will also be faced with drawing diagrams on your own, whether that be using a diagram to help with your own understanding, developing a diagrammatic template for using with others to elicit 'data', or creating diagrams to communicate findings to others. So you also need to attend to your own diagramming practice as well as with others. Most diagrams that we create ourselves are done on pieces of paper first and may require several attempts for us to be satisfied, whether or not we ever share them with another person. The reason for that is that the rigour of drawing a diagram, iterating through several versions and of clearly specifying the purposes and assumptions behind the diagram, can be enough to change our own thinking about a situation or what we want to do. The act of drawing influences our thinking and our thinking influences what we draw, including all the issues of whether the diagram is for personal use or might be shared with others, and the implications that sharing it with others raises. Of course, just drawing a diagram to help our thinking is of little use in environmental sustainability if it is not shared with others, or if we are unable to convey that changed thinking to others through non-diagrammatic means. Most of the examples shown in this book are about getting others to create and debate diagrams that are relevant to their situation and their understanding of it.

Working with others

Involving others with diagrams comes in two main forms: co-creation of a collective diagram and using a diagram as the focus for a mediated discussion of the situation that the diagram represents. Both techniques can be very powerful in helping those involved to gain a shared understanding of a situation as it draws out the different perspectives they may have and also for developing a negotiated set of actions for moving on (although in many cases, the fact that thinking has been changed can lead to changed action and behaviour without the need for it to be made explicit in a set of written action points). Drawing or using diagrams with one other person, or groups of people, requires the same attention to inter-personal and group processes when discussions are around written documents. With one-to-one sessions you need to use the diagram as a prompt and decide whether you are adding to the diagram or the other person is, all the time checking that the other person is happy with the diagram. With group sessions, everyone needs to be given the opportunity to contribute and to suggest changes or additions to the diagram. A difference though is that a major record of the discussion – the diagram – is visible to all at the time for further comment whereas notes of a meeting come afterwards when participants may be less inclined to comment on them. It is important therefore to have someone dedicated to the task of drawing, or give everyone a turn with the pen. It can also be very helpful to have a neutral person facilitate the proceedings as this will be more informal than many meetings but still requires someone to manage the process fairly and defuse any tensions that may arise. In addition, it is necessary to think about the ethical issues involved in working on, for or with others as part of a study and recognising your own part in the process. This may include agreeing how contributions are acknowledged, or whether contributions are not acknowledged, so that sensitive comments are not attributable to one person but to the group as a whole. The latter is often done under the Chatham House Rule.[1]

Using diagrams for data analysis and presenting findings

Many diagrams are only seen by the creator or creators, or a few other people who work with it and these can often be messy and complicated to follow unless you were involved in the process of creation or had a record of its creation. Sometimes using a structured template diagram as the starting point can help with this. However, there will be times when a diagram is included in a report or used as part of a presentation, and in these cases there is a need to make the diagram as easily understood as possible, given that the reader may be unfamiliar with the style and rules governing the type of diagram being used.

Diagrams that arise from a data elicitation stage can be used in a number of ways as part of the analysis and synthesis into reportable findings. One step is to take the sometimes rough and ready diagram and create a clean version that is much easier to follow for the researchers, the participants and project funder. This translation from 'draft' to 'final' version has to be handled carefully and can be greatly aided by either notes or audio recordings of the discussion as the group is generating the diagram and/or notes or audio recordings of a plenary when one or more members of the group explain the diagram and their thinking behind it. The same issues of translation and fidelity arises when analysing several similar diagrams for synthesising into a single, composite diagram.

Diagrams for communication need to follow conventions that are widely understood. A diagram developed for communication:

- is large, clear and well laid out;
- has colour and/or shading for emphasis;

- has a title which describes the purpose of the diagram; and
- has a key to the meaning of all the symbols used in the diagram.

Annotation, notes and/or narrative may be necessary but in general you should use two simple diagrams instead of one complicated one, or show how a diagram is built up in stages.

Mapping and professional facilitation

A further important consideration is that while the use of diagrams can reduce potential biases as they make the research process more transparent (Buckley and Waring, 2013), it is necessary to be mindful of the power relations involved, both between researcher and participant and between the participants themselves. This is particularly important in workshop settings where certain contributors may seek to dominate the task and where using professional workshop facilitators can prove invaluable for ensuring equality in the contribution of views, particularly for research on more controversial issues. Also, unlike us as researchers, they serve as independent mediators without a stake in the project.

Mark Yoxon of Inform, the professional facilitators used in the projects discussed in Chapters Three, Four and Six, notes:

> In essence facilitation is "to make easy" or "ease a process." With effective planning, light touch guidance and management the facilitator's goal is to ensure that the group's objectives are met, with clear evaluation, good participation and full buy-in from all involved. The key responsibility of a facilitator is to create a workable group process and an environment in which it can flourish, and in doing so help the group reach a successful decision, solution or conclusion. To facilitate well, the facilitator must first understand the group's desired outcome(s), and the background and context of the event. In practice this means:
>
> - Designing and planning the group process, and selecting tools and techniques that best help the group progress towards that outcome(s)
>
> - Guiding and managing the group processes to ensure that:
>   - There is effective participation and full inclusion

- As much as possible, participants achieve a mutual understanding and agreement
- That all contributions are considered and included in the ideas, solutions and decisions that emerge from the event
- Participants take shared responsibility for the outcome(s)
- Ensure that outcomes, actions and questions are properly recorded and followed up.

To be an effective facilitator there is always a challenging balance to achieve. The facilitator needs to sense when to take a leadership role and when to be neutral and take a back seat.

Facilitation requires a very particular skills set which the Inform partners – Mark Yoxon and Mo Shapiro – have gained over 40 years international experience in facilitation, training and stakeholder dialogue. Academic researchers, on the other hand, are not necessarily very skilled in what is required.

Conclusions

Diagrams can be very important additions to systems-based studies and participatory and action-oriented research in helping understanding and helping with interventions to create systemic change in general, while diagramming in particular is a helpful tool for use where multiple disciplines are associated with supporting environmental sustainability. First, it is a tool that helps our understanding of complex inter-relationships involved in environmental sustainability issues. Second, it helps with interdisciplinary conversations by facilitating engagement of different perspectives on sustainability. Third, diagramming provides a vehicle for transdisciplinarity – a language for mediating between experts and non-experts which can help in transforming situations of environmental sustainability (Lyall et al, 2015). Fourth, large scale participation in conversations is helped more by diagrams than lengthy text documents, because they capture much of the essence of a situation in a compact way and are easier to create in groups. Fifth, diagramming can be stimulating and engaging such that often it is the processes involved around the diagram or map that is more important in describing and effecting change in environmental situations for the participants than the diagram itself.

This chapter has only had space to provide a brief overview of common diagram types we have used and how to draw them; however, the case study chapters that follow provide more detail on their use in different environmental contexts and with different stakeholders. If you are looking for more details on diagram types and how to draw them we have listed some other sources of information on these and other forms of diagrams in Box 2.2. You will also see that the examples provided in the case study chapters come in three main forms. Some are photographs of a diagram produced by research participants that has been taken as a record of what they have done. Some are versions of participant diagrams redrawn by the researchers to make them more legible and then photographed. Some are (re)drawn by the researchers on a computer for presentation to others or for use in publications. We hope this range of examples helps illustrate the many points made in this chapter about the various uses of diagrams when researching environmental sustainability situations and the inherent 'messiness' and creativity that can flow from producing them.

Box 2.2: Additional sources of information on diagramming

There are very few books that deal with systems diagramming or related types of diagramming and any that are will be noted in the various book chapters. Other books, as noted in Chapter One, deal with visual methods for research in one form or another. For web-based material on systems diagramming and related diagramming techniques look at the following:

1. Extracts from The Open University's study pack on diagramming on OpenLearn: www.open.edu/openlearn/science-maths-technology/computing-and-ict/systems-computer/systems-diagramming/content-section-0
2. An animated tutorial from the Systems Group at The Open University: http://systems.open.ac.uk/materials/t552/index.htm
3. An interactive media guide to diagrams from The Open University available on OpenLearn: www.open.edu/openlearn/money-management/management/guide-diagrams
4. Two extracts from an Open University Development Management module on OpenLearn: www.open.edu/openlearn/science-maths-technology/computing-and-ict/systems-computer/diagramming-development-1-bounding-realities/content-section-0 and www.open.edu/openlearn/science-maths-technology/computing-and-

ict/systems-computer/diagramming-development-2-exploring-interrelationships/content-section-0

5. Wikipedia articles on diagrams and concept mapping: http://en.wikipedia.org/wiki/Diagram and http://en.wikipedia.org/wiki/Concept_map

6. The Mindtools site: www.mindtools.com/pages/article/newTMC_04.htm

7. A document from ICRA: www.icra-edu.org/resources/266/systems+diagrams+-+guidelines

In addition to the above material on diagramming, The Open University's OpenLearn platform also contains many free courses and other educational resources on systems thinking and environmental sustainability, derived from its many modules and teaching programmes.

Notes

[1] Under the Chatham House Rule, information disclosed during a meeting may be reported by those present, but the source of that information may not be explicitly or implicitly identified – see www.chathamhouse.org/about/chatham-house-rule

References

Anderson, V. and Johnson, L. (1997) *Systems Thinking Basics: from concepts to causal loops*, Cambridge, MA: Pegasus Communication.

Armson, R. (2011) *Growing Wings on the Way: Systems Thinking for Messy Situations*, Axminster: Triarchy Press.

Blackmore, C. (ed) (2010) *Social Learning Systems and Communities of Practice*, London: Springer.

Bronte-Stewart, M. (1997) 'Using diagrams and Muller-Merbach's framework to teach systems theory', *Systemist*, 19(3): 174–86.

Buckley, C.A. and Waring, M. (2013) 'Using diagrams to support the research process: Examples from grounded theory', *Qualitative Research*, 13(2): 148–72.

Buzan, A. (1974) *Use Your Head*, London: BBC Publications.

Chapman, J. (2004) *Systems Failure: why governments must learn to think differently*, London: Demos.

Checkland, P. (1999) *Systems Thinking, Systems Practice*, 2nd edition, London: Wiley.

Checkland, P.B. and Haynes, M.G. (1994) 'Varieties of Systems Thinking: the case of Soft Systems Methodology', *Systems Dynamics Review*, 10(2–3): 189–97.

Carter, R., Martin, J. and Munday, M. (1984) *Systems, Management and Change: a graphic guide*, London: Harper and Row.

Capra, F. (1997) *The Web of Life*, London: Harper Collins.

Hughes, J. (ed.) (2012) *SAGE Visual Methods*, London: Sage Publications Ltd.

Ison, R. (2010) *Systems Practice: How to act in a Climate Change World*, London: Springer, and Milton Keynes: Open University.

Ison, R. and Blackmore, C. (2014) 'Designing and Developing a Reflexive Learning System for Managing Systemic Change', *Systems*, 2: 119–36.

Lane, A. (2002) *Systems Thinking and Practice: Diagramming*, 2nd edition, Milton Keynes: Open University.

Lane, A. (2013) 'A review of diagramming in systems practice and how technologies have supported the teaching and learning of diagramming for systems thinking in practice', *Systemic Practice and Action Research*, 26: 319–29.

Lane, A. and Morris, R. (2001) 'Teaching diagramming at a distance: seeing the human wood through the technological trees', *Systemic Practice and Action Research*, 14(6): 715–34.

Lyall, C., Meagher, M. and Bruce, A. (2015) 'A rose by any other name? Transdisciplinarity in the context of UK research policy', *Futures*, 65: 150–62.

Meadows, D. (2008) *Thinking in Systems: A Primer*, London: Earthscan.

Midgley, G. (2007) 'Systems thinking for evaluation', in R. Williams and I. Imam (eds), *Systems Concepts in Evaluation: An Expert Anthology*, Point Reyes, CA: EdgePress, pp 11–34.

Morris, R. M. (2009) 'Thinking about systems for sustainable lifestyles', *Environmental Scientist*, 18(1): 15–18.

Oreszczyn, S. and Lane, A. (2012) *Mapping knowledge exchange in the UK Hedgerow management system: A report on a workshop held at the first International Hedgelink Conference*, Staffordshire University, Stoke on Trent, UK, 3–5 September, Milton Keynes: The Open University.

Ramage, M. and Shipp, K. (2009) *Systems Thinkers*, London: Springer.

Reynolds, M. (2011) 'Critical Thinking and Systems Thinking', in C.P. Horvath and J.M. Forte (eds), *Critical Thinking*, New York: Nova Science Publishers, pp 37–68.

Reynolds, M. (2013) 'Managing systemic risk using systems thinking in practice', *AWERProcedia Advances in Applied Sciences*, 1: 217–24.

Reynolds, M. (2014) 'Triple-loop learning and conversing with reality', *Kybernetes*, 43(9/10): 1381–91.

Reynolds, M. and Holwell, S. (eds) (2010) *Systems Approaches to Managing Change: a practical guide*, London: Springer

Senge, P. (1990) *The Fifth Discipline: The Art and Practice of the Learning Organisation*, London: Doubleday.

THREE

Researching agri-environmental problems with others

Sue Oreszczyn, Les Levidow and Dave Wield

Editors' introduction

Working towards sustainable agriculture often involves working on contested or controversial issues with others. They involve a complex mix of people, all with their own opinions and ways of seeing the world, such as civil society organisations, policymakers and companies. All the agri-environmental projects (those concerned with the environment but carried out in agricultural contexts) discussed in this chapter involve controversial issues, such as the introduction and development of GM crops, the potential power of large biotechnology companies, the increased use of biofuels, water and intensification of agriculture. As with the next chapter (Chapter Four), this chapter discusses the use and value of mapping techniques in these highly contested environmental research contexts. However, unlike Chapter Four the projects drawn on here were all large scale, multi-partner, European projects. The processes and mapping techniques were chosen for specific purposes, according to the needs of the different projects, the context and type of participants involved and their strategic aims. They also represent the development of the authors' approaches to engaging with people and demonstrate the way that the approach has changed over time as they have sought ways to enable participants to engage in the research process more fully. Thus while the final project discussed in this chapter is less about mapping, it is included because its unusual funding arrangements enabled a different mode of research participation that provided useful insights for the more action-oriented research we advocate in this book.

Introduction

Several of the mapping techniques presented in this book have evolved from their use in business and organisational knowledge management (for example, Eden, 1988; Huff, 1990), as have the theories from which they draw, such as communities of practice (Lave and Wenger, 1991), networks of practice (Brown and Duguid, 2001) and tacit versus explicit knowledge (Collins, 2010; Polyani, 2015 [1958]), discussed in more detail in Chapters Four and Seven. These techniques and theories are concerned with how informal or tacit knowledge is generated and managed in organisations and have been used by consultants and practitioners as well as academics to link theory and practice (see for example, Huff and Jenkins, 2002). The mapping techniques used by the projects in this chapter were, likewise, originally devised by people who were paid to help companies clarify their strategic options. As you will see, the research projects adapted these techniques and used them for analysing different people's, groups' or organisations' perspectives on environmental issues. Importantly, they also used them to help establish very different relationships with their stakeholders.

The projects in this chapter particularly address the way that social science has been challenged to provide a more solid and less disparate evidence base for making policy decisions (Lyall et al, 2004; Oakley, 2001, Nutley, 2003; Solesbury, 2001). The first two project examples, Policy Influences in Technology for Agriculture (PITA) and Precautionary Expertise for GM Crops (PEG), were conducted at a time when, despite efforts by researchers to give more attention to dissemination and end-user needs, few research projects actually attempted to directly involve policymakers within the research process itself. They represented a step forward in thinking about how participants, in this case companies and senior policymakers, may be more involved. The third, more recent, project discussed – Cooperative Research on Environmental Problems in Europe (CREPE) – goes one step further, not only more actively involving participants, but also attempting to work with them as equal partners.

Mapping with companies

In this first example on policy influences in technology on agriculture (PITA),[1] project participants were treated more as informants than partners in the project: partly as a result of the thinking in methodological approaches at the time and partly as a necessary way of working with major multinational companies with little time for researchers. Cognitive maps (see Figure 3.1 and also Chapter Four) were constructed for, and from, individual company monographs and material supporting these monographs. The maps mapped the strategic thinking behind the development of new technologies and also the corporate thinking of the companies on environmental sustainability. Good examples of these maps maybe found in the Monsanto Monograph (Chataway and Tait, 2000).[2]

Behind PITA was the notion that technological innovation in the agrochemicals, biotechnology and seeds industries has the potential to deliver more socially and environmentally sustainable farming systems. However, although a range of European policies could contribute to these outcomes, in practice they often counteract one another. The PITA project conducted an integrated analysis of policies and market-related factors and investigated their impact on the strategies and decision making of companies (multinationals and small and medium enterprises) and public sector research establishments. It also considered the implications of these decisions for employment, competitiveness and environmental benefits in Europe. The overall aim of the project was to contribute to the development of sustainable industrial and farming systems and an improved quality of life by encouraging the development and uptake of 'cleaner' technology for intensive agriculture (see Tait et al, 2001).

Monographs and maps

A focus on technology strategies and trajectories allowed us, in our detailed study of 14 major multinational companies (including seven of the top ten global agro-chemicals and seeds companies), to consider the drivers that influence innovation from the perspectives of the companies. We found cognitive mapping to be useful for highlighting the thinking of key actors in decision making about new technologies and this was used as a key form of analysis.

Cognitions may be described as the belief systems used by individuals to perceive, construct and make sense of their world (Swan, 1997). The term 'cognitive mapping' is used to describe a set of qualitative modelling techniques that attempt to portray these cognitions. The particular technique used for this project was developed by Eden (1989) and is based on Kelly's Personal Construct theory (Kelly, 1995 [1955]). The technique has since been developed and used extensively in consultancy situations, particularly for mapping strategic thinking in companies (see, for example, Huff and Jenkins, 2002). It is designed to capture in a diagram the thinking on a particular issue of an individual or an organisation. Eden and Ackerman (1998) argue that it is not meant to be a precise model of cognition, but rather a technique that translates Kelly's theory into a useful tool enabling the representation of the part of the person's (or organisation's) construct system that they are willing or able to reveal.

Cognitive maps have the advantage of enabling links between concepts to be made to illuminate on the reasoning behind an issue. They can highlight the importance of particular beliefs within a view, that is by showing which concepts have highly developed reasoning behind them. The maps do not assume a linear model of reasoning from worldview through to specific beliefs and then actions: they do not assume that beliefs are necessarily hierarchical – some may appear further down the diagram as a result of specific actions or instruments. Reinforcing mechanisms can be identified through feedback loops. Each cognitive frame (perspective) can be set out on one sheet of paper (see Figure 3.1).

The main advantages of using the cognitive mapping technique for analysis within the PITA project were that they:

- provided a way of presenting the individual researcher's analysis to a large team, making the large amount of information more accessible;
- provided useful reminders of the contents of each monograph;
- captured the essence of a company's world view through highlighting connections between aspects such as innovation, markets, and so on;
- established the relationships between aspects of thinking;
- enabled comparisons to be made between and across the companies;
- through the links between concepts, highlighted aspects of the companies' views that may not be immediately obvious when reading the monograph;
- highlighted the differences in individuals views when mapping the interviews; and
- identified strands of thinking and clusters of concepts which represent key themes.

There are, however, potential difficulties with them in that links may not always be that clear, therefore the researcher may be making assumptions about links. The maps present the drawer's particular view of the situation, participants' reflections on the maps are therefore important, and the maps can be used as a basis for discussion, as noted in Chapter Two. Also, the maps can get complicated at the lower level of detail – separate maps may be drawn to get round this.

For the overall project analysis, four or five cognitive maps were produced for each company using the material collected, for example from interviews or company information, or produced in monographs written for each company. These researcher produced maps provided a foundation for further higher level integrated analysis to be carried out by the research team. They presented each company's thinking on key aspects of concern in the PITA project – innovation, policy and environmental sustainability. Overview maps attempted to provide an overview of a company's strategic thinking and to capture the essence of that company's worldview, while the cognitive maps drawn directly from interviews with company representatives resulted in maps depicting personal views held by key decisions makers within their organisation. Thus the maps described the company's self-perceptions as perceived by the researcher or author of the monograph and represent a snapshot, at a particular moment in time, of the worldview of a particular company.

While it is possible to draw the maps by hand, and this may be particularly useful in an interview situation, the large number of maps generated by the project were produced using the computer software Decision Explorer.[3] This software was developed specifically for capturing and exploring the complexity of qualitative information and may be used in groups, such as workshop situations, as well as individually. The software enables the mapping of concepts and the relationships between them and can be used to explore different perspectives on complex issues. As cognitive mapping techniques do not represent mental models in the psychological sense and data collection (such as interviewing techniques) can influence what is revealed, each monograph, together with the maps, was sent to the company concerned for comments and to ensure their views were being accurately portrayed.

Figure 3.1 shows one example of the many maps drawn during the course of the project. This example focused on the environmental elements of concern to one major multinational company based mainly in Europe. We found that European companies were more dependent on the European context and were more sensitive to European political and regulatory cultures, including the more active stakeholder approach demanded by European citizens.

As you can see, the maps consist of concepts linked by arrows or lines. Links describe relationships between concepts. Along with the concepts, they form a line of argument, a description of a problem or the components of a strategy. A concept is expressed as a short statement covering a single idea or notion, for example assertions about part of a strategy, causes of a problem or means of improving a situation. The links between concepts can cover a range of different types of relationship, causal, connotative or temporal. They may also

Figure 3.1: Example of a company's cognitive map from the PITA project

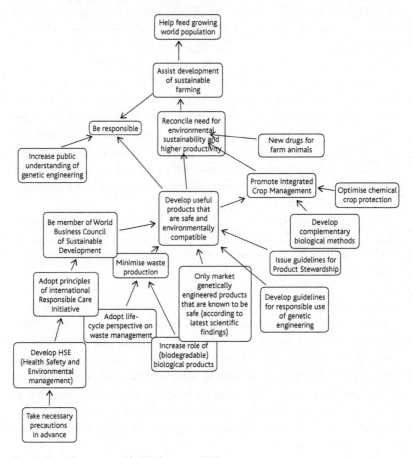

Source: From Oreszczyn with PITA Partners, 2001

be positive or negative. The statements, or concepts at the top of the maps represent the company's aspirations or goals, with strategies for achieving these goals represented below them.

Findings and reflections

The maps generated a wealth of data and findings and these may be found in the project documents.[4] One example relevant here is the maps revealed the way that almost all the companies in our sample had used the concept of sustainability to describe their vision of the interactions between agriculture and the environment. Underlying this view was the notion that new innovations were important for feeding a growing world population while at the same time protecting biodiversity. They felt they were making a contribution to the sustainability of farming systems as their whole crop strategies supported high yielding agriculture while at the same time reducing pesticide use and developing 'cleaner' pesticides. This was their particular view at the time and others, such as environmental groups, viewed things differently. Therefore, an important feature of cognitive maps for contentious environmental issues is that they can help diverse groups of people with different views understand the thinking behind others' views. They demonstrate the complexity and level of sophistication of thinking behind people's beliefs. They help avoid presenting people's views as for and against positions, which can be over simplistic and misleading. They point to why particular positions taken by people regarding a particular issue are as they are and might be difficult to move, but also indicate where minds might meet to find ways forward.

The maps were particularly useful for setting particular views or strategies of the companies within their wider context. A company's view on environmental sustainability formed just one aspect of their thinking. What the maps were able to reveal was how their thinking on the environment linked in with their thinking about research strategies more generally and also the wider company view. Interestingly each company had a very particular worldview, often associated with their particular kind of leadership. Presenting the maps back to the companies can provoke interesting conversations around how they view themselves as well as ensuring that the researcher has accurately reflected their thinking.

Companies can be difficult to engage in research on environmental sustainability unless it is something that they are particularly interested in or it is important to their business. Environmental issues are often contentious and companies have to be mindful of how they are perceived by their customers. Significant attempts were made to try and build relationships with the companies being studied. In some cases this was successful and ongoing relationships were formed, while for others they simply did not want to be involved. Where some companies in a project are reluctant to be interviewed, cognitive mapping enables secondary data to be combined with primary data to develop maps of the companies' thinking and strategies. In circumstances where interviews are not possible, mapping the secondary material available may be the best that can be achieved. However, because of the visual nature of the maps, offering them to companies (or other hard to reach participants) for comment and their reactions can be a useful way of engaging them with what you are doing.

Finally, despite the research being carried out some time ago, company interest in these maps remains to this day, demonstrating the way the maps may enable longer term reflection by both researchers and participants. One particularly interesting encounter took place in late 2013 in the headquarters of one major global company. A new generation of company senior strategists saw our cognitive maps on their company for the first time and commented on their usefulness and timeliness even after 15 years.

Scenario mapping with policymakers

In this section we turn to the use of scenario mapping in a workshop that was carried out with senior policy actors for a research project concerned with precaution and GM crops in the UK (Oreszczyn, 2004, 2005). The workshop formed part of a larger European project looking at precautionary expertise for GM crops across Europe (PEG)[5] and was seen by us as a tool for better linking policy and research – the importance of which was noted in Chapter One. We also believed that the workshop had the potential to promote a learning process that involved all those engaged in the research and not just the researchers, something that was seen as particularly pertinent given the wide range of views on whether or not the UK should grow GM crops. Scenario mapping (see also Chapter Six) is particularly suitable for the exploration of environmental issues that tend to be complex, feature a wide range of views and stakeholders and involve long-term consequences. As a useful tool for foresight exercises, they are a technique used by many of the world's successful businesses and national governments to improve long-term decision making.

There are many different scenario methods ranging from those based on techniques utilising a high degree of specialist expertise – such as the large computer models used to consider climate change[6] to more informal and participatory futures planning workshops such as those used to consider future landscapes (see, for example, Reed et al, 2013), or the Harman Fans used in Chapter Five. It is not our intention here to provide a review of these but to explain a process that we employed because of its suitability for working with senior policy actors in our research.

Most scenario building exercises construct plausible scenarios, although not necessarily using mapping techniques, by identifying the key variables and by considering the roles of the different actors involved. That is, they identify the components of a scenario that may change and therefore influence the future being studied. They can be used to reveal the trade-offs that would need to occur or the way interactions between policies and attitudes can result in different futures. They also consider how different people or groups may influence these components or respond to any changes in them. Many different futures may be generated by considering different timescales along a given path to a particular future.

A UK scenario workshop

As with our other projects, the PEG research team were keen to involve policy actors[7] at an early stage of the research, and throughout the research process, to ensure that the research outcomes were as relevant as possible to current policy decisions. The one day workshop, held in 2003, was designed to capture some of the complexity of views on the situation in the UK at the time, and to consider potential dynamics and interactions among policy actors that are not necessarily obvious from interviews with individuals but may be important for decision making (see, Oreszczyn, 2003; Oreszczyn and Carr, 2008).

For us as researchers, the scenario approach offered a participatory element to engage with users of the research and ensure that our research questions and findings were embedded in the policy process itself. It provided a policy analysis tool that was an immediate check on the likely response of stakeholders to the policy implications of research findings; a way of checking out any assumptions we, the researchers, may have made about other people's views; a way of making sure our research was policy relevant; a means of revealing aspects we may have neglected; and material for informing the later stages of our research. Further, for controversial topics, such as GM crops, it offered a way for different stakeholders to explore different policy scenarios in an open, imaginative and non-confrontational way – it provided a 'safe' environment in which people could air issues of concern.

We considered it important that this exercise should not be regarded simply as a process of benefit only to the researchers. Therefore, for the participants, the mapping workshop offered an opportunity to influence the research to ensure that it addressed their priorities or concerns; an opportunity to learn about our research findings early on; an opportunity to network with people from other departments or institutes who faced problems or decisions similar to their own and an opportunity to be exposed to views not necessarily found in their usual environment. The number of high profile policy actors that the workshop attracted, and who remained engaged throughout the day, indicated that what we were offering was of interest or use not just to us researchers, but also to the participants.

Using three policy scenarios

During the PEG workshop, participants were asked to use their respective expertise to explore three different policy scenarios about GM crops and to generate maps. Rather than creating scenarios within the workshop process, which would take time, these three scenarios were chosen by the research team and presented to the participants. The policy scenarios were a tool for considering the causes and consequences of commercialisation of GM crops. Rather than choose scenarios far into the future, as recommended by many authors, drawing on the views expressed in earlier interviews with policy actors as part of the project, we chose three scenarios which we considered plausible policy options for present decision makers.[8] The scenarios were deliberately worded as simple one line statements, and were somewhat vague and ambiguous, to encourage participants to think creatively and develop their own storylines for the scenarios through discussion. Keeping them simple also meant that participants unfamiliar with scenario planning would readily understand them. The chosen scenarios were:

1. Commercialisation is postponed further.
2. Limited commercialisation goes ahead.
3. Commercialisation goes ahead.

A letter of invitation to the workshop was sent to over 60 key stakeholders with influence on the decisions being made about GM crops in the UK at the time. They covered a broad range of expertise – farmers' groups, industry, government officials and committee members, consumers groups, and NGOs. The event itself attracted 20 participants from a range of backgrounds, all of whom were involved in the policy process either directly as a member of a government department or advisory committee, or through their position within their organisation (see Oreszczyn, 2003, for full details).

The mapping process

The workshop was managed by a professional facilitator; this was essential for such a contentious topic and where participants covered the full spectrum of views on genetic modification, as noted in

Chapters Two and Four. A background document was sent to the participants before the workshop giving details of our research so far and enabling participants to comment on our early findings. This together with an introductory talk around a 'rich picture' depicting the main issues (see Figure 3.2) set the scene for the scenario exercise. As noted in Chapter Two, and further described in Chapters Seven and Eight, rich pictures have their origins in Soft Systems Methodology developed by Peter Checkland (1981), where they are used to gain an understanding of a human activity system. This particular picture summarised the main topics in the briefing document sent to the partners before the workshop in a cartoon-like form.

A further introductory talk was also given by one of the participants before dividing the participants into three groups – one for each of the scenarios. Each group was asked to consider the possible causes and consequences of that scenario. So that the groups could share their ideas, this discussion was followed by a 'carousel' activity, whereby each group moved round the room to add to the ideas posted by the other groups about their scenarios. This allowed all groups to contribute ideas to all three scenarios. Further it saved time, as each group was able to add ideas without having to have a full discussion on each scenario. Groups were encouraged to consider as many causes and consequences as possible for each scenario and these were written on sticky notes where all members of the group could see them. When they had considered all three scenarios in turn, each group returned to their initial scenario to sort all the causes and consequences into themes before giving a short presentation explaining these themes to the other groups. Participants were asked to identify gaps in the scenarios, to think about possible interactions of causes and consequences and possible unintended consequences, and to consider how various actors might respond. Once the maps were complete, each group gave a short presentation on their scenario map to the other groups. Importantly, each participant was able to present their own viewpoint by adding a new sequence if their view was not consistent with those of the rest of the group. The final maps represented an amalgamation of the group's views, so that not all participants necessarily agreed with all the views on each scenario map.

Despite the limited amount of time available for the scenario exercise, a rich variety of causes and consequences were identified and mapped. The large number of consequences generated for each scenario highlighted the complex and interacting consequences involved in any decision for GM crops. They therefore indicated the

Figure 3.2: The rich picture used at the beginning of the workshop with policy actors in the PEG project

Source: Author: PEG workshop background document

difficulties with making any policy decision. Figure 3.3 shows an example of one map generated by the participants.

Following the workshop, a draft report was produced by the researchers and sent to the participants together with copies of the scenario maps drawn on the day. This enabled any further comments from the participants to be included within the final report. Full details of the process and all the maps may be found in the workshop report (Oreszczyn, 2003). Here we now note some of our observations that may be useful to those using this type of mapping technique.

Reflections on the process

Careful consideration needs to be given to the scenarios presented to participants. In our workshop we realised that the scenario title allocated may have influence on how the group functions. For example, consideration of Scenario 1 appeared easier than Scenario 2 or Scenario 3 because Scenario 1 involved a continuation of the present situation. Further, the scenarios differed in how easy they were for participants to construct. For example, Scenario 2 was more difficult for participants so there are fewer links in this scenario map as the group ran out of time. Initially participants made little headway on the causes and consequences because much time was spent discussing what the term 'limited' meant in this context. There were also discussions about how to structure the scenario map since it was felt many of the issues could be described as both a cause and a consequence, for example, public concern. Thus, while participants considered Scenario 2 difficult to interpret, importantly, the discussions generated by trying to resolve this difficulty raised issues that might occur for this scenario in practice. In the third scenario, there was considerable disagreement. Critically, consequences could be determined by the success or failure of a small number of regulatory mechanisms, such as segregation and labelling. However, views differed on what outcome would count as 'success' or 'failure'. This demonstrated that, although difficult to capture, the discussions around the scenarios were as important as the map building exercise itself.

The final discussion provided a valuable part of the joint learning process between researchers and participants. The issue of the validity of the scenario exercise in particular was raised, as some participants were concerned there was no way of testing the accuracy of the scenario map statements. Berkhout and Hertin (2002) have also noted that this is a common criticism, particularly from scientists who may not feel comfortable about using an inherently subjective framework. However, although scenarios may be plausible they are not designed to be verifiable. It was also suggested that more weight might be given to particular views according to the evidence available to support those views. For example, since there is wide scientific agreement that gene flow will occur, this view could carry more weight. Tools and

Figure 3.3: Example of a scenario map from the PEG Project: Scenario 1: Commercialisation is further postponed

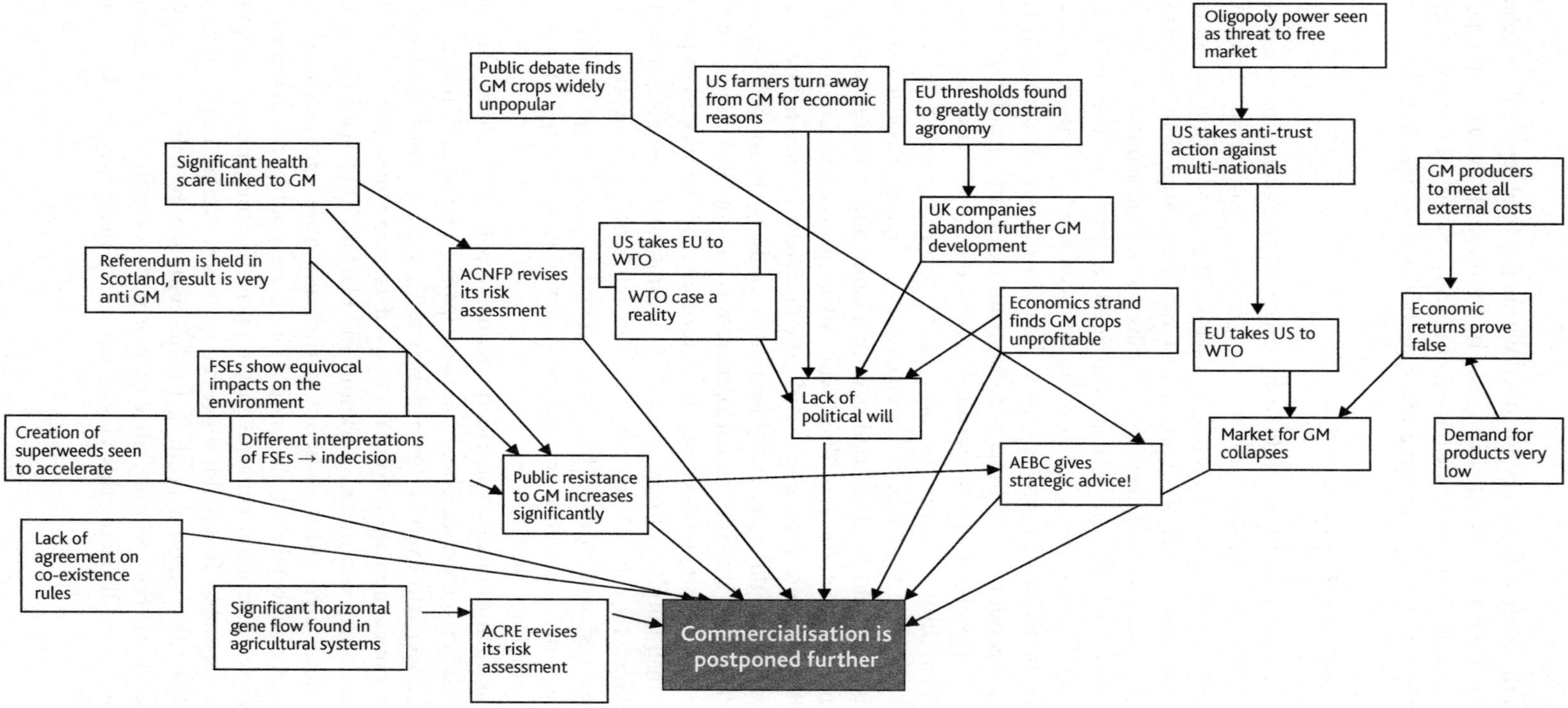

(continued)

Source: Oreszczyn (2003)

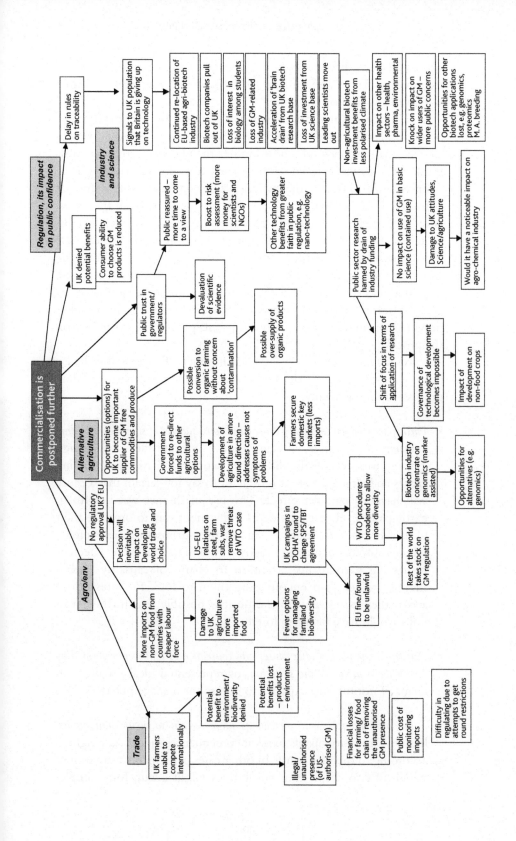

Commercialisation is postponed further

Regulation, its impact on public confidence

- Delay in rules on traceability
  - Signals to UK population that Britain is giving up on technology
    - Continued re-location of EU-based agri-biotech industry
    - Biotech companies pull out of UK
    - Loss of interest in biology among students
    - Loss of GM-related industry
    - Acceleration of 'brain drain' from UK biotech research base
    - Loss of investment from UK science base
    - Leading scientists move out

Industry and science

- UK denied potential benefits
- Consumer ability to choose GM products is reduced
- Public trust in government/ regulators
  - Public reassured – more time to come to a view
    - Boost to risk assessment (more money for scientists and NGOs)
    - Other technology benefits from greater faith in public regulation, e.g. nano-technology
  - Devaluation of scientific evidence

- Non-agricultural biotech investment benefits from less polarised climate
  - Impact on other health sectors – health, pharma, environmental
  - Knock on impact on wider users of GM – more public concerns
  - Opportunities for other biotech applications lost, e.g. genomics, proteomics M.A. breeding

Alternative agriculture

- Opportunities (options) for UK to become important supplier of GM free commodities and produce
  - Possible conversion to organic farming without concern about 'contamination'
    - Possible over-supply of organic products
  - Government forced to re-direct funds to other agricultural options
  - Development of agriculture in a more sound direction – addresses causes not symptoms of problems
    - Farmers secure domestic key markets (less imports)

- Public sector research harmed by drain of industry funding
  - No impact on use of GM in basic science (contained use)
    - Damage to UK attitudes, Science/agriculture
    - Would it have a noticeable impact on agro-chemical industry
  - Shift of focus in terms of application of research
    - Governance of technological development becomes impossible
      - Impact of development on non-food crops
  - Biotech industry concentrate on genomics (marker assisted)
    - Opportunities for alternatives (e.g. genomics)

- No regulatory approval UK? EU
  - Decision will inevitably impact on Developing world trade and choice
    - US–EU relations on steel, farm subs, war, remove threat of WTO case
      - UK campaigns in 'DOHA' round to allow SPS/TBT agreement
        - WTO procedures broadened to allow more diversity
        - Rest of the world takes stock on GM regulation
        - EU fine/found to be unlawful

Agro/env

- More imports on non-GM food from countries with cheaper labour force
  - Damage to UK agriculture – more imported food
    - Fewer options for managing farmland biodiversity

Trade

- UK farmers unable to compete internationally
  - Potential benefit to environment/ biodiversity denied
    - Potential benefits lost – products – environment
  - Illegal/ unauthorised presence (of US-authorised GM)
    - Financial losses for farming/ food chain of removing the unauthorised GM presence
    - Public cost of monitoring imports
    - Difficulty in regulating due to attempts to get round restrictions

approaches exist that can be used to weight variables in this way (for example, Schlange and Juttner, 1997); however, there was not time within this workshop to do this.

In Chapters One and Two we noted the importance of accommodating a diversity of perspectives, the nature of this exercise allowed many voices to be heard rather than assuming that scientists speak with one voice. While some participants felt concerned over the open-ended character of the exercise, others commented that this was a strength of the exercise, as there is no clarity on many of the issues. Another participant remarked that future uncertain consequences must be taken into account by government policy and that the exercise throws up a host of issues people are concerned about and that the government has to take on board. Another commented that the diagrams may also be useful for identifying potential interventions and practices relevant to a participant's situation. Thus this final session provided an important opportunity for all participants to reflect on the process.

As researchers we also observed a number of aspects that had a bearing on the final scenarios maps produced and on scenario building processes more generally:

• *Participants tended to classify causes and consequences of scenarios according to themes*, for example, regulatory issues, market issues, social issues. This, in part, reflects the difficulties people can have in identifying causes and effects where it is difficult to say for certain that a cause will have a particular effect. The use of themes was helpful to participants in that it provided a convenient way to organise their ideas. However, in terms of one of the purposes of the exercise, which was to encourage creative thinking, it had the effect of restricting participants' attention to chains of causality within themes, rather than encouraging them to look for interactions across themes. Given more time it is possible that further cross links would have been explored.

• *Participants tended to offer causes and consequences that were informed by an idealised model of the situation*, or represented ideal situations in terms of institutional capacity to control or manage practices.

• *Some consequences were viewed as more certain to occur than others*, leading some participants to ask if consequences should be weighted according to their certainty. In other cases participants were unsure which of two contrasting possibilities might occur, for example, more, or less intensive agricultural; more, or less sustainable practices. Although the combined expertise of the participants was considerable, many consequences lay beyond consensual predictions and some elements of the GM debate were striking by their absence from the maps. The under-representation at the workshop of certain types of expertise is likely to have limited the diversity of ideas represented in the maps.

- *Participants often identified contradictory chains of causes and consequences.* This probably reflects uncertainties associated with GM crops. One advantage of scenario mapping is that it enables contrasting understandings or predictions to be represented alongside another within the same map. Many of the chains of consequences also reflected the personal individual expertise or interests within the group. For example, Scenario 3 had a chain relating to investment in the UK science base which half-jokingly ended with the consequence 'I still have a job'.

- *The process highlighted where people agreed and disagreed.* Differences of opinion were generally accommodated through the generation of a new line of causes or consequences on the scenario map. However, much commonality of issues was also highlighted. There was, however, a tendency for participants to become stuck in arguments over the consequences of a particular scenario. Also, in some cases the process of scenario building was slowed down by participants attempting to correct the 'misconceptions' of another group member. Some members of the groups were more dominant than others and there were cases of participants attempting to police the ideas by removing sticky notes describing ideas that they considered to be inaccurate or untrue. This mirrors the way processes (or institutions) can become blind to possible/plausible causes or outcomes of decisions. It also emphasises the need for good workshop facilitation.

The scenario mapping exercise reveals a number of common issues concerning mapping techniques. It demonstrates the way that mapping can be useful in revealing what otherwise might remain implicit, for example what would count for success or failure. However, it also highlights a common problem with cause and effect diagrams in that they are not necessarily that easy for people to construct, particularly if there is uncertainty about the link between causes and effects. It also highlights the way that people tend to believe the map is of something real 'out there' rather than a device for thinking about/representing what people think about the scenario or issues surrounding it. The queries about accuracy of a map demonstrated this tendency by some participants and their tendency to think as if there is an objective truth that could be found to guide action.

Improving links between policy and research

Despite the limited amount of time available, the scenario exercise generated a space for communication and therefore potentially a space for learning. Our workshop was particularly timely, amid public debate on the need for a policy decision around GM crops and speculation about an EU moratorium. This relevance to participants helped in attracting high-level policy actors. However, as also noted in other chapters, there are no guarantees about who will participate and this can lead to an incomplete picture with certain views being underrepresented or not represented at all. It is likely to help if there is something obvious that the participant may gain from the experience. For the policy actor participants our workshop provided an opportunity for contact with one another in a less formal setting than the office and enabled them to consider their own views in relation to others. As the workshop coincided with the period of the 'formal' public debate on GM in the UK, we were able to contribute to these activities. However, while this had many advantages, such as creating significant interest by policymakers in our research, it also meant that key stakeholders were in demand for many different events at the time of our workshop. As a result, some groups, particularly the NGOs and farmers, were not well represented and consumer groups were not represented at all.

As also noted by Lyall et al (2004), research rarely provides definitive solutions for decision makers. What the workshop did provide was policy relevant insights into decision making for GM crops that may be used to inform policy discussions as well as our research. However, as Lyall et al (2004) also note, research where the users of the research are not passive recipients is difficult to evaluate. Reflection therefore plays an important role. The final discussions, reflections on the day provided by one of the participants, feedback on the day and on the workshop report, all contributed to a reflective process – not just by the researchers but also the participants. Yet, while informal feedback from participants suggested that most enjoyed the experience and welcomed the opportunity to come together to discuss issues of common concern, only a few people found time to comment in detail on the final workshop report.

Like other authors in this book, it has been our desire to use mapping techniques to 'ground' our research to ensure it is relevant to those who may wish to use it and also to involve participants in our research in a more participatory way. In the following sections we reflect on our experience of researching with people in a European Commission funded project – 'Cooperative Research on Environmental Problems in Europe' (CREPE). Going beyond participation or collaboration in the general sense, research cooperation has been given specific meanings, especially for critical perspectives on knowledge production and orientations. This project stems from a concept paper sponsored by DG Research, where 'cooperative research' was defined as 'a form of research process which involves both researchers and non-researchers in close cooperative engagement' (Stirling, 2006: 9). It requires 'constant attention to transdisciplinary engagement with stakeholders and public constituencies in order to explore the driving aims and purposes, the alternative orientations, and the wider social and environmental implications of research and innovation' (Stirling, 2006: 32).

While mapping was not a central feature, the CREPE project is included here because it demonstrates the direction in which our research has moved. It provides both a novel and practical example of how non-academics, in this case civil society organisations (CSOs), and academic researchers can work together as more equal partners to find policy solutions to environmental sustainability issues and raises several issues of general concern for participatory research processes.

Partners rather than participants

Researching with people, even if it is action-oriented research (see Chapter One), generally only has funding for the academics involved. In CREPE, the unusual funding arrangement, whereby all project partners (academic and CSO) received equal funding, meant that rather than the academic partners providing a space for research, we worked together – CSO researchers and academic researchers – to devise the project, develop the processes and find ways of working together. The project management involved the whole team and reflection on our processes, by all partners as we went along, was a key part of what we did (Oreszczyn et al, 2010).

The CREPE project was funded by the European Commission over three years and involved researching different policy options for European agricultural futures. The thematic focus of the project was sustainable development, especially environmental issues arising from agricultural practices and innovations. As an ambiguous concept, 'sustainable development' provided an entry point for the diversity of perspectives on societal futures. CREPE was designed to question dominant agendas and to open up alternative pathways for sustainable development (Levidow and Oreszczyn, 2012). A taxonomy of three approaches to sustainable development was developed as a common framework, a device for enabling us to work together as researcher partners and provide a common approach to analysis. Partners had the freedom to develop their own techniques for their individual studies, suitable to their particular contexts, while the common analytical framework provided coherence to the project as a whole.

Within CREPE there was a wide variety of activity over the three year period (from 2008 to 2010), with different levels of engagement, varying research topics and various levels of expertise and experience of doing cooperative-type research. For each of the project partners, their own studies extended and linked their stakeholder networks, for example, among other CSOs and local organisations, enabling them to be better equipped to participate in policymaking for sustainable futures. The partnerships within CREPE meant that all project partners, both academic and non-academic, could play the role of change agents.[9]

We also related co-production of knowledge to communities of practice (Lave and Wenger, 1991; Wenger et al, 2002). As the CREPE project developed, networks of practice emerged as useful for thinking about the complex processes and interactions among the distributed members of the project team and their distributed networks (Hinchliffe et al, 2014). These theoretical concepts are explained further in Chapters Four and Seven.

Project processes

CREPE had a particular way of working because of the nature of the more equal partnership of project participants. To begin, the project coordinator approached a wide range of CSOs on diverse topics. The CSOs that were strong candidates already had some experience in research on agri-environmental issues. Six CSOs were chosen as partners for the project. Each work plan for the research proposal was then developed through discussions between the CSO and the coordinator. A further unique aspect of CREPE was that one work package was devoted solely to analysing the cooperative research process within the whole project (see Oreszczyn et al, 2010). This relied on the project having processes to enable constant reflection. The cooperative processes within CREPE were complex and operated both at the level of the overall project, where partners worked together to deliver the CREPE project, and at the level of the individual studies that each partner implemented. Individual and collective reflection were therefore important. Different methods of reflection were used appropriate to the processes in the different partners' projects.

The academic coordinators of CREPE initiated and led on the development of the cooperative research processes and were on hand to assist with the variety of methods used. They provided guidance to partners on appropriate literature that may inform their cooperative practices; and facilitated discussion and reflection on cooperative processes. Each partner recorded their cooperative practices in order to share with the project team and contributed to an evolving and practice based understanding of these processes. Feedback sessions at the end of project meetings enabled partners to reflect on the meeting process and the outcomes, and all partners were expected to comment on draft reports of other partners' studies at project meetings. An advisory group also helped to inform and reflect during the research process.

Three key reflective methods were used:

1. *Diaries:* Within the individual partner's studies reflection on the cooperative processes involved all partners keeping a 'cooperative research diary' detailing the ways in which cooperative research aspects of the individual projects were being handled and practised. Entries to the diaries detailed who they cooperated with, how they developed their cooperative research and what worked well and what worked less well. Partners were encouraged to record descriptive accounts, recording activities, conversations, difficulties, tensions, excitement and so on.

2. *Interactive workshops:* Workshop activities were an important part of CREPE enabling partners to engage with each other and their networks face-to-face. They were a common element used in partner meetings and across the project. Workshops varied in their format and methods, some involved mapping, for example the Force Field Analysis (Lewin, 1951) described in Chapter Six and depicted in Figure 6.3, while others did not. Methods were chosen according to the partners' studies aims. Each CSO held a stakeholder workshop with members of their networks and beyond. In this way the project drew in a wide and diverse group of people helping to broaden the CSOs and researcher networks. Some workshops also involved experts with experience in the topic under study as a means to gain

their advice or longer term involvement. The workshops were also designed to develop our cooperative research. So towards the end of the CREPE project, two project-wide workshops were held – one on the EU-level policy issues with senior policy makers in Europe, and the other on the cooperative research processes. Both encouraged wider comment by stakeholders on the findings of the project and helped to inform the final reports.[10]

3. *Critical moments' reflection:* Towards the end of the project an exercise was conducted whereby partners were asked to reflect back on their experience of participating. This exercise was adapted from Critical Moments Reflection Methodology (McDowell et al, 2005). CREPE partners were asked to reflect on what were the 'critical moments' for their study and the most important element (or elements) from their experience of working on CREPE. These could be moments of change when situations or feelings became better or worse, or turning points, either good or bad, such as: surprises; the emergence, or solution, of a difficult problem; the disturbance of a strongly held belief; change in a key component of the context of the research, and so on. In this reflection process partners were also asked to comment on the key lessons learned for their research, their organisation or for themselves personally; how what we had done together may be improved on; if they had suggestions for future efforts; or if they felt there were aspects of doing cooperative research that needed further investigation.

Reflecting on process and practice across all three projects

The merits or otherwise of the mapping techniques we used have been discussed in previous sections. What follows notes some of the issues raised by our experiences. Rather than simply reflections on our mapping methods, these reflections relate to the whole participatory process of which mapping was an essential part and particularly draws on analysis of the cooperative research processes within CREPE (Oreszczyn et al, 2010).

Early engagement of academic partners with non-academic partners was an important feature of the co-production of environmental knowledge, allowing them to be involved in shaping the initial design of the research. Early engagement becomes vital if those to be engaged with are to see the purpose of the research and therefore be willing to commit the time and energy required, particularly if they are not being paid. As an example, one of the CREPE partner studies did not involve a partner at the conceptual stage of their study. Consequently, this study experienced difficulties in finding CSOs interested in the topic, which was not recognised by the CSO as a major issue in generic terms. Whereas academics can readily see the importance of practitioner input into research, the practitioners may not be framing their issues in this way; in this case the CSO was more interested in specific issues relevant to their current campaigns.

Different identities, cultures and understandings cannot be ignored. Although a time consuming process for both academics and participants/partners, the processes and practices we used paid particular attention to relationship building and therefore to the way different cultures can create misunderstandings or conflicts. It was, however, noticeable in CREPE that the very different political-organisational cultures being brought together did not lead to disagreements – rather the opposite. The differences enabled partners to learn from one another. Something similar was found when building the scenario maps for the PEG project where, despite very different views, ways were found within the mapping process to accommodate all views equally. However, for partners to engage in co-production in projects with researchers and apply these in their own work, they need to be clear about what they are attempting to achieve together. In all the projects this involved an initial learning process that enabled mutual understanding about what they and we were each attempting to do, as a clearer basis for the joint activity – such as mapping. In CREPE this involved obtaining some initial common ground and mutual understanding in the early partners meetings using Force Field Analysis, mentioned earlier. Such interactive exercises at partners meetings helped with understanding the concept of cooperative research, how it relates to similar concepts and what research techniques to use and why. For the PEG project it involved early reporting back by the researchers to the policymakers on preliminary findings and detailed explanations of our use of techniques. In contrast, the lack of mutual understanding in some instances in the more conventional PITA project led to some company monographs (and cognitive maps) lacking primary data from interviews with key personnel.

Mutual learning was important in all the projects but took different forms. Within CREPE there was an emphasis on trying things out and then discussing with others, through our reflection processes, what worked, how it worked, what failed and what could be improved. In contrast, the less participatory and more researcher led nature of PEG and PITA relied more heavily on the mapping to play an important role in the learning process; for example, the mapping experiences helped participants to reflect on their own unique situation in light of others' experiences and to have a conversation about it.

Enabling spaces for relationship building and strengthening networks were important for learning to occur; spaces that allowed for both group learning and individual learning. Mapping facilitates such learning but works best as one of many learning spaces within a project. The projects in this chapter offered a diversity of learning spaces. Processes in CREPE facilitated a much greater degree of learning than the other projects. Both the PITA and PEG projects involved methods to gain feedback from participants; however, PITA involved fewer learning spaces and so it was generally the researchers who learned. In PEG the workshop facilitated learning among the policymakers through the scenario building activity. In this case there was a degree of learning facilitated among the participants as well as the researchers. These aspects are reflected in Figure 1.1 in the introduction to the book.

Diversity of experience and expertise was important and mutually beneficial. In CREPE partners were able to offer one another both moral support and their particular expertise in both the processes and research areas. As noted by one participant, 'The opportunity to work with formal research helped us achieve a social and thus political recognition that could not have been reached without this support.' (CREPE Work Package 8). Working with academics meant that CSOs were able to produce research that not only enabled them to be taken more seriously but also to produce outputs with rigour – although not necessarily in the sense of a conventional academic definition of rigour. Thus, working with academics helps formalise the local or tacit knowledge of the non-academics. Further, participants with less experience of academic research can learn how research is done by academics by doing it with us. Participants were also able to benefit from, and be drawn directly into, the academic and policy networks of the researchers. In different ways, the PEG and CREPE projects went beyond the normal scope of academic research, seeking out inside knowledge that can have great relevance to policy issues. Working together enabled academic researchers and non-academics to make more explicit the existing relationships, networks and ways of operating. Making them more explicit helps participants to consider how best to utilise the potential.

Flexibility is a necessary aspect of this way of working. More participatory projects make substantial demands on people's time and effort; CREPE provides a good example of the general need for funding bodies and academic researchers to have a greater degree of flexibility than perhaps would normally be the case to accommodate the particular difficulties of working with non-academics and practitioners. Practitioner organisations and businesses are less stable organisations than academic institutions, so significant changes from the original plans are often required. Changes in staff within the organisation you are working with can also result in changes in expertise. All of the projects had to deal with events beyond their control. Further, practitioners are rarely working to the same timescales as academics and other demands on their time are often more pressing. While research is a central part of an academics' role, for practitioners it is often an additional practice and an unfamiliar one.

More equal stakes was a particular feature of the CREPE project and played a crucial role in its success. The joint stakes placed on partners in CREPE meant that they were on a more equal footing with the academics than is normally the case. This strengthened CSOs' capacity to participate in research activities, for example by enabling more staff time or new posts to be funded for such activities. However, it is important to note that the stakes do necessarily differ, for example, because the rewards can be less obvious for CSOs or other research participants than for academics. In contrast, the PITA and PEG projects had to rely on much goodwill from the participants for their success. Particularly in the case of PITA, the kind of evidence gathered and so results achieved were very much dependent on who agreed to take part.

Diversity is necessarily a feature of the research process and methods employed. This has implications for any standardised guidelines, assessment tools or precise management methods. A clear message from our experiences is that no one size fits all. This adds weight to the argument made by Huxham and Vangen (2005: 34) in their work on collaboration, that there is 'no simple prescription for best practice' and that this style of working requires the use of descriptive theory based on action-oriented research rather than formal assessment procedures. Further, there is not necessarily a strict, clear distinction between co-produced research and conventional research processes as both may be used within a particular study.

Final thoughts

The examples in this chapter highlight the way the co-production of environmental knowledge that mapping can facilitate has important roles beyond answering research questions. New relationships extend knowledge networks and promote learning among stakeholder groups, while also redefining the problems to be researched, thus opening up policy assumptions and societal futures. However, the three projects described here demonstrate how thought needs to be given to the way that different groups of people may need different approaches to involving them both in a research project and in a mapping process. While we have noted the trend in researching *with* people rather than *on* people and indeed our own desire to engage people more in our research, it is not necessarily appropriate or desirable to fully engage participants in what you are doing. Time constraints in particular can limit the type and extent of mapping approach used and breadth of expertise in contributions. New researchers frequently comment that they feel concerned about how they will get their participants and whether they will be turned down. And as Lyall et al (2015) note, there is also a high risk of 'engagement fatigue' when submitting proposals with stakeholders as the majority of research proposals do not get funded. Yet our experience suggests that most actually do not turn you down so long as they are interested in what you are doing and it feels relevant to them. So it does mean that it is important to try to involve people early on and to be clear about any unfamiliar mapping techniques you may want to use. It is also important not to underestimate the difficulties of doing this type of research. The participatory processes and mapping workshops we used in these projects require facilitation and communication skills that are not necessarily well developed among researchers in the normal course of their work.

Acknowledgements
The authors would like to thank the funders of the three research projects in this chapter, the European Commission, and all the research partners and other participants who contributed to all the projects' success.

Notes
[1] PITA was funded by the European Commission between 1998 and 2001 and involved partners in Denmark, France, Germany, Netherlands, Spain and the UK, see project website: https://web.archive.org/web/20071026070534/http://technology.open.ac.uk:80/cts/pita/

[2] Map 5 in the Monsanto Monograph provides an example of one manager's thinking on sustainability. Company Monographs may be found at http://dpp.open.ac.uk/research/projects/policy-influences-technology-agriculture-chemicals-biotechnology-and-seeds-pita

[3] http://banxia.com

[4] PITA project documents may be found at https://web.archive.org/web/20071026070534/http://technology.open.ac.uk:80/cts/pita/.

[5] Precautionary Expertise for GM Crops (PEG) was funded under the European Community Research Programme: Quality of Life and Management of Living Resources Key Action 111-13: socio-economic studies of life sciences, Project QLRT-2001-00034. The workshop was designed to inform the UK part of this wider study. The PEG project analysed how current European practices compare with different accounts of the precautionary principle in seven EU member states. Similar workshops have been held with senior policy actors in each of the countries involved. The PEG project had research partners in Austria, Denmark, France, Germany, Spain, and the Netherlands. Project website: https://web.archive.org/web/20110911214048/http://technology.open.ac.uk/cts/peg/

[6] See http://www.ipcc.ch

[7] In this research we take a broad view of the term 'policy actors'; considering it to refer to all those engaged in contributing to the policymaking process.

[8] Subsequently, Scenario 2 went ahead. A single crop, a GM forage maize variety (Chardon LL), produced by Bayer CropsScience was considered safe and effective and given the go-ahead for commercialisation in principle. However, the company decided not to commercialise their already five-year-old crop.

[9] The eight project partners included the UK, Spain, Italy, France, Netherlands. For full details, see http://web.archive.org/web/20161021185449/http://crepeweb.net/

[10] The workshop reports may be found at the CREPE project website: http://web.archive.org/web/20161021185449/http://crepeweb.net/

References

Berkhout, F. and Hertin, J. (2002) 'Foresight Futures Scenarios: Developing and applying a participative strategic planning tool', *Greener Management International*, 37: 37–52.

Brown J.S. and Duguid P. (2001) 'Knowledge and Organization: A Social-Practice Perspective', *Organization Science,* 12 (2): 198–213.

Chataway, J. and Tait, J. (2000) *PITA: Monsanto Monograph*, Annex C11, Milton Keynes: The Open University, http://oro.open.ac.uk/49393/

Checkland, P. (1981) *Systems Thinking Systems Practice*, Chichester: Wiley.

Collins, H. (2010) *Tacit and Explicit Knowledge*, Chicago and London: The University of Chicago Press.

Eden, C, (1988) 'Cognitive Mapping', *European Journal of Operational Research*, 36: 1–13.

Eden, C. (1989) 'Using Cognitive Mapping for Strategic Options Development and Analysis (SODA)', in J. Rosenhead (ed), *Rational Analysis for a Problematic World*, Chichester: Wiley, pp 21–42.

Eden, C. and Ackerman, F. (1998) *Making Strategy: The Journey of Strategic Management,* London: Sage Publications.

Kelly, G.A. (1995) [1955] *The Psychology of Personal Constructs*, Norton: New York.

Hinchliffe, S., Levidow, L. and Oreszczyn, S. (2014) 'Engaging cooperative research', *Environment and Planning A*, 46: 2080–94.

Huff, A. (1990) *Mapping Strategic Thought*, London: Wiley.

Huff, A. and Jenkins, M. (eds) (2002) *Mapping Strategic Knowledge*, London: Sage Publications.

Huxham, C. and Vangen, S. (2005) *Managing to Collaborate: The theory and practice of collaborative advantage.* London: Routledge.

Lave, J. and Wenger, E. (1991) *Situated Learning: Legitimate peripheral learning*, Cambridge: Cambridge University Press.

Levidow, L. and Oreszczyn, S. (2012) 'Challenging unsustainable development through research cooperation', *Local Environment*, 17 (1): 35–56.

Lewin, K. (1951) *Field Theory in Social Science*, New York: Harper and Row.

Lyall, C., Bruce, A., Firn, J. and Tait, J. (2004) 'Assessing end-use relevance of public sector research organisations', *Research Policy,* 33: 73–87.

Lyall, C., Meagher, L. and Bruce, A. (2015) 'A rose by any other name? Transdisciplinarity in the context of UK research policy', *Futures,* 65: 150–62.

McDowell, C., Nagel, A., Williams, S.M. and Canepa, C. (2005) 'Building knowledge from the practice of local communities', *Knowledge Management for Development Journal*, 1 (3). http://journal.km4dev.org/index.php/km4dj/article/view/44.

Nutley, S. (2003) 'Bridging the policy/research divide: Reflections and lessons from the UK,' keynote conference paper for 'Facing the Future: engaging stakeholders and citizens in developing public policy', 23–24 April, National Institute of Governance, Canberra.

Oakley, A. (2001) *Evidence-informed Policy and Practice: Challenges for Social Science.* Manchester: Manchester Statistical Society.

Oreszczyn, S. (2003) *Precautionary Expertise for GM Crops (PEG): UK National Workshop Report*, Milton Keynes: The Open University, http://oro.open.ac.uk/48293/

Oreszczyn, S. (2004) *UK: Precaution as Process, PEG project UK National Report*, Milton Keynes: The Open University, http://oro.open.ac.uk/48292/

Oreszczyn, S. (2005) 'GM Crops in the United Kingdom: precaution as process', *Science and Public Policy*, 32 (4): 317–24.

Oreszczyn, S. and Carr, S. (2008) 'Improving the link between policy research and practice: Using a scenario workshop as a qualitative research tool in the case of genetically modified crops', *Qualitative Research*, 8 (4): 473–97.

Oreszczyn, S. with PITA Partners (2001) *PITA Project, Annex C2: Policy Influences on Technology for Agriculture*, Cognitive Maps of Company Monographs. Milton Keynes: The Open University.

Oreszczyn, S., Levidow, L. and Hinchliffe, S. (2010) *Cooperative research processes in CREPE, WP8 report of CREPE project*, Milton Keynes: The Open University, www.crepeweb.net

Polanyi, M. (2015) [1958] *Personal Knowledge: Towards a Post-Critical Philosophy*, London: Routledge.

Reed, M.S., Kenter, J., Bonn, A., Broad, K., Burt, T.P., Fazey, I.R., Fraser, E.D.G., Hubacek, K., Nainggolan, D., Quinn, C.H., Stringer, L.C. and Ravera, F. (2013) 'Participatory scenario development for environmental management: A methodological framework illustrated with experience from the UK uplands', *Journal of Environmental Management*, 128: 345–62.

Schlange, L.E. and Juttner, U. (1997) 'Helping managers to identify the key strategic issues', *Long Range Planning*, 30 (5): 777–86.

Solesbury, W. (2001) 'Evidence Based Policy: Whence it Came and Where it's Going'. Working Paper 1. Queen Mary University of London. London: ESRC UK Centre for Evidence Based Policy and Practice.

Stirling, A. (2006) *From science and society to science in society: Towards a framework for co-operative research*, Report of a European Commission workshop, 'GoverScience', 24–25 November 2005, http://eurosfaire.prd.fr/7pc/bibliotheque/consulter.php?id=308

Swan, J. (1997) 'Using cognitive Mapping in Management Research: Decisions about Technical Innovation', *British Journal of Management*, 8: 183–98.

Tait, J., Chataway, J. and Wield, D. (2001) *PITA Project: Policy Influences on Technology for Agriculture: Chemicals, Biotechnology and Seeds, PITA Final Report*, Programme European Commission-DG XII, Project No. PL 97/1280 Contract No. SOE1-CT97-1068, Milton Keynes: The Open University, http://technology.open.ac.uk/cts/pita

Wenger, E., McDermott, R. and Snyder, W.M. (2002) *Cultivating Communities of Practice*, Boston, MA: Harvard Business School Press.

FOUR

Mapping agri-environmental knowledge systems

Sue Oreszczyn and Andy Lane

Editors' introduction

In this chapter we (the editors) draw on our experiences over many years of investigating knowledge exchange processes across three research projects that mostly deal with agri-environmental knowledge systems with contentious issues for stakeholders (farmers, policymakers, researchers, businesses and NGOs) to explore, as was the case in Chapter Three. The first project discussed considers UK farmers' understandings of new technologies and the influencers on them. We then took this work forward into subsequent projects that analysed complex knowledge flows in a number of different contexts – agriculture, health, food, international development and hedgerow management systems. We reflect upon how our use of diagramming and our relationships with participants in our research methods evolved through the three phases of the first project and into the subsequent projects, as is also the case in Chapters Five and Eight. We discuss not only how we drew on tried and tested mapping techniques – cognitive maps and Harman Fans – but also the mapping techniques we devised specifically for the projects. As well as drawing on theories about participatory approaches to research as described in Chapters One and Two, the projects also particularly drew on theories about communities of practice, explained further in Chapter Seven.

Introduction

As discussed in Chapter One, it is important to not only find out about different people's perspectives when considering solutions to issues concerning environmental sustainability, but also bring together different types of knowledge. However, more than that, it is important to consider how, or indeed whether, knowledge is exchanged between people and then acted upon. The majority of this chapter discusses an Economic and Social Research Council (ESRC) funded project that used an increasingly more interactive approach, and mapping techniques, to research with farmers. We were interested in not simply their understandings of genetically modified (GM) crops and new technologies more generally, but also how these understandings came about. That is, who influenced their decision making process, in what way and how knowledge exchange might be improved. We discuss the mapping techniques we used and devised. We then consider two subsequent projects that worked with conference participants (academics and practitioners) to look further at knowledge flows and which developed mapping methods for capturing knowledge exchange. We conclude with our thoughts on key issues for using mapping successfully when researching similar topics and in particular the responses of participants to the mapping.

Researching *with* farmers and their networks

The context for much of our joint research over 20 years has been farmers and farming systems in the UK. As owners and land managers farmers are vital to both providing a sustainable environment and sustainable food supplies. While as a necessity farmers farm for profit, they also view themselves as custodians of the land and today many have become very conscious of their impact on, or contribution to, environmental sustainability. A key driver for improvements in farmers' environmental awareness in the UK has been the need for the protection of important wildlife and their habitats from intensive farming methods. Increasingly, there are additional concerns around global climate change and the potential impacts on future food security. New innovations, for instance new farming practices or the use of new technologies – such as GM crops – are viewed by many as a way of meeting these environmental challenges. However, it is only recently that researchers have been interested in researching these developments from the farmer's perspective. To see how they are making their decisions, what or who is influencing their decisions about adopting new innovations, and how best to help them (Klerkx and Proctor, 2013; Oreszczyn et al, 2010, 2012a).

All too often innovations have been provided for farmers by others without sufficient regard for the farmers' own practices and contexts. This is in contrast to innovations and practices being developed *with* farmers, using their experiential knowledge to shape those innovations and practices both before and after adoption and implementation. The differing perspectives of the many actors, and in particular the perspectives of farmers versus other actors, leads farmers to use knowledge management practices that mix and match information from a variety of trusted sources to suit the needs of their farming business. If external knowledge and innovations are to support the scientific input to sustainable intensification of agriculture (Royal Society, 2009) then they must also be matched with an understanding of the practices and contexts in which they are to be deployed.

With this in mind, in our research with farmers over many years, we have been keen to ensure that our findings are grounded in the actual practices of the people involved, thus making the findings more relevant to those participating in the study and policymakers who may use the research findings. We have sought to find ways of involving farmers as more active participants in the research. Our desire has been to research *with* farmers and their wider networks as key stakeholders in the situations we are studying, rather than *on* them as objects of study, and to do so from the outset of the research process wherever possible. We have drawn heavily on ideas from participatory and action-oriented, research (see for example, Chevalier and Buckles, 2013; Hemant et al, 2013) and grounded theory (Charmaz, 2014; Glaser, 1994) to inform our modes of data gathering and analysis. These approaches fit well with our broader use of systems approaches in our scholarship. What follows describes particular projects as examples of how we have attempted to put some of our thinking about research into practice as well as describing the mapping techniques involved.

Farmer understandings, communities and networks of practice

'Farmers' understandings of GM crops within local communities' was conducted over three years between 2004 and 2007. The project was concerned with obtaining a more complete picture of the introduction of a new and contested technology in the UK, GM crops, and focused on farmers' understandings in the context of new technologies more generally, and of farmers' networks. The research aimed to get away from polarised arguments for or against GM crops (see Defra, 2003; Pidgeon et al, 2005) by focusing on the context of decisions about employing new technologies by those who will potentially use them first-hand: non-organic, larger scale commodity crop growers. Three successive phases of the project over three years used an increasingly participatory, relationship building approach with participants to ensure that our findings were relevant to users. We wanted to understand through these three phases first their experiences of these crops, second who and what their main influences were, and third what were the wider issues and influences involved. Each of the three, increasingly more participatory phases involved the use of interactive mapping techniques to capture and represent the main findings in a holistic manner for feeding back and forwards to the various participants (see Oreszczyn, 2005a, 2005b, 2005c).

While our research drew on systems thinking, and the ideas discussed earlier, we also drew on theories about situated learning (Lave and Wenger, 1991) and communities of practice (Wenger, 2000, 1998; Wenger-Trayner and Wenger-Trayner, 2015). Communities of practice are groups of people who share a common pursuit, activity or concern. Although all members do not necessarily work together, they form a common identity and understanding through their common interests and interactions. Over time, they accumulate knowledge, tools and informal ties as they learn together. Chapter Seven discusses these ideas in more detail.

As a broader concept, and so perhaps more relevant to the distributed nature of the farmers in our project, we also drew on ideas from theories about networks of practice (Brown and Duguid, 2000; Teigland, 2003). These recognise that similar practices may be shared by individuals, within and outside an organisation. Social proximity depends on much more than simply geographical location per se. Networks of practice have the same features as communities of practice (their subset) but may have weaker ties. What binds the network together is shared or common practice which lead to shared know-how (Brown and Duguid, 1991, 2001; Hustad, 2010). Such networks of practice can particularly be built by shared problem solving (Wenger et al, 2002). Members of a network of practice may never meet or know each other, yet they share a common culture and activities; they are capable of sharing knowledge and social identity. As the farmers' understandings of GM crops project evolved, 'networks of practice' and particularly the extended concept of 'web of influencers on practice' (see Oreszczyn et al, 2010) became useful concepts for analysing the distributed nature of farming businesses, their support businesses and other practitioner groups. Together, farmers' networks of practice and their web of influencers represent the whole environment in which learning may occur, and so provide insights into their social learning system.

Building trust

At the time of the research, much of the debate surrounding the science and technology of genetically modified organisms had focused

78

on the policies and practices of national governments and international organisations or on the acceptability of GM products with consumers. Little work had been done at the local level, particularly with respect to farmers, who would be the primary users of GM crop technology. For the Farmers' Understandings project, we felt it important that our research should therefore be grounded in farmers' actual experiences and everyday practice. Building trust, in ourselves and the research process, with our research participants was thus a priority for the project and was especially important because of the nature of the running controversy over GM crops.

Overall, we tried to treat the participants as valued partners in the process and not simply as research subjects. As with the projects described in Chapter Three, it was also considered important to engage with potential users of the research from the policymaking arena from the outset and for the duration of the project to ensure that our research was both relevant and trusted. A representative from the National Farmers Union (NFU) administration, the secretary of the Supply Chain Initiative on Modified Agricultural Crops (SCIMAC) and a farmer board member of the NFU agreed to contribute to the project in an advisory capacity. They met with us on a regular basis, helped with implementing the design of the project, which required the support of a very particular group of farmers who had been involved in UK farm scale trials of GM crops, and also commented on the project outputs.

Interviews and cognitive mapping: Phase 1

As we wished to interview farmers with experience of growing GM crops, the project focused on non-organic, larger scale, commodity crop farming, although the farmers interviewed were varied in terms of what they grew and their farming approach. The initial group of farmers were chosen because they had been involved in the Farm Scale Evaluations (FSEs) for GM herbicide tolerant crops (see Defra, 2007). A second group of farmers was then selected who were situated locally to these farmers, but who had not been involved in the FSEs. Groups of farmers were selected from the east and west sides of the country to see if there were any significant regional differences, although the precise locations were dependent on the location of the FSEs. Essential to this process was the involvement of our project advisors who provided us with the local contacts who could help us with getting the farmers' permission to contact them. It is important to note here that it was farmers' understandings of new innovations that we were particularly interested in, and how they came to those understandings through their influences and networks. This was therefore a particular group of farmers – commodity crop farmers, that is those most likely to take up a new innovation such as GM crops. Also, we were limited by the number of farmers who had been engaged in the FSEs and by the number who would agree to participate in our research, which was on a sensitive subject. However, as we were concerned with in-depth understandings and relationship building over time, smaller numbers were appropriate to what we wanted to do.

Semi-structured telephone interviews were carried out with 30 farmers who had agreed to participate at this stage of our research (see Oreszczyn, 2005a). These interviews were important as the first point of contact for involving the farmers in later stages of the project. They provided an opportunity to start to build up trust in both ourselves and our approach to the research. At this stage we particularly emphasised the way we were concerned about seeing things from their point of view and helping to facilitate them putting their view forward in a more formal way.

Analysing the interviews thematically, we found that these farmers were weighing up the pros and cons of GM crops and considering how they would fit into their farming business as a whole, in exactly the same way as they would weigh up any new technology. In this respect GM crops were considered no differently from a new conventional crop. However, in reality individuals' views are not made up of isolated themes but connected lines of thought. Cognitive maps of individuals' views were therefore drawn up from the interview data – in a similar manner to those described previously in Chapter Three – and subsequently shown to them for validation (see Figure 4.1). These maps captured the connections and linkages in an individual farmer's thinking, thus drawing together all the separate threads outlined in the themes. In this way views on particular issues could be placed in their context. As in Chapter Three, key issues, aims or goals appeared at the top of the maps, and below mapped the thinking behind those aims or goals.

The interviews and associated maps depicted the farmers' stories. Being able to compete in world markets was a key issue, demonstrated by the way that it was placed at the top of all their cognitive maps. New technologies were viewed as important for 'moving forward' and any new crops were considered a particularly advantageous step at a time when there are few new major agricultural breakthroughs. These maps of individual views were then used in the second stage of the project, with a smaller group of farmers, to consider in more depth some of the issues the interviewed farmers had raised.

Figure 4.1: Example cognitive map of a farmer's view

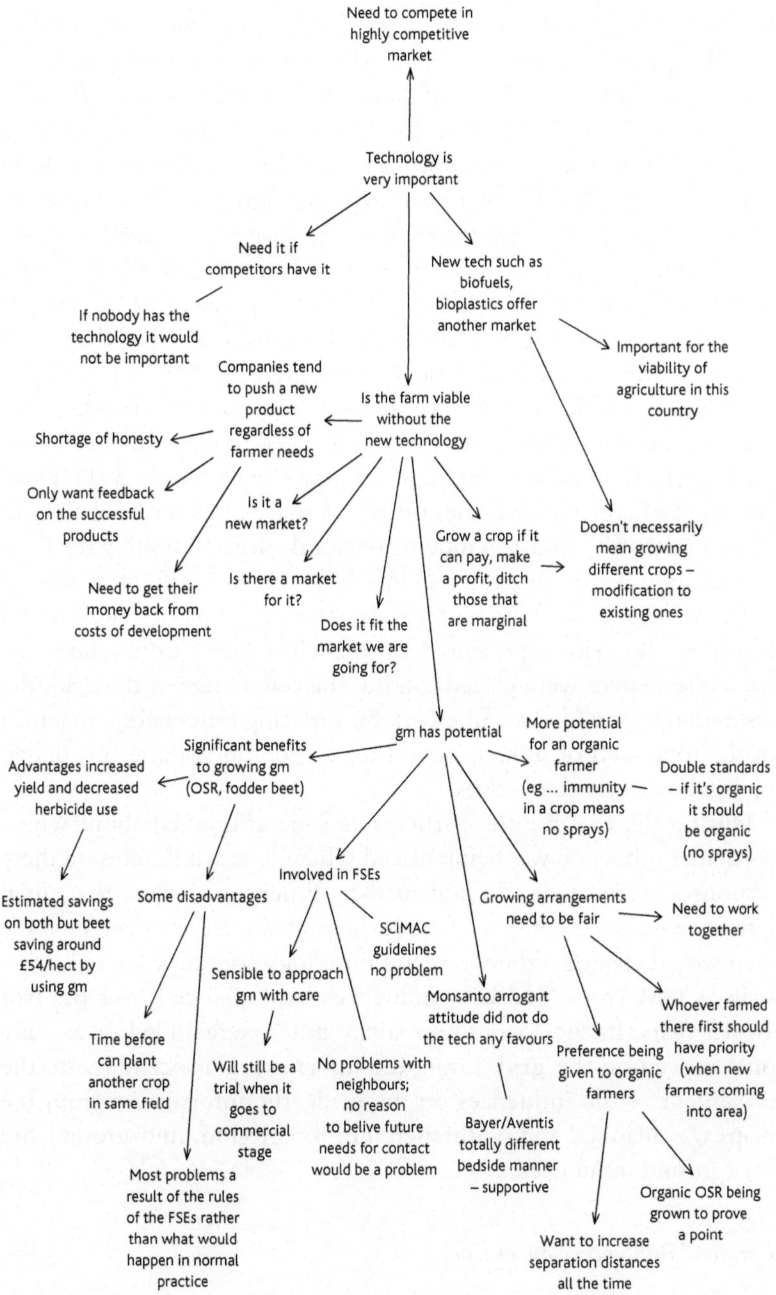

Source: Oreszczyn (2005a)

Mapping networks of influencers: Phase 2

Following the telephone interviews, 20 farmers who had said they were happy to be involved further in the research, were selected from three regions of the country. Of these we were able to visit 17 farmers, 11 of which were involved in the FSEs. Six of these visits involved interviews with the farmer and someone else connected with farm decisions, for example, their farm manager, agronomist or a relative.

At the start of each interview the cognitive map drawn from the initial telephone interviews in Phase 1 was discussed with the farmer and any corrections or additions to the maps were made. In this way we created a more accurate representation of what they were saying. In this phase we particularly wanted to know more about the farmer's influencers. So we devised, and piloted, an interactive mapping exercise whereby farmers were asked to place the influences on their decision making on a circular grid – see Figure 4.2. This grid consisted of concentric circles on an A1 sheet of paper labelled with an arbitrary scale from 1–6 moving outwards, with 'Running the farm as a business/Farm decision making' at the centre. Influences viewed as having a larger impact on farm decisions were placed close to the centre of the grid (represented by a labelled sticky note) and those having less effect were placed towards the outer edge of the grid (the scale merely provided a framework for ordering influences). So a map of the total web of influencers on their decision making was drawn up by the farmer themselves.

During the exercise the participants were also asked about why a particular influence was being placed where it was and notes on these responses were made. To add further dimensions, once the initial influence map was completed the participants were then asked how the map would change if they were just thinking about new technologies, such as GM crops, and how influences have changed over the past 10–15 years. In these cases new sticky notes were added or existing ones moved on the grid. Using the information associated with the placement of the influences on the grids, the information from the maps was analysed and synthesised into foreground, mid-ground and background influences.

Farmers' influencers on practice

We found that although farming is a more geographically-isolated occupation than many other occupations, farmers regularly interacted with a wide number of individuals and organisations in their web of

Figure 4.2: Example influence map constructed by one of the farmers involved in the farm scale evaluations for GM crops

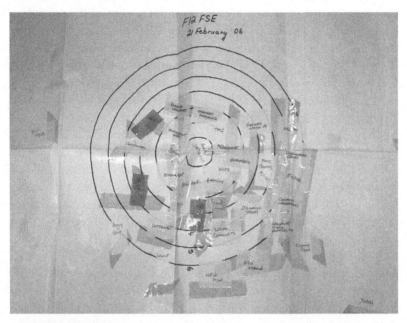

Source: Oreszczyn (2005b)

influencers. This strong web of influencers gave farmers access to a rich knowledge and information environment. They had common concerns and showed a remarkably similar set of views. The maps provided a visual representation of just how many other people and organisations who are not farmers contribute to their learning and knowledge management. The mapping exercise also highlighted how it was often key individuals in organisations that had the most influence rather than the organisation itself. From the material gathered in this phase a second report was produced and sent to the participants for comment before being more widely distributed, although as with the previous report from Phase 1, few comments were received. A further meeting was held with our advisors to discuss the findings from the second phase of the project and to seek advice on a workshop planned for Phase 3.

Mapping the future: Phase 3

Phase 3 of the project also used mapping to explore better ways to support farmers' decisions by exploring with farmers and their influencers where practices or policy may need to change and in what ways. This phase drew on the findings from the other phases of the project to inform a workshop that brought together farmers and key members of their web of influencers. The aim of the workshop was to bring together farmers and other decision makers to explore thinking within groups that may bring out issues that interviews with individuals miss, but that may be important for understanding current and future farm decision making. We considered it important that this exercise should not be regarded as a process that was only of benefit to the researchers. For participants we hoped the workshop would offer an opportunity to share understandings of potential futures for new technologies and scientific developments, including GM crops, and to have a direct input into a project designed to inform UK policymaking. It also offered them an opportunity to learn about our research findings so far, to ensure that it addressed their priorities or concerns, and to network with people with similar interests to their own.

To provide a structure to the workshop, we initially considered several methodologies. We needed a mechanism that would allow inclusive and open discussion of the key issues and ultimately represent and record the outcome of those discussions in a time-sequenced way. At the suggestion of our workshop facilitator, we decided that the Harman Fan method developed by Willis Harman and described in detail in his book *An Incomplete Guide to the Future* (Harman, 1979) provided an appropriate way to achieve these objectives. Like the cognitive mapping technique used in Phase 1, Harman Fans can be used to display complex topics in a relatively simple way and show connections and interactions between issues, rather than simply drawing out themes (see Figure 4.3). However, they also enable a temporal analysis of likely wide-scale future developments or scenarios. The method was designed to identify different future situations of a system, to organise these situations based on whether they were perceived to occur sooner or later and then identify possible pathways that might lead to a particular situation occurring.

A letter of invitation to the workshop was sent to 30 farmers from our original interviews and 30 members of key organisations in their networks or 'community of influence'. Of these it attracted 25 participants – 10 farmer participants and 15 non-farmer participants. As with the GM crops project in Chapter Three and discussed in Chapter Two, the workshop was managed by a professional facilitator and the workshop process adopted the Chatham House Rule – to encourage an open discussion. Following introductions, a talk on the project so far was given by one of the researchers. A background

Figure 4.3: Example of a Harman Fan compiled by the participants in the final workshop of the farmers' understandings of GM crops project

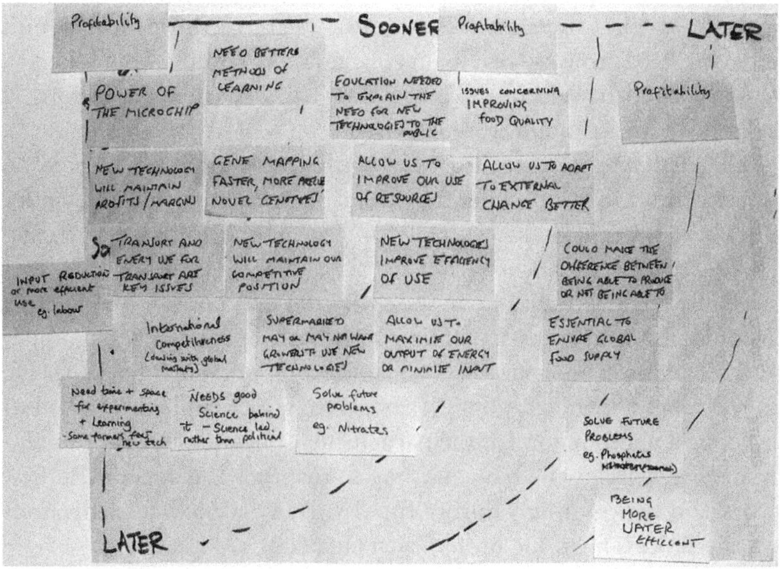

Source: Oreszczyn and Lane (2005c)

document summarising the project had been sent to the participants beforehand to entice them to attend. Two senior crop researchers then gave a presentation on technological innovations and scientific developments past, present and future. These talks set the scene for the group activities that followed, as well as acting as a way to attract participants to the workshop in the first place.

Using the Harman Fan

Following the introductory scene-setting presentations, the participants were split into four groups (labelled Tomatoes, Broccoli, Potatoes and Corn), according to the icons on their name badges that had been provided on arrival. In one group, the participants were all farmers, in a second group they were all non-farmers, and in the third and fourth groups farmers and non-farmers were mixed, to provide a rough check on whether or not the composition of the group affected the issues raised.

Participants in two of the four groups were asked to write on sticky notes their answers to the question 'New technology in agriculture: why is it important and what does it mean for the farmer?' Participants in these two groups were also asked to think about any wider aspects of new technologies. Participants in the other two groups were asked to write down on sticky notes their answers to the question 'GM crops: what are the issues around growing GM crops?' Participants in these two groups were asked to think particularly about the issues they had experienced personally and those they thought might exist.

All participants were provided with instructions and asked to discuss their question collectively and place their sticky notes onto flip chart paper on which a Harman Fan template for the question had been drawn. Participants were asked to agree whether the issues needed to be dealt with now, soon, or later and position the post–its accordingly (see Figure 4.3). The groups were encouraged to consider and discuss as many issues as possible for each question. At each stage in the process the fans and flip charts were photographed and used to produce a photo report for the participants. This was sent out to them immediately following the workshop so that they had a record of their work and that of others during the day. Box 4.1 provides reflections on the process from the professional facilitator we used.

Box 4.1: Facilitator thoughts...

Mark Yoxon (www.inform-global.com)

This was the second time that we had used the Harman Fan as an organising device for a facilitated workshop and we have continued to use the technique for other successful events. I think it is very effective because the fan itself provides clear and broad brush strokes which participants then populate to map future scenarios and possible pathways towards them. Without the fan my feeling is we could still have developed answers to the project's key questions and this might have left the project team the task of overlaying these responses with some kind of time referencing. This would probably mean that despite their best efforts, project team bias would inevitably be superimposed on delegate outputs.

Mapping using the Harman Fan meant that the delegates were involved in all stages of the process and the required workshop design criteria were met effectively. What the project team were left with at the end of the day was much more than mere building blocks to work with. Active engagement with the participants resulted in the emergence of an agreed skeletal structure for the next steps of the work. These critical raw materials represented participant wisdom and expertise and their own take on how the issues might roll out into the future. In this way I believe the aims and objectives of the workshop were met very effectively, with participant energy and enthusiasm throughout the event and stronger relationships for follow-up activities.

Future changes

Building on the outcomes of the other phases of the research, the workshop discussions and activities confirmed the findings from the two previous phases and also suggested a number of proposals for future changes in the farmers' web of influencers that might improve how new technologies and scientific developments are pursued and supported. The research identified a need for:

- An enabling environment that is responsive to farmers' needs, with clear, consistent and long-term policy signals about the future of agriculture, to allow farmers time to adapt to changing demands.
- Improved connections between farmers and consumers.
- Greater awareness among policymakers, regulators, scientists and the supermarkets of what farmers can and cannot do.
- Independent, trustworthy, sources of research and advice for farmers.
- The valuing of farmers' informal and experiential learning, for example in the shaping of agricultural research.

The findings from the workshop also suggested ways to improve the systems of support available to farmers in their decisions about new technologies: horizon-scanning on behalf of farmers to synthesise information, look at the potential of new technologies, and develop clear long-term directions for agriculture; better co-ordinated and more widespread initiatives for marketing and promoting new technologies used in agriculture; government-sponsored intermediaries qualified in and knowledgeable about agriculture to improve the links between government policies, scientific research and the grassroots.

These findings were presented in a full report on the workshop that was drafted and sent to the participants asking for their comments and, importantly, space within the report was deliberately left free for their additional contributions (Oreszczyn, 2005c).

Taking forward what we learned

As we have just seen, our research identified the way that key people, rather than organisations, played an important role in farmers' networks of practice. These key influencers were able to span the boundaries between the farming network of practice and other communities or networks of practice in farmers' web of influencers. We found that the exchange of knowledge across the boundaries between policy, research and practice in the farming context tends to be one way. For example, farming guidance and farming research reports tend not to be discussion documents, rather, they focus on recommendations or policy options. This leaves no room for dialogue. Ideally knowledge should flow in both directions, so also flowing between farming practice at the ground level and government policy and research, rather than simply experts gathering knowledge and transmitting that information. Another point to highlight here is that policy briefings and research reports are also largely non-visual and the information contained in them inevitably hides much of the complexity around the issues raised in the research.

One of the developments while we have been undertaking this type of research with farmers has been the growing interest in knowledge brokerage and knowledge exchange practices. The concern is that large bodies of knowledge are generated for policy use, or to improve practices in agricultural and environmental management, yet this knowledge is not always deemed useful, appropriately communicated or being used by the 'right' people. Equally, changes in organisational structures and responsibilities can lead to fragmentation of effort in knowledge creation and exchange across a large number of people (Klerkx and Proctor, 2013) and/or create complex knowledge management challenges for key advisors. Thus, we saw a need for a better understanding of existing knowledge actors and their connections to enable improvements in knowledge flows. In the following parts of this chapter we reflect on two workshops, with different groups of stakeholders and settings, that sought to consider these issues further. They are also workshops that we managed to get accepted into the programmes of existing conferences involving relevant practitioners, through discussions with the conference organisers. They were not part of a large funded project so this meant that we did not need to set up special events and work out who to invite.

Mapping health, food and international development knowledge flows

The first workshop was designed to address the question: How context dependent are models for brokering? For example, are the models the same for food systems or agriculture as for health? The workshop was held at a conference in December 2010 called Bridging the Gap between Research Policy and Practice: The importance of intermediaries (knowledge brokers) in producing research impact. We mapped the complex interactions among knowledge brokers in three different contexts – health, food and international development using a mapping template we had devised. Our method was designed to capture and map out the thinking of participants and identify which people and what types of knowledge are involved in brokering and the nature of the exchange between those involved (see Oreszczyn and Lane, 2012c).

The workshop lasted for an hour and included nine participants from the larger event, plus ourselves. Following a short presentation on the aims of the workshop (to capture knowledge exchange in particular contexts by mapping who is involved and the knowledge exchanges that take place) an example map from our own context – agriculture – was provided in a PowerPoint slide. Participants were then divided into small groups with similar interests and provided with sheets of A3 paper with blank boxes arranged for them to collectively fill in with the knowledge users, the knowledge brokers and the knowledge creators in their particular context. These basic components of a map were then used to produce models of knowledge brokering/exchange systems, from their experiences, for group discussion (see Figure 4.4).

The maps served as a mediating agent to capture some of what was being discussed in a structured way. Each group decided what the context they were discussing would be and one participant (or two participants if their context were the same) from each group led the discussion by identifying the key institutions/people in their contexts. Then, in discussion with others in their group, the participants added arrows to map direction, nature and strength of knowledge exchanges. One person from each group presented their map, and thinking behind it, for discussion with the rest of the participants to enable contrasts and similarities to be drawn out. Four broad contexts were discussed in the workshop – agriculture, food security, the health service and international development.

Figure 4.4: Example of a knowledge flow diagram drawn by participants of the conference on hedgerow futures

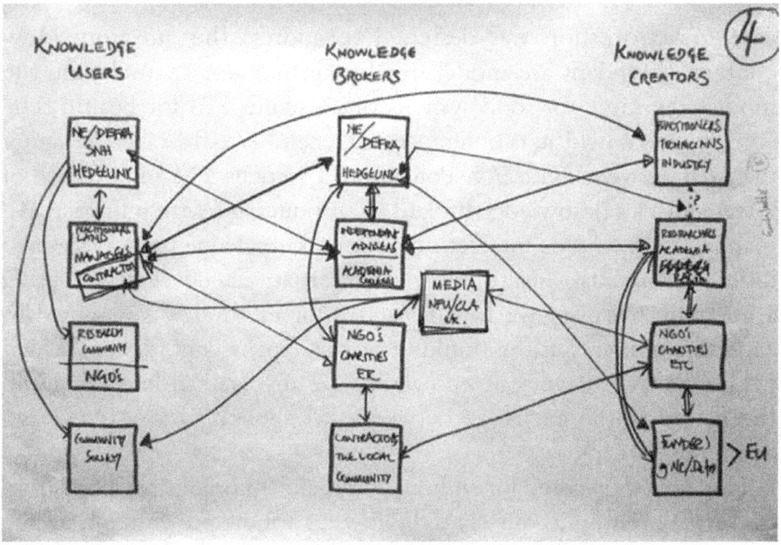

Source: Oreszczyn and Lane (2012b)

Issues raised by the mapping

The mapping exercise was constrained by the short time available. We only managed to capture a broad sense of the issues involved and were unable to map all the links and capture all the relationships involved. Neither were we able to consider what participants meant by brokering or being an intermediary, knowledge, information and understanding, and neither was learning addressed. Despite these constraints, the maps highlighted the lack of a holistic, circular or joined up approach to knowledge flows and exchanges in the different contexts. They showed the way that intermediaries operate at different scales and levels and this may affect their ability to be effective and trusted individuals. Also that knowledge brokering encompasses a variety of activities some of which may be competing. For example, the knowledge intermediaries in the workshop had very particular roles, in some cases, so many roles that it may limit their ability to be effective boundary spanners. Although the maps oversimplified what are complex interactions, they also demonstrated the tendency for knowledge flows to operate one way – from 'professional' creators 'at a distance' to the 'local' users.

The workshop therefore had its limits and was just the beginning of a process to explore issues of context; a more substantive study was needed to both test out the robustness of the mapping techniques and tease out some of the issues the workshop raised about knowledge flows and obtain a fuller analysis. This workshop design and experience with the mapping template was then used to inform a further workshop that aimed to capture and map the thinking of participants on the key components of a knowledge management system for farm hedgerows.

Mapping hedgerow knowledge flows

Our second example of mapping knowledge flows is through another conference workshop, held as part of a UK conference on Hedgerow Futures (Oreszczyn and Lane, 2012a). Hedgerows are a small component of the landscape and a small part of landscape and wildlife management, but a highly conspicuous one. They are different from other wildlife habitats, such as ponds, as they have legal protection and a strong sociocultural role as part of our rural landscape and heritage (see Oreszczyn and Lane, 2000). The workshop was designed to capture the thinking of conference participants on the management of hedgerows. In this case we had 37 participants which represented the majority of those attending this specialist conference. We used our bespoke mapping tool to get these participants to identify which people and what types of knowledge are involved in a knowledge management system for hedgerows in the UK. The mapping exercise offered an opportunity to capture some of the wider experience and thinking of the conference participants in a less formal but structured way. In contrast to policy briefings or research reports, it also offered a way to feed into policymaking more directly as some participants were also policymakers and the 'collective' results from those participants could also be used directly to inform their work.

The workshop process

Using a number of phases, participants were asked to map the various knowledge exchanges and the nature of the exchanges between those involved (see Oreszczyn and Lane, 2012b). First, using a blank template diagram, we asked participants to identify people or organisations that are currently seen as knowledge creators, brokers and/or users (some people or organisations may do more than one) for hedgerow management in the UK. Second, we invited the participants to identify the links and capture the relationships between these various 'actors' and explore the different forms of knowledge (in terms of both content and medium used). Third, we invited participants to indicate, in an ideal world, where there may be gaps in the system they had mapped out or where there needed to be changing knowledge practices on the part of some of the actors.

The workshop lasted for an hour and we divided the 37 conference participants into four groups of 8–10 people. The maps were designed to serve as a mediating agent to capture some of what was being discussed in a structured way. As the workshop was timetabled at the end of the first day we had assumed that only a relatively small number of the conference participants would wish to participate and there would be only two groups, thus enabling us to sit with them to fully listen to and document their conversations as they created the maps. In the event most of the conference wanted to participate so we had to forgo collecting the fine detail of conversations in favour of obtaining more maps, although we did move separately from group to group to check their progress and answer queries.

Following a short presentation on the aims of the workshop (to capture knowledge exchange taking place in hedgerow management systems), participants were divided into the four groups. Each group 'elected' a scribe who often led the discussion as well as writing down the thinking of the group on the sheets of A2 paper. As indicated above, first, each group identified the key institutions/people from their perspective. Then, in discussion with others in their group, added arrows to map direction, nature and strength of knowledge flows. The groups were also asked to consider what key aspects should change when considering the situation at present. At the end of the session the work of each group was briefly outlined by the authors of this report in a presentation to the rest of the participants, along with the group's leaders providing explanations of their map.

Knowledge flows and exchanges

The maps reflected the different group's discussions with the patterns shown in each of the maps drawn, highlighting key issues that were raised by the groups. Although there were many similarities in the maps, the emphasis on different participants in the knowledge exchange network in each map varied, reflecting the different interests and experiences of the participants at the conference, which included policymakers, researchers and practitioners. Taken together, the maps, and associated discussion points, provide an overall picture of the actors and knowledge flows in the current hedgerow management system as seen by many of those actively involved in it.

The maps depicted the complexity of the knowledge exchanges within the hedgerow management system. The multiple connections, the variety of roles that some organisations have (for example as user, broker and creator), the large number of people or organisations involved, how dispersed and distributed it is. The group that were able to go the farthest with the activity, and place the types of interaction on their map, also indicated the importance of the type of knowledge exchange and how it differed. As we had found with our previous projects, the weight of the flow of knowledge was from knowledge creators to knowledge users, with most passing through brokers or intermediaries. Where the knowledge did flow back in the other direction, the need was expressed for such links to be improved and strengthened. Importantly, practitioners and brokers exchanged knowledge more on a face to face basis, while more formal, written knowledge flowed between creators and brokers.

While no clear way forward transpired from this short activity, a number of important implications for policy emerged. A number of participants reflected on the way the current situation was far more complex and fragmented than in the past, with users unclear where to go for the knowledge they need – something our previous research had also noted (Oreszczyn et al, 2010). Neither was it clear if that knowledge was being guided by the needs of users. The lack of knowledge flow from users to creators implies it was not. Further, a number of organisations were perceived to have more than one role, which could have serious implications, as noted earlier in this chapter, as too many roles can limit an organisation's or person's ability to become useful intermediaries by diluting their effectiveness.

The maps captured and highlighted the variety of perceptions on who has a role to do what. This was important as such variety will have an effect on the knowledge flows within the hedgerow management system. It will result in differences in assumptions about who is responsible and different expectations about who should be doing something. Further, that people placed different things in different places on the maps could also indicate there is a lack of clarity over the different roles they should or could take, this is particularly likely to occur if roles are not made explicit, formalised and documented.

A number of changes were highlighted as ways to improve on how things are currently done. These included improvements in communication with people on the ground; a greater role for independent advisors; better use of the media, and so on, although we were unable in the time available to explore the detail of how these changes could be put into practice. While this activity focused on hedgerows, the maps also implied there is a need to improve links between farmers, researchers, policy actors and the public to foster or enable improvements in knowledge flows within farm management systems more generally.

Reflecting on the workshop

The interest shown by the participants at the conference for what we were attempting to do far exceeded our expectations. We were only given an hour's slot at the end of the day, and the limited time meant that participants were not able to fully complete their maps, yet we were able in that short time to capture important views and points for policymakers to consider. Conventional conference formats, where 'experts' make their presentations to others, serve to convey knowledge in a top down, uni-directional way, and are still the usual way of doing things. Providing an activity, such as this workshop, offers a way for people to engage with one another in a much more direct way and to learn from one another. It also allows some of the more informal, tacit knowledge gained through practice to become formalised and opened up for discussion.

However, the activity was more of an experiment than we had originally planned and we had not anticipated the overwhelming response our workshop would receive – particularly as it was at the end of a very full first day. While participants were able to benefit from exchanging their thinking, we as researchers were unable to capture all the richness of those conversations as participant observers. If we had been better prepared we could have had recording devices available for each group to use. So we had to rely much more on the diagrams themselves and the plenary presentations made by one or two members of each group. Participant feedback and comment on this workshop report was therefore particularly important.

Reflections on our projects

Much learning goes unrecognised and is not made apparent, particularly when tacit in nature. Mapping can formalise the tacit knowledge, enabling both formal and informal knowledge to be useful for solving an environmental problem or developing a new innovation. The mapping exercises set out in this chapter enabled participants to discuss their views in relation to others and draw out aspects that would not otherwise have been apparent. Implicit or informal relationships and knowledge flows became more obvious while the conversations around the mapping exercises enabled the researchers to ensure that they correctly and adequately portrayed people's thinking. Where each stage was able to inform the following stage of the research, the research could be led in a direction that was relevant to the participants' concerns.

Participants value an opportunity to be informed about the design and/or preliminary findings of the research at an early stage of the research. While not all wished to be more involved and work with each other and the researchers to make a contribution, those who did appreciated it. For example, many of the farmers noted how they appreciated the use of a more participatory methodology that sought the inclusion of their view, as users, into the broader societal conversations or to broaden the high-profile conversations, beyond for/against arguments about new technologies. They also valued the interactive, relationship building nature of the research approach. In particular, there were a number of complimentary comments and e-mails following the workshop. As one participant noted, "I found the subject and methodology of the day fascinating. I had never experienced that approach before and it was intriguing to see the thought processes that it puts you through" and "It (our workshop report) makes interesting reading and bits will be of particular interest to certain organisations within agriculture. I enjoyed taking part in the survey".

Importantly, while some participants may be initially hesitant as they are being asked to do something unfamiliar, once involved in the process they tend to enjoy it. Thus, not only does the interaction between people promote learning and knowledge exchange between participants, it does so in an entertaining way. The process also provides them with tools they can take away and use for themselves. However, it is important not to reify the diagramming technique itself or to give too much weight to the diagram produced as often its value, as in the farmer influence mapping, comes from being a mediating tool for structuring a conversation between participants as much as being useful qualitative research data that can be used for further analysis.

Limitations

It is clear that the number of people you are able to involve in these processes is limited by the number of researchers involved. Second, it generally does not support rapid data collection. Producing visual data, and bringing people together to do so, is very time consuming. Participants need to be primed beforehand with knowledge, not just about the research project but also the visual process you are asking them to undertake – which can be quite complicated and unfamiliar. Third, such visual mapping methods can be challenging to analyse as the complexity of the maps and diverse nature of the data makes it different to organise and to spot patterns and themes. Fourth, even with a short study, but certainly with long studies, the degree of relationship building that is needed is very time consuming to set up and to manage. As also noted by Eppler (2006), different mapping methods offer different benefits and constraints themselves, and so employing combinations of methods can play to the strengths of each one and have more impact than just using one, as was the case in the knowledge mapping studies.

Like most research reporting, we have tended to set out what we did as though it was a logical process and sequence of events that proceeded unhindered. However, as with the projects mentioned in other chapters, at various stages adjustments had to be made. For example, in our original proposal we had assumed that farmers would be affected by what their local communities thought and we had planned to carry out two small local workshops with farmers and members of their local community. However, early on in our research we found that the local public community has very little influence on farmers' decision making and thinking about new technologies. The project therefore limited its focus to the farmers' direct influencers from within the agricultural community, rather than attempting to draw in the wider public community.

We learned that it was important to recognise the competing demands on participants' time and try to work with them and to appreciate that different methods work for different people. Farmers, for example, like to be visited on their farms; this then made drawing them into a workshop easier as they came to understand the point in what they are being asked to do. With professional groups, attaching your activities to an existing event works well. Almost inevitably there will be some key people in demand for other events or with significant workloads that prevent their participation, and other ways need to be found to draw in their perspectives into the research.

Making an impact

Some direct evidence of impact from our research can be observed, for example, other researchers have picked up and used our model for their own research contexts (see for example Ingram et al, 2014) and the farmers project was described by a social science commentator at one event we spoke at as "an innovative contribution in an area that has been under researched up to now". Recently, reflecting back on the farmers' understandings project, Helen Ferrier, Chief Science and Regulatory Affairs Adviser for the NFU and one of our project advisors noted:

> 'Farmers and growers are an incredibly diverse group of individuals, with their farm businesses and farming systems varying considerably not only between sectors but also within. They overlay their personal views, interests and beliefs with the experiences, needs and perspectives they build up running their businesses, often with a long family history of living and working in farming communities. This makes it very challenging if not impossible to generalise and genuinely represent everyone, especially on a thorny subject such as GM crops. This was especially true in 2004 when the polarised and heated debates and sensationalist media coverage still coloured most discussion about GM. The voice of those farmers who actually had experience of growing GM crops in the UK was easily drowned out, and it was difficult for us to persuade commentators to talk more widely about the benefits of new agricultural technologies. Being involved in this project allowed us to get a greater insight into how our members' experiences and networks shaped their views. It also enabled us to highlight, through pointing to academic literature, the extremely important message that GM was not a special case in farmers' minds but would simply be another option they could choose from when making cropping decisions. This concept of choice for the farmer and also the fact that British farmers operate as part of a global supply chain for food and feed remains to this day a central part of NFU biotechnology policy.' (Helen Ferrier, 27 September 2016)

Generally, however, it is difficult to judge whether or not your research has made much, if any, difference. Often impacts take years to play out, particularly if they are around fundamental changes in the way people think. This makes things difficult in a climate where researchers are increasingly asked to demonstrate to research councils and other funders what the impact of their research will be or what it has been. Improving environmental sustainability requires people to learn, be innovative and often to think in different ways, which raises the question of how can we evidence this? There is also the assumption that impact is a positive thing yet there may well be negative impacts, particularly for contentious topics. When the ESRC, as funders of the Farmers' Understandings project, put out a press release on our project, it led to a series of challenges from anti-GM groups and campaigners that we had to deal with (Lane, 2008).

Reporting on our research not only involved the usual reporting mechanisms, such as project reports, but also policy briefings (see Oreszczyn et al, 2007). However, such briefings are necessarily short and do not portray the complexity of the issues involved. By involving policymakers in our research through our mapping exercises, we were able to alert them to some of this complexity. We were able to not only develop our (academic) knowledge further but also to facilitate or contribute to learning by others. The inclusion of maps in our reporting can also help to draw attention to our research processes as well as our research findings.

Of particular importance for policy and practice were the way the mapping exercises in this chapter drew attention to the different ways that participants can view knowledge exchanges. Also, the way that despite efforts to the contrary, in many cases knowledge flows remain essentially one way – from those who produce the knowledge to those who use it. For example, our research noted that there is little appropriate connection between both the scientific research occurring in the agricultural science community of practice, and in agricultural policy development, with the day to day agricultural practices and long-term plans of farmers (see Oreszczyn et al, 2007; Lane et al, 2007). Revealing the main obstacle is the predominant practice and culture of transmitting knowledge, that is experts produce the research findings; brokers explain it to those that 'need' it, rather than mutual sharing and/or co-creation. While our mapping approach does not overcome this practice, it does expose it, or show it to be largely lacking.

Acknowledgements

The authors would like to thank all participants for taking the time to participate in this research. In particular we should like to thank Hedgelink UK for their assistance with knowledge mapping; our project advisors – Helen Ferrier (National Farmers' Union) and Daniel Pearsall (SCIMAC); Marlene Gordon, our research secretary; and Mark Yoxon our professional facilitator.

Farmers Understandings of GM Crops research was funded by the UK Economic and Social Research Council (www.esrc.ac.uk) under its Science in Society Programme, award number RES-151-25-0046. The research was in association with Innogen, the Institute for Innovation Generation in the Life Sciences (www.innogen.ac.uk).

References

Brown, J.S. and Duguid, P. (1991) 'Organizational Learning and Communities-of-Practice: Toward a Unified View of Working, Learning, and Innovating', *Organization Science* 2 (1): 40–57.

Brown, J.S and Duguid, P. (2000) *The Social Life of Information*, Harvard Business School Press.

Brown, J.S. and Duguid P. (2001) 'Knowledge and Organization: A Social-Practice Perspective', *Organization Science*, 12 (2): 198–213.

Charmaz, K. (2014) *Grounded Theory*, 2nd edition, London: Sage.

Chevalier, J.M. and Buckles, D.J. (2013) *Participatory Action Research: theory and methods for engaging inquiry*, Abingdon and New York: Routledge.

Defra (2003) *GM Nation?* UK National Government web archive, http://webarchive.nationalarchives.gov.uk/20081023141438/http://www.defra.gov.uk/environment/gm/crops/debate/index.htm

Defra (2007) *The Farm Scale Evaluations*, UK National Government web archive, http://webarchive.nationalarchives.gov.uk/20080306073937/http:/www.defra.gov.uk/environment/gm/fse/

Eppler, M.J. (2006) 'A comparison between concept maps, mind maps, conceptual diagrams, and visual metaphors as complementary tools for knowledge construction and sharing', *Information Visualization* (5): 202–10.

Glaser, B.G. (1994) *More Grounded Theory Methodology: A Reader*, California: Sociology Press.

Harman, W.W. (1979) *An Incomplete Guide to the Future*, New York: Norton.

Hemant, R.O., Hall, A and Sulaiman V.R. (2013) (eds) *Adaptive Collaborative Approaches in Natural Resource Governance: Rethinking, Participation, Learning and Innovation*, Abingdon: Routledge.

Hustad, E. (2010) 'Exploring Knowledge Work Practices and Evolution in Distributed Networks of Practice', *Electronic Journal of Knowledge Management*, 8(1): 69–78.

Ingram, J., Maye, D., Kirwan, J., Curry, N. and Kubinakova, K. (2014) 'Learning in the permaculture community of practice in England: an analysis of the relationship between core practices and boundary processes', *Journal of Agricultural Education and Extension*, 20 (3): 275–90.

Klerkx, L.W.A. and Proctor, A. (2013) 'Beyond fragmentation and disconnect: Networks for knowledge exchange in the English land management system', *Land Use Policy*, 30: 13–2.

Lane, A. (2008) 'GM crops ate my hamster!' *Sesame,* 23: 34 [Newsletter for Open University Students].

Lane, A., Oreszczyn, S. and Carr, S., (2007) *Farmers' understandings of genetically modified crops within local communities,* ESRC End of Award Report, RES-151-25-0046. Swindon: Economic and Social Research Council.

Lave, J. and Wenger, E. (1991) *Situated Learning: Legitimate Peripheral Learning,* Cambridge: Cambridge University Press.

Oreszczyn, S. (2005a) *What farmers say about new technologies and GM crops: a report on the initial telephone interviews,* Swindon: Economic and Social Research Council, www.researchcatalogue.esrc.ac.uk/grants/RES-151-25-0046/read

Oreszczyn, S. (2005b) *What farmers say about influences on their decisions about farming, new technologies and GM crops: a report on the farm visits,* Swindon: Economic and Social Research Council, www.researchcatalogue.esrc.ac.uk/grants/RES-151-25-0046/read

Oreszczyn, S. (2005c) *New technologies and scientific developments: exploring better ways to support farmers' decisions: phase 3 workshop report,* Swindon: Economic and Social Research Council, www.researchcatalogue.esrc.ac.uk/grants/RES-151-25-0046/read

Oreszczyn, S. and Lane, A. (2000) 'The Meaning of Hedgerows in the English Landscape: Different stakeholder perspectives and the implications for future hedge management', *Journal of Environmental Management,* 60, 101–18.

Oreszczyn, S. and Lane, A. (2012a) 'Agri-environmental knowledge management and networks of practice a background paper', in J.W. Dover (ed) *Hedgerow Futures: Proceedings of the first International Hedgelink conference,* 3–5 September, Staffordshire University, Stoke-on-Trent, pp 203–06.

Oreszczyn, S. and Lane, A. (2012b) *Mapping knowledge exchange in the UK hedgerow management system, Report on a Workshop held at Hedgerow Futures,* Milton Keynes: The Open University.

Oreszczyn, S. and Lane, A. (2012c) 'The Role of contexts in knowledge brokering systems', Workshop Report from Bridging the Gap between Research Policy and Practice: The importance of intermediaries (knowledge brokers) in producing research impact, ESRC Genomics Network, 7 December, Milton Keynes: The Open University.

Oreszczyn, S., Lane, A. and Carr, S. (2007) *Farmers' Understandings of Genetically Modified Crops within Local Communities,* Innogen Policy briefing 10, ESRC Genomics Network, www.innogen.ac.uk/downloads/Farmers-Understandings-of-GM-Crops.pdf

Oreszczyn, S., Lane A. and Carr, S. (2010) 'The role of networks of practice and webs of influencers on farmers' engagement with and learning about agricultural innovations', *Journal of Rural Studies*, 26: 404–17.

Pidgeon, N., Poortinga, W., Rowe, G., Horlick-Jones, T., Walls, J. and O'Riordan, T. (2005) 'Using Surveys in Public Participation Processes for Risk Decision Making: The Case of the 2003 British GM Nation? Public Debate', *Risk Analysis*, 25 (2): 467–79.

The Royal Society (2009) *Reaping the benefits: science and the sustainable intensification of global agriculture*, Royal Society Policy document 11/09, https://royalsociety.org/~/media/Royal_Society_Content/policy/publications/2009/4294967719.pdf

Teigland, R. (2003) 'Knowledge Networking: Structure and Performance in Networks of Practice', PhD dissertation, Stockholm Schools of Economics, Sweden.

Wenger, E. (1998) *Communities of Practice, Learning, Meaning, and Identity*, New York: Cambridge University Press.

Wenger, E. (2000) 'Communities of Practice and Social Learning Systems', *Organization* 7 (2): 225–46.

Wenger, E., McDermott, R. and Snyder, W.M. (2002) *Cultivating Communities of Practice*. Boston: Harvard Business School Press.

Wenger-Trayner, E. and Wenger-Trayner, B. (2015) 'Introduction to Communities of Practice', http://wenger-trayner.com/introduction-to-communities-of-practice/

FIVE

Using visual approaches with Indigenous communities

Andrea Berardi, Jay Mistry, Lakeram Haynes, Deirdre Jafferally, Elisa Bignante, Grace Albert, Rebecca Xavier, Ryan Benjamin and Géraud de Ville

Editors' introduction

In this chapter we are told the story of longstanding and ongoing research on natural resource management working with Indigenous forest communities in South America. The authors included here represent the range of people that Andrea Berardi and Jay Mistry, as lead authors, have worked with over the years. Their biographies can be found at the front of this book and reading these is considered by the lead authors to be important for a full understanding of their research story. The authors consider their experiences, their challenges and the ethics involved in what they did. Like the other examples in this book, their research drew heavily from systems theories and, as with previous chapters, the authors describe the way that their research processes evolved over time. In this case, moving away from their quantitative origins and becoming increasingly more visual and inclusive over time. This chapter places diagramming within the wider context of visual approaches more generally. Going beyond diagramming, the authors explain how they developed visual techniques relevant for their particular context, including (and combining) video, drawings and photo stories as well as diagramming. Here they explain the way that their approach and use of visual techniques helped to strengthen the capabilities of marginalised people.

Introduction

For over 15 years, the authors of this chapter have been engaged with the Indigenous communities of the North Rupununi, Guyana, in working through complex natural resource management dilemmas.

Over time, we have developed a critically reflective approach to collaborative research with Indigenous community members in order to evaluate the type of research methods and techniques we apply, to reposition power relationships in the research processes, and analyse the immediate and long-term impact of the research intervention on participants. Why do researchers and participants engage in the use of visual methods? What are their differential motivations and how does this affect decision making during the research process? Who participates in and benefits from this research? What is the role of technology? How are Indigenous people's rights and knowledges taken into account and advanced? How do visual methods contribute to transformative change and social justice? With what limits?

Like other chapters in this book, in this chapter we discuss our transition from an expert led research approach, which was dominated by quantifying research methods imposed by non-Guyanese academics, towards increasingly more participatory, qualitative and visual approaches, and the challenges that we faced in this transition.

Not all of the authors of this chapter were involved at every stage of research (although all participated in Project Cobra – see below, and all participants are now part of the Cobra Collective – for more information about the work of the Cobra Collective, visit www. cobracollective.org), and not all of the individuals contributing to our evolving practice are listed as authors. However, the composition of chapter authors represents the range of perspectives that were involved over the years, and our aim here is to try and represent these perspectives within our narrative. Only individuals that have agreed to be named as co-authors in this publication are named in the text. The author's biographies are particularly relevant here and may be found in the Notes on Contributors section at the front of the book. These biographies demonstrate the personal motivations and experiences underpinning the research and reflections outlined in this chapter.

The way this chapter was developed took into account the specific circumstances of the co-authors and their preferred working practices. An initial call for co-authors was sent out by Andrea to 12 individuals. The ones that responded positively are the co-authors described in the Notes on Contributors section at the front of the book. Andrea then initiated a number of email discussions by asking individuals their views on a number of questions, including:

What motivates you to use visual techniques, such as drawings, photos or videos?
How do visual techniques affect the way we work together?

How do visual techniques affect the way we engage communities during the research?

Who do you think benefits from the use of visual techniques?

What do you think is the role of technology in the use of visual techniques?

How are communities' rights and knowledges taken into account and advanced when we use visual techniques?

How do visual techniques contribute to positive change, including sustainability and justice, within communities?

What do you think are the limits of visual techniques?

Co-authors were asked to illustrate their responses with specific examples based on their experiences of having worked together in one or more projects in the North Rupununi. These responses, and the discussions that ensued, provided the foundations for the chapter, which was drafted by Andrea. Drafts were sent out to the co-authors and critical readers for comments, and Andrea tried his best to address these. The result is what you are about to read.

The context: North Rupununi, Guyana

The North Rupununi, a region approximately 8,000 km² in size (almost equivalent to the area of Yellowstone National Park in the USA, or the Greek island of Crete), is one of the most biodiverse hotspots of the world, and also home to the Makushi and Wapishana Indigenous groups. It is located in the south-west of Guyana, South America, and is characterised by a mosaic of wetland, savanna and rainforest ecosystems determined in large part by the seasonal flooding of the Rupununi River, a major tributary of the Essequibo River, which drains into the Caribbean Sea. The North Rupununi is home to an estimated 7,500–8,000 Indigenous community members which have traditionally thrived through direct sustainable exploitation of their natural resources. Contact with the outside world has been challenging in the past, and continues to be challenging now. Depending on the weather and its state of maintenance, a 450 km unpaved laterite road through almost uninterrupted and scarcely populated rainforest connects the North Rupununi to the coast, where the majority of Guyana's 746,000 people live. Politics in the region is complex. Since colonisation by Europeans, the Indigenous communities of the North Rupununi have been increasingly disempowered with a gradual erosion of resource user rights (see Mistry et al, 2009a, for an in-depth account of the region's environmental history). In 1969, shortly after Guyanese independence from its British colonial masters, an attempted uprising in order to gain greater autonomy for the region was brutally put down by Guyanese military forces, and the region became a backwater for many decades as the Guyanese government poured resources into developing the coast while essentially leaving Indigenous communities to fend for themselves.

With the opening up of Guyana to international trade and investment in the 1990s, the North Rupununi communities have increasingly come under intense pressure to abandon their traditional land use practices in support for ecotourism, mining, oil exploration, logging and commercial fishing and agriculture. However, the historical exclusion of the Indigenous communities from the decision making process has continued, due in part to their inability to access and develop information about their own region and the political and policy process determining access and user rights. In particular, the use of the written English language underpinning most decision making processes, as exemplified through legislation that controls access to, and beneficiaries of, the region's natural resources, has effectively excluded Indigenous participation in the decision making process.

Engagement in decision making is also challenged by a myriad of other factors, including limited educational prospects and tough working conditions: high temperatures and humidity; exposure to diseases combined with poor medical facilities; low security; alcoholism; limited infrastructure; nepotism; the emigration of the most able youth; cultural loss; and feelings of helplessness in many that remain. These are just a few of the issues that communities face in their day-to-day struggle for survival. In addition to the grave social challenges, the region is increasingly facing chaotic weather patterns frequently oscillating between extreme droughts and floods. Climate change, combined with population growth, permanent settlement and the introduction of technologies such as fishing nets and chainsaws, has depleted many natural resources, with individuals having to travel further afield and work harder for less return. As exemplified by the following statements given by Rupununi residents in MacDonald (2014), community members are finding it increasingly difficult to maintain traditional livelihoods, while the attraction to collaborate with non-Indigenous stakeholders in less sustainable commercial practices and/or fall into a downward spiral of alcohol abuse, violence and depression, are increasing in the region:

'when people go to Brazil, they adapt the, they kind of adapt to the, to the lifestyle of the Brazilians. They have practices that is unacceptable when they return to the villages, like for example, criminal acts. Acts of violence.' (Wapishana community leader, quoted in MacDonald, 2014: 90)

'[youths] got into alcohol and drugs and gang violence, so when they come back here, that is what they tend to come back with. And that is really something, you know, harmful to the community.' (Makushi elder, quoted in MacDonald, 2014: 90)

'our culture is almost dying, I must say in all the communities, so. Some people are not, very few people are hunting, very few of our youths could, let's say for example, make the handicrafts, make our staple foods, very few, they now rely on the older folks to, you know, make it more conveniently ... The traditional way of life is, is basically under threat.' (Wapishana community leader, quoted in MacDonald, 2014: 91)

The development of a systemic, participatory and visual research approach

The following is an account of how our systemic, participatory and visual research approach has emerged over more than 15 years of collaborative working in the North Rupununi.

The account reflects on our evolving practice as systems practitioners. Systems thinking and practice has been central to our practice right from the first research project, but our approach has changed over time, reflecting the historical changes in systems thinking and practice through 'hard', 'soft' and 'critical' approaches (Checkland, 1981) and Andrea's developing understanding of the field as a result of him joining the community of systems researchers within The Open University in 2002. Initially, we very much adopted a 'hard systems' approach (see Chapter Two), focusing on identifying key 'cause and effect' relationships and the resulting emergent properties within systems 'out there'. We then began adopting 'soft systems' techniques and concepts, with more emphasis on surfacing distinct systems of interests by engaging with a wide range of stakeholders. And finally, we began introducing 'critical systems' techniques (Ulrich, 2005; Reynolds; 2011), where we explored the impact of power relations in determining how systems of interests are operationalised in the real word (and how these could be influenced in order to promote the interests of the most marginalised).

Concurrent with our evolving systemic and participatory approaches, we began to weave into our research practice a range of visual techniques. Our research engagement in the North Rupununi overlapped with the growing academic interest in applying visual research within participatory research with Indigenous communities across the world. Our interest in applying visual research went beyond the use of diagramming techniques. Visual research is a wider field of qualitative research that uses imagery, such as photography, video, diagrams, maps and sketches, to record, analyse, reformulate and communicate knowledge (Boedhihartono, 2012). We saw participatory visual methods as a means to giving a 'voice' to Indigenous people: supporting social change through raising awareness of issues; building capacity to engender action; and as a potentially powerful vehicle for influencing decision makers at local, national and global levels. For example, 'countermapping', where Indigenous participants develop their own maps of traditional landscape use in order to contest official designations that undermine Indigenous interests, has been successfully applied to demarcate Indigenous territories (Peluso, 1995; Taylor, 2008). Indeed, Nietschmann (1995) asserts that:

> More Indigenous territory has been claimed by maps than by guns. And more Indigenous territory can be reclaimed and defended by maps than by guns.

First contact (1999–2000)

The genesis of our long-term collaboration in the North Rupununi emerged in 1999 when an anthropologist working in the region contacted Jay, just a year after beginning her work as a lecturer at Royal Holloway University of London – her first full-time academic post. The anthropologist relayed an urgent request by Indigenous community leaders for help with investigating water quality in the region, and its effects on wildlife and human health. An expedition was swiftly organised also involving Andrea, who had just completed his PhD. Over a three-week period and with the support of an Indigenous researcher (now an internationally renowned wildlife cameraman), the expedition set about testing water samples from a wide variety of sources (ponds, streams, rivers and community wells) used by community members either for fishing or for drinking/ washing. The resulting analysis showed, within the limitations of the sampling (including the chemicals tested, the time frame and the spatial distribution of sample points), that the low concentration of harmful chemicals identified in the water suggested that the cause for the perceived drop in fish catches may have been as a result of other factors. However, some wells had very high acidity levels due to the presence of acid sulphate sediments in the subsurface. Water extracted from these wells could result in toxic contamination from dissolving water receptacles if these were made of, for example, aluminium (Mistry et al, 2004).

Darwin Project (2003–2005)

Clearly, a more in-depth and longitudinal study needed to be carried out to investigate the local concerns for dwindling fish catches, so, with community encouragement, the initial expedition was followed up with a major three-year £135,000 project involving intense biophysical and ecological monitoring of the region's wetlands, with the ultimate aim of developing an integrated conservation and development management plan for the region (Mistry et al, 2008, 2010a). Andrea, Jay, Lakeram and Deirdre were the co-authors involved in this project. Halfway through the project, significant disagreements emerged within the academic team coordinating the research. This was fuelled by Andrea's disillusionment with the top-down, natural science led approach which exclusively focused on collecting numerical data, and his fears that a prescriptive management plan would offer very few chances of being implemented in the region. In essence, the disagreement centred around the distinction between 'doing things better' and 'doing better things' (Ackoff, 2004). The prescriptive data collection was not working according to plan as a result of extreme logistical difficulties, illnesses within the fieldwork staff (malaria is rife in the region) and low morale. One view was simply to plough on, continue with the approach that everyone was familiar with, and try to apply some 'fixes' where possible, that is 'let's just do things better'. Another view was to completely abandon the quantitative data collection altogether, and instead embark on an intensive programme of community engagement, that is 'let's do better things'. After heated and open discussions comprising all research team members, including Indigenous contributors, a major rethink in the research approach was initiated. Lakeram, working then as an Indigenous researcher on the project, and Deirdre, the project manager, both still in their early to mid 20s, played key roles in mediating between the conflicting academic perspectives, and were to take on increasingly significant leadership roles in future projects. The compromise essentially involved a significant reduction in the time and energy expended on data collection (we decided to focus on the most accessible sites and we ended the monitoring before the prescribed date). We also introduced a community engagement programme alongside the establishment of decentralised decision making within the project. An account of the issues and the emergence of new principles for community engagement and research practices are published in detail in Mistry et al (2009b).

One of the key principles emerging from the rethink was a commitment by the research team to have positive and timely impacts on the ground through direct engagement with community perspectives and aspirations. This involved academic team members pledging a long-term commitment, and prioritising the building of trusting relationships, with the North Rupununi communities. The nature of subsequent research projects therefore departed from the typical scientific investigation, which is usually situated in a controlled time-delimited intervention involving pre-established activities and deliverables, with the principal aim of producing published research whose recommendations would hopefully be adopted by 'others'. Instead, the new approach focused heavily on community participation, not only by having the interventions emerging from community aspirations and adopting appropriate processes of community engagement, but also in looking at how information was recorded and shared. Summarising this transformative moment in our research approach, the big realisation was that the management 'plan' for the North Rupununi wetlands would not be located within a nicely bound, text-based, colour printout. Instead, the management of the North Rupununi wetlands would be embodied within the people we engaged with and their evolving practices. The focus therefore shifted towards building communities' skill sets for dealing with the complex natural resource management situation. This was not, however, a 'they all lived happily forever after' tale, as an honest assessment of the major challenges facing the community-led initiative identified what seemed to be unsurmountable barriers. In Mistry et al (2010a), we used a 'system viability' framework for developing and applying indicators to assess the long-term prospects of our management process having any impact, and nearly all indicators were below the 'viability' threshold. We had a lot of work to do.

Post-Darwin and ECOSENSUS Projects (2005–2008)

The follow-on to the Darwin Project involved another substantial grant of £108,000 focusing on building capacity for natural resource management in the North Rupununi region and Guyana as a whole. The emphasis changed from counting 'things', such as getting individuals to monitor changes in the number of individuals of a certain species in a certain waterbody, to building capacity within individuals for managing complex and messy social-ecological situations that were outside of their traditional 'comfort zone'. The 'North Rupununi Adaptive Management Plan' would not be situated within a printout, but within the embodied capacities of people. This is not to dismiss the value of quantitative measurement in natural resource management, but the view was that after decades of quantitative 'top-down' research in the region (for example, Lowe-McConnell, 1964; Eden, 1970; ter Welle et al, 1993; Castello, 2001; Mistry et al, 2004, 2008; Read et al, 2010; Pickles et al, 2011; Taylor et al, 2016), it was time to try out something different, incorporating community participation. A full account of our first attempt at this, applying 'problem-based learning' for building capacity in working through complex problems can be found in Mistry et al (2010b).

This shift in approach also denoted a shift in the power balance: counting 'things' was great for rapidly churning out papers in high impact journals but virtually useless for supporting the Indigenous communities in their natural resource management dilemmas. Indigenous community members told us they were perfectly able to monitor their own environment using their traditional ecological knowledge, with occasional support from specialists (as exemplified by our water survey described above). The key message was that community members wanted the research to support their own needs rather than the needs of foreign researchers and their careers. So, directly engaging with the messy, complex reality and traditional knowledge proved to be a major challenge for the academics involved, but did result in higher levels of community engagement and practical outcomes on the ground. The challenges were many – some stemming from our own inexperience and lack of understanding, and others emerging as a result of the time, money, energy and patience that participatory process require, often moving in directions way beyond the original objectives stipulated by the funders. We were now 'doing better things' but in a situation where we needed to 'do these better things better'!

Notwithstanding the challenges, the shift in approach resulted in a major endeavour to produce practical assets that community members could actively use to advance sustainable livelihoods. So, for example, we experimented for the first time in the collaborative production of visual materials, such as ecotourism maps and a photographic guide highlighting the wildlife and natural landscape of the North Rupununi wetlands (Wetlands Partnership, 2008a, 2008b). The maps were an especially engaging activity that involved enthusiastic community participation, and this inspired a parallel project that went into much greater depth in exploring the potential of mapping for supporting decision making in natural resource management (see the discussion of the 'ECOSENSUS Project' below).

We began to explore modes of communication that community members would find more engaging and could manage and control themselves in order to influence decision making at local, regional, national and international levels. Our initial strategy was to investigate the potential of Geographical Information Systems (GIS). As opposed to static and simplified paper-based maps, a GIS enables users to create their own map layers, and overlay these in order to analyse, for example, change over space and time within the landscape, and potentially contribute to natural resource management planning, such as, for example, the identification of non-fishing zones.

It was evident that the natural resource management dilemmas within the North Rupununi wetlands were 'spatial' – they involved complex spatial interactions between, for example, stakeholder interests; resource distribution, use and management; land tenure and access; and potential conflicts between land conversion for commercial purposes, such as logging, mining and oil exploration, and other land uses such as traditional subsistence and ecotourism. Spatial decision making in the North Rupununi was, and continues to be, characterised by multiple and often conflicting objectives, inherent unpredictability and decentralised control. But crucially, it is also visual decision making: community members are regularly observed picking up sticks and drawing maps on the ground. Andrea, in collaboration with Lakeram, wanted to explore the possibility of using information and communication technology (ICT) tools to enhance the ground-based sketches. Dealing with these issues required firstly a shared understanding between stakeholders and secondly, appropriate access to spatial information by stakeholders who traditionally may have little experience of ICTs.

Thus, our first serious foray in the use of participatory visual tools was ECOSENSUS (Ecological/Electronic Collaborative Sense Making Support System), a pilot project undertaken over a timescale of 18 months (2005–2007) with a budget of just under £45,000 and supported by the Economic and Social Research Council (ESRC) in the UK (Berardi et al, 2006). One of the main challenges that we identified with GIS tools is that they failed to 'embed' the complex discussions behind every map. However, we wanted to avoid having a visual tool incorporating text-based functionality for capturing the discussions. Our aim was to minimise the challenges revolving around participants' literacy levels, which went beyond just spelling and grammar, but also involved clashes between Indigenous and Western worldviews that could not be represented if participants were forced to engage in the English language, especially when writing it. Instead, we wanted to explore the possibility of integrating a visual argumentation mapping tool within the GIS. Thus, the overall aim of ECOSENSUS was to develop an integrated GIS/visual sense making tool and then to develop the practice and understanding in the use of these tools for managing complex spatial problems (always within the very real context of natural resource dilemmas in the North Rupununi).

The ECOSENSUS project had, as its primary activity, the task of integrating two key software tools: Compendium (an open source dialogue/argument mapping tool)[1] and UDIG (an open source GIS tool).[2] Compendium had been developed over a 20 year time span into a powerful tool for visually mapping discussions among participants. The key purpose of such mapping is to develop a shared understanding among a diverse group of people. Compendium uses a simple visual language composed of a defined set of symbolic icons representing distinct elements of a discussion: questions; ideas; arguments in favour; arguments against; and decisions. In essence, Compendium serves as a 'sense making' diagramming tool: helping users to make sense of their experiences and thoughts through a straightforward and visual structuring of knowledge.

In ECOSENSUS, we wanted to support fluid movement between spatial mapping on the one hand, and visual argumentation mapping on the other. The idea was to develop a set of icons within the GIS tool which represented the most significant natural resources within the North Rupununi. Figure 5.1, for example, shows a number of drawings by Lakeram sketched during the project, representing some important natural resources of the North Rupununi. But we also wanted to make the software more accessible to the Indigenous communities. So, for example, on the behest of Lakeram, the icon representing the 'decision' within Compendium was changed from a hammer and block (inspired by the judicial process in Western countries) to a handshake – a powerful realignment of the decision making from a hierarchical process (a judge making a decision imposed on others), to a more equitable 'handshake' agreement among parties. This demonstrates the necessity of not presupposing participants' symbolic representations within diagramming techniques, especially rich picturing. Although

Figure 5.1: Lakeram Haynes's sketches with symbolic representations of key natural resource management areas of the North Rupununi

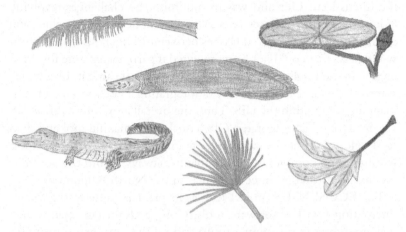

Notes: From top-left to bottom-right: Ite' palm (representing areas where palm thatching could be collected for roofing), giant waterlily (representing areas with a high density of ponds for fishing), Arapaima fish and black caiman (representing areas with a high concentration of wildlife), Kokerite palm (representing areas for the collection of handicraft material), and cassava (representing areas within the rainforest for rotational farming plots)

there is a tendency to use 'ready-made' clipart symbols and/or imagery downloaded from the web, our experience indicates the significance of freehand drawing in representing participants' genuine perspectives.

The various icons representing key natural resources were digitised and added as a toolbar within the GIS software, enabling a user to click and drag these onto a base map of the North Rupununi. By double-clicking on a natural resource icon, a sense making map would open up in Compendium, where users would be presented with a series of questions to help them work through the issues for that particular natural resource within that particular locality (Figure 5.2). Each sense making map could also be nested with other sense making maps so as to weave together the complex decision making processes for the region as a whole.

In integrating the GIS and argumentation mapping, we wanted to avoid seeking a technocentric approach to working through natural resource management dilemmas but rather to support the process of critical and participatory inquiry. Inspired by approaches such as Soft Systems Methodology (Checkland, 1981) as discussed in Chapter Two and Critical Systems Heuristics (Ulrich, 2005), we attempted to direct the visual argumentation mapping through a series of questions directly informed by these two approaches (see Reynolds et al, 2007, for further details). Although the process worked well when it was

Figure 5.2: Screenshot of the Compendium-uDig integration

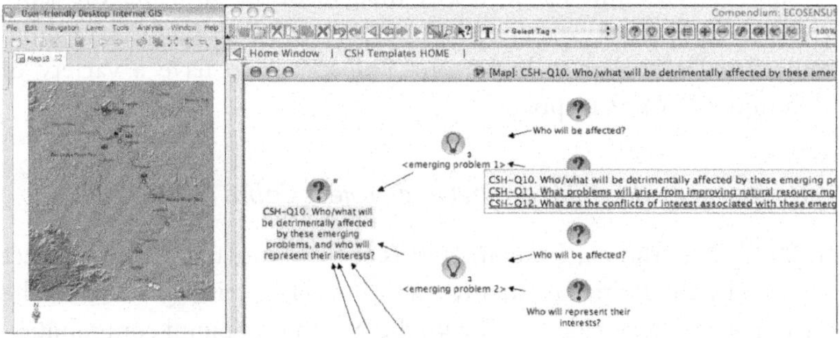

facilitated by a team member in a face-to-face setting, the Guyanese participants struggled to continue using the ECOSENSUS software tools and process beyond these facilitated face-to-face meetings. The reasons were apparently as a result of the challenges of using quite sophisticated software tools in a difficult environment, with intermittent electricity, for example, disrupting computer-based work.

The challenges with the infrastructure may have been the most readily reported difficulty by the participants, but more nuanced issues were surfaced when discussing the visual argumentation tool. Indigenous cultures in the region are familiar with iconic representations, as many locations contain petroglyphs and cave drawings, and, until recently, many still practised symbolic body painting. However, social memory is primarily maintained through oral narration, which frequently lacks the structure of a linear and logical 'argument' as perceived in Western cultures. In the eyes of Westerners, Indigenous discussions are perceived to be circular, meandering, repetitive, indirect, long and/or appear to go off topic. Nailing down isolated, logically consistent, coherent and short argument chains (as required by the Compendium argument mapping software and SSM/CSH questions), in the limited timeframe available, was therefore very difficult to do without help from a non-Indigenous facilitator. The importance of facilitation, particularly for contentious issues, has been noted in the previous chapters; however, in this case the research team were concerned about the influence of the facilitator if 'speaking on the behalf of communities' rather than enabling communities themselves to express their views. The conclusion from ECOSENSUS was that the team would abandon argumentation mapping in future initiatives, and seek alternative visual means for working through complex natural resource management dilemmas which could be more directly controlled by the communities themselves. The lesson that we learnt from ECOSENSUS was that not all visual techniques, however facilitated and participatory, are suitable for all contexts, so rather than insisting on using the same visual technique in all cases and/or persevering after much struggling, sometimes it is best to move on. The key is to have a variety of techniques at one's disposal.

Participatory video pilot project and Project Cobra (2007–2015)

In 2007, Jay, Andrea, Lakeram and Rebecca initiated a small project (funded by the British Academy over 18 months with £7,000) on the use of participatory video (PV) with the North Rupununi communities. The motivations for the project resulted from discussions with local community leaders and elders where it became clear that the historical context of the region was an important influence on current natural resource management practices, and their wish for the experiences of the elders to be recorded for future generations before they died. We had also been reflecting on our research practice as a result of the ECOSENSUS pilot, and exploring the idea of simpler, more direct visual forms of participatory engagement with local communities (less reliant on sitting in front of a computer clicking on icons). We were particularly interested in investigating how social memory, expressed through shared oral narratives that influence collective thoughts and actions, influenced natural resource management practices in a way that enabled local communities to take greater ownership of the research process, present their views authentically, and provide an immediate and accessible dissemination output in the form of films. Over the PV project period, five Indigenous facilitators were trained in PV (including Lakeram and Rebecca), supported by Jay and Andrea. The team worked through iterative action research cycles of discussion and practical PV filming, editing and screening with different community members, and developed two themed films for feedback and further development. Full details of the PV process and results are provided in Mistry and Berardi (2012) and Mistry et al (2014).

This PV work was taken a step further when an opportunity to showcase how Indigenous communities were sustainably managing their natural resources came about. Project Cobra[3] was a European Commission funded project (€1.9 million, 2011–2015) led by Jay, with the aim to work with Indigenous communities in the Guiana Shield region of South America to identify, record and share their own solutions to emerging social-ecological challenges. Project Cobra involved ten research, civil society organisation and business partners across Europe and South America, and pulled together all the co-authors of this chapter (see Notes on contributors): Jay, Andrea and Elisa representing academic institutions; Lakeram, Grace, Rebecca and Ryan representing Indigenous communities; and Deirdre and Géraud representing civic society organisations. Although we worked with various Indigenous communities of the Guiana Shield, the most in-depth research took place with the Makushi and Wapishana of the North Rupununi, Guyana, which was led by Lakeram, Grace, Ryan and Rebecca. Using the visual methods of PV and participatory photography (PP), the Indigenous researchers on the Project Cobra team helped communities explore their current survival strategies with the aim to identify local solutions or 'best practices' that could be shared with other Indigenous groups. Like PV with video, PP is a technique for eliciting participants' perspectives through the still image. The project produced numerous films and photostories which can be found on the project's MediaGate,[4] but as part of the participatory visual process, there were other outputs including storyboards and spray diagrams. Storyboards, for example, were used in the planning process for the production of films and photostories, but were also used to explore how the future of the community might develop through different scenarios. The use of storyboards is picked up again in Chapter Six. A critical aspect of PV and PP is that, at regular intervals, the wider community was able to feedback through evening screenings of the videos and photostory printouts resembling graphic novels. This allowed the research team to adapt the content of these outputs through iterative cycles of feedback.

Although the photo and video technology required significant skills levels to operate, these were on a much more practical level compared to the GIS and sense making tools. Lighting, picture framing and sound were the main challenges here. We also significantly simplified the process underpinning the 'narrative' that had to be captured through visual means. Instead of asking participants to work through a simplification of SSM and CSH, we adapted another systems approach, Orientor Theory (Bossel, 1999) into a simple framework for exploring the survival strategies of communities. Our adaptation, termed 'system viability' (Berardi et al, 2013, 2015), asked participants to explore six distinct strategies for facing up to challenges within their environment: resisting temporary change; adapting to permanent change; developing efficient processes for dealing with scarce resources; developing flexible strategies for dealing with a heterogeneous environment; focusing on immediate existence needs; and engaging in partnerships with others. Once films and photostories, capturing the range of community survival strategies, were developed by the communities, these were analysed by the whole team (academic and Indigenous researchers) to identify community indicators of wellbeing. These indicators were then represented in the form of spray diagrams, as large A1 posters, to present back to the communities for feedback and refinement (see Figure 5.3 for an example of the final agreed output).

In this case, engagement with the spray diagrams was much simpler and straightforward compared to the argumentation mapping. In essence, we used the spray diagramming technique as a summary and classification tool for the indicators that emerged. During the feedback and refinement process, Lakeram, Grace, Rebecca and/or Ryan would go through the various branches of the spray diagram, explaining to participants the meaning of each component (often reminding them how the components were identified from the PV and PP outputs) and requesting feedback on whether the participants were happy with the components' names and their positioning within a particular branch. Participants were also asked whether there were any indicators, which had been represented within the PV and PP outputs, that they felt had been missed out and should be represented within the spray diagram. However, the technique only worked through face-to-face facilitation, and the resulting diagrams were never used again by the communities after the facilitated indicator refinement exercise. The video and photostory outputs, on the other hand, have continued to be powerful assets, both within the communities and externally.

The final indicators selected were then used to identify the 'best' survival strategies communities had developed. These included traditional farming practices, traditional fishing practices, community self-help practices, and cultural transmission practices. These 'best practices' were then filmed in greater detail and promoted in six Indigenous communities from six different countries in the region: Brazil, Colombia, Venezuela, Guyana, Suriname and French Guiana. The aim of the knowledge exchange was to inspire recipient communities to apply some of these best practices, and, in turn, document their own best practices for wider dissemination. An account of the process can be found in Mistry et al (2016) and Tschirhart et al (2016).

The videos produced during this process continue to have a life beyond Project Cobra. For example, they have been used as advocacy tools to lobby national politicians in Guyana and Venezuela. Some communities have even continued to document additional best practices for wider dissemination. At the community level, the difference between the continued interest in the videos and photostories, compared to the limited interest in the spray diagram

Figure 5.3: Example of an indicator spray diagram produced for Apoteri village, North Rupununi, Guyana

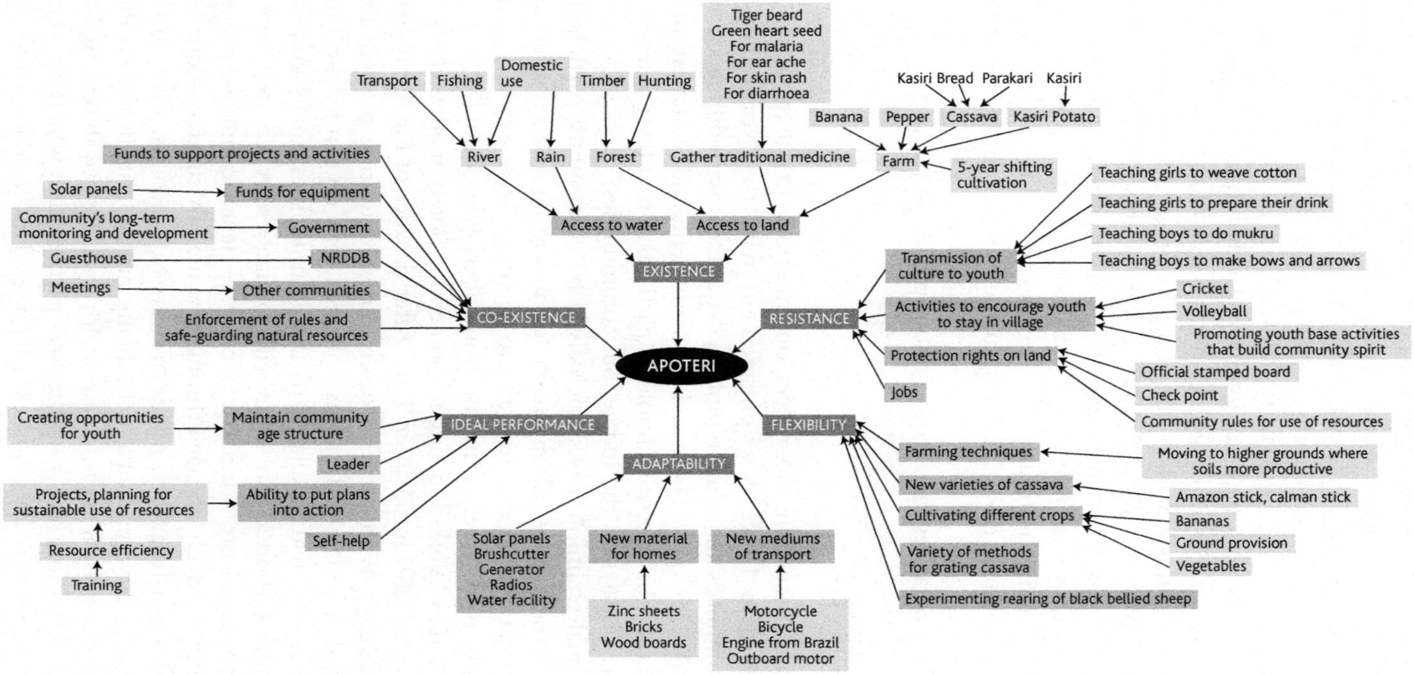

Source: Berardi et al (2012)

outputs (which were supported by the communities only within the timeframe of Project Cobra), is, at one level, relatively straightforward. Community members continue to have a fascination with watching videos and seeing pictures of themselves, family members, friends and significant individuals from their own communities, just as we occasionally look back at pictures and videos of significant moments with our own lives. Project Cobra was one of the few opportunities that communities had to film and photograph themselves, and these assets have remained as DVDs and printouts circulating within the communities. The spray diagrams, on the other hand, represent an academic exercise that might come in useful to decision makers at some stage in the future, but there is certainly no demand for these diagrams to be circulating within the communities at this moment in time.

This concludes the account of our process so far.

Discussion

In this discussion, we reflect on questions that have arisen from more than 15 years of engagement with the North Rupununi communities and our attempts to experiment with different forms of visual techniques. These include the benefits and limitations of visual methods, the role of technology, participation in the process and the wider impacts on the Indigenous communities.

Visual techniques were perceived by community participants to be a straightforward approach for recording and communicating information. They were found to be an attractive way of getting the attention of wider community members who would otherwise be affected by 'workshop fatigue' (something noted in other chapters and discussed later in Chapter Ten). After decades of foreign researchers turning up within their communities requesting participation in workshops, where data was collected, but no immediate tangible output was made available to the communities, many community members reported frustration with foreign researchers and expressed a wish to avoid any workshop. In our experience, community members are more actively engaged through the use of visual techniques – they do not just listen or provide answers to questions, they do things, they are active participants by being protagonists in the creation of immediate visual assets. As a rule, for example, we always tried to put together a short film from the day's participation which was screened in the evenings. This, in turn, encouraged more people to participate the next day. Crucially, visual methods are seen as giving a more realistic, genuine and wider picture of the situation, stimulating broad discussions and critical thinking:

> 'So many things come up you wouldn't expect while using visual methods: people's perspectives, stories about the place, and not necessarily the same things would come up during a traditional interview'. (Elisa)

Indeed, by "seeing the world through peoples own eyes and views of the world" (Jay), visual techniques allow us to see people 'in action' and it brings us closer to their problems, their lives. Visual techniques are seen to enhance participation and there are ripple effects throughout the community: the research is perceived to be more intimate and builds trust in that it allows community members to "correct the work that's been done" (Rebecca). There is also something about the immediacy of the product. You have something to show at the end of a day's work: a map, a diagram, photographs or video. Non-visual research approaches often leave you 'empty-handed' – you need to go away with your hidden audio interviews and notes, often leaving nothing behind in return for the community's participation.

Even within the research team, working with visual techniques creates a more relaxed atmosphere, fostering creativity and helping to see problems from different perspectives. While in some phases of the research it allowed team members to work more closely (for example when editing videos), visual techniques also encourage team members to break out from the closely knit research team and interact with the wider community. Crucially, because visual methods were perceived to be 'fun' not only for participants, but also for the research team, individuals felt more motivated in their work, "creating a positive outlook on the outcome of the work" (Grace).

However, visual techniques are not without their challenges. Although the data collected through the methods are more representative of people's views and ways of knowing the world, they can be highly contextual and sometimes personal, so require considerable time to interpret. For example, identifying indicators of community wellbeing from the visual materials produced by the communities required at least three iterations of consultation and feedback. As Grace emphasises, visual techniques are "difficult to access in a short time". When digital equipment is involved, in the cases of PV and PP, there are issues with community members learning how to use equipment, and technical difficulties (for example, lack of electricity, humidity, problems in storage) that can hinder community participation. In addition, visual methods have a range of ethical concerns. Protecting communities' rights and knowledge can be done through following free, prior and informed consent processes, where it is clear to participants what is being visually captured, how, for whom and where it is being disseminated. In Project Cobra, where Indigenous participants were involved in making videos and photostories of their most successful practices, a visual consent form outlining this information was developed and administered to all participants by the Indigenous researchers. As Elisa says:

> 'their [community] rights and knowledges are taken into account if they have the freedom to decide what to film/ photograph, how to do it, how to edit and share the final product. In other words if the communities own the visual output'.

Nevertheless, the fact that community members directly contribute to the visual products also means that they can easily be identified in videos, photographs and drawings. This could expose them to retaliation by those individuals and/or groups, both within and outside the community, if they are openly critical about an issue. On the other hand, we observed that in many of the videos, photostories and drawings, community members were selective with what they disclosed. This could be in response to worries about reprisals, but more commonly was to protect intellectual property. Visual materials could reveal the presence and/or location of natural resources to outsiders who may then exploit these unsustainably and/or remove the rights of Indigenous communities to continue with their traditional livelihoods. As Lakeram points out "visuals are one part of an information sharing or presentation. But what is not provided is the specific of a knowledge which protects the rights to the knowledge". Ownership of visual products, is therefore, of utmost concern, and negotiating how and where material is stored and access rights is key for deciding if visual outputs can be made public, or whether they remain within the custody of communities.

Our use of technology was perceived to be a double-edged sword. ICT, such as videos, photography and associated gadgets such as projectors, made it much easier to engage participants who were unable to read or write, while cutting down on the effort needed to record and communicate in a very challenging environment where physical products such as paper can very quickly degrade. It also "adds to the beauty of the presentation allowing one to get connected and feel involved in an activity" (Lakeram). We are often amazed by the level of community turnout in the evening screenings of the videos, or involved with discussions around spray diagramming indicator posters, encouraging both the team and participants alike to produce more artistic, entertaining and beautiful outputs that could showcase a community and its environment to the outside world. Technology was also valued as a way of recording the knowledge of an older generation for posterity that would otherwise be forgotten, and for facilitating the exchange of knowledge between communities.

But technology was also perceived to be an expensive 'Western' product especially distracting youth from traditional livelihoods. Often, engagement with these technologies, such as with the ECOSENSUS project, would involve a lot of effort and expense, and produce very little of enduring value, apart from the lessons learnt. A frequent observation in the North Rupununi is broken equipment lying around, rusting and deteriorating in the open air or half-burnt in waste pits. Although less enticing for participants, harder to manage for the researchers, and not so easy to copy and share, paper-based visual approaches would at least be a low-cost and non-toxic alternative. However, we also recognise that younger participants, as in all cultures, had a fascination, and a capacity to rapidly familiarise themselves, with technology. So techniques such as PV and PP did provide the allure for youngsters in learning how to operate cameras and edit the imagery on laptops. The big challenge was to try to sustain these tools beyond the lifetime of the project. So, for example, video and photographic equipment has been used by the Indigenous researchers to record weddings in return for a small payment.

Our ultimate aim in the use of visual techniques has been to contribute to some form of positive change, including sustainability and justice, within the North Rupununi communities. "Visual techniques can help redress power inequalities between Indigenous people and external stakeholders, giving Indigenous people a tool that can contribute towards self-determined development" (Jay). We have seen within Project Cobra that identifying local solutions or 'best practices' for natural resource management using visual methods and producing visual products that could be shared with other Indigenous groups, engendered a sense of pride among community members. A counter-narrative to the commonly held deficit model within Indigenous communities – we need help, we are helpless, the visual products showcased community owned solutions – 'we have solutions from which to overcome challenges and there are others that can learn from us'. Indeed, the videos and photostories produced in the North Rupununi inspired the six other Indigenous communities in Brazil, Colombia, Venezuela, Guyana, Suriname and French Guiana with whom they were shared to take action to address their own similar challenges. For example, the community in Suriname was experiencing a loss of community cohesion as a result of the influx of a cash economy, and no-one was willing to repair a bridge connecting two parts of the community, used by children on a daily basis for going to school, without being paid. The North Rupununi video of self-help (volunteer work for community good) sparked a huge debate in the community on community values, leading to a workplan for restoring the bridge, which was eventually completed within three months.

Visual techniques can also have a positive effect by allowing communities to record events as a form of transparency. They are "a powerful tool in bringing about factual information and especially sharing for the benefit of those who are directly impacted in the various areas in a community setting" (Lakeram). There are many cases where, for example, government officials come to Indigenous communities to discuss specific issues, which are then seldom acted upon. Visual techniques provide a form of transparent governance where communities have information in an accessible form that can be used to hold people to account by:

> 'giving more voice to communities, allowing them to reach different audiences at different scales, by empowering communities in the use of new techniques which can be used to pursue communities goals, to become more visible to policymakers, to make their claims' (Elisa).

Conclusions

Despite the many challenges we have faced to date in using visual techniques, we continue to support the approach in our current work and advocate its potential for strengthening the position of marginalised groups, such as Indigenous peoples, to maintaining their cultures and environments. However, while trying to communicate our findings on the power of visual communication, many individuals within our research team have experienced significant prejudice from within the wider academic community and decision makers. The lack of 'numbers' and the perceived 'amateurish' products were not seen to be of value within professional circles and it is a struggle for the outputs to be appreciated by decision makers outside of the Indigenous communities we worked with. Thus, the benefits of visual research are perceived by our team as being directed more to the communities themselves and it is a struggle to break out and use the visual outputs to influence wider decision making. As a result, we have been forced to fall back on the usual products in order to 'translate' the visual outputs into an impact outside of the communities: peer reviewed academic publications; keynote speeches by senior team members; glossy reports and professionally produced videos reworking the visual materials produced by communities. We are aware that making policy and decision makers more open and responsive to visual products and more specifically, to take on board the issues raised within these products and act upon them, is a key area that we have to persevere in.

Notes

[1] Full details on Compendium can be found at http://compendiuminstitute. net

[2] UDIG stands for User-friendly Desktop Internet GIS and full details about it can be found at http://udig.refractions.net

[3] Full detail of the COBRA project can be found at www.projectcobra.org

[4] Project COBRA's MediaGate can be found at http://projectcobra.org/media-gate/

Acknowledgements

We would like to express our deepest gratitude to the North Rupununi community members that have supported our research endeavours. We would like to thank all past and present researchers and 'critical friends' that have contributed to the various projects described in this chapter and the Guyanese institutions that have hosted us so warmly, including the North Rupununi District Development Board, the Bina Hill Institute, the Iwokrama International Centre, and the University of Guyana. We also appreciate the courage of funding bodies that have increasingly supported our visual and participatory research with Indigenous communities. Last, but not least, we ask our loved ones to forgive us for our long absences from home. I hope this chapter has helped explain what your daddy, mummy, wife, husband, brother, sister, son and daughter were up to during those very long weeks and months of absence from home.

References

Ackoff, R.L. (2004) 'Transforming the systems movement', *The Systems Thinker*, 15 (8): 2–5.

Berardi, A., Bachler, M., Bernard, C., Buckingham-Shum, S., Ganapathy, S., Mistry, J., Reynolds, M. and Ulrich W. (2006) 'The ECOSENSUS Project: Co-Evolving Tools', Practices and Open Content for Participatory Natural Resource Management, Second International Conference on e-Social Science. 28–30 June, Manchester.

Berardi, A., Tschirhart, C., Mistry, J., Bignante, E., Haynes, L., Albert, G., Benjamin, R., Xavier, R. and Jafferally, D. (2013) 'From resilience to viability: a case study of Indigenous communities of the North Rupununi, Guyana', *EchoGéo* (24), http://echogeo.revues.org/13411

Berardi, A., Mistry, J., Tschirhart, C., Abraham, J. and Bignante, E. (2012) Report on the cross-scalar interactions and compatibilities governing sustainable development and ecosystem service management of the Guiana Shield, Cobra Project, Milton Keynes: The Open University, http://projectcobra.org/wp-content/uploads/D2.1Reportoncross-scalarinteractionsandcompatibilities3.pdf

Berardi, A., Mistry, J., Tschirhart, C., Bignante, E., Davis, O., Haynes, L., Benjamin, R., Albert, G., Xavier, R., Jafferally, D. and de Ville, G. (2015) 'Applying the system viability framework for cross-scalar governance of nested social-ecological systems in the Guiana Shield, South America', *Ecology and Society*, 20 (3): 42, www.ecologyandsociety.org/vol20/iss3/art42/

Boedhihartono, A.K. (2012) *Visualizing Sustainable Landscapes: Understanding and Negotiating Conservation and Development Trade-offs Using Visual Techniques*, Gland, Switzerland: IUCN and James Cook University.

Bossel, H. (1999) *Indicators for sustainable development - theory, method, applications*. A report to the Balaton Group. International Institute for Sustainable Development, Winnipeg, Manitoba, Canada.

Castello, L. (2001) 'Stock assessment and management of the Arapaima in the North Rupununi, Guyana', Instituto de Desenvolvimento Sustentável Mamiraua, Amazonas, Brasil.

Checkland, P. (1981) *Systems Thinking, Systems Practice*, Chichester: John Wiley and Sons.

Eden, M.J. (1970) 'Savanna vegetation in the northern Rupununi, Guyana', *Journal of Tropical Geography*, 30: 17–28.

Lowe-McConnell, R.H.L. (1964) 'The fishes of the Rupununi savanna district of British Guiana, South America', *Journal of the Linnean Society of London, Zoology*, 45: 103–44. doi: 10.1111/j.1096-3642.1964.tb00490.x

MacDonald, K. (2014) 'Rupununi Imaginaries', PhD dissertation, Graduate Program in Geography, York University, Toronto, Canada.

Mistry, J. and Berardi, A. (2012) 'The challenges and opportunities of participatory video in geographical research: exploring collaboration with Indigenous communities in the North Rupununi, Guyana', *Area*, 44 (1): 110–16.

Mistry, J., Berardi, A. and Mcgregor, D. (2009a) 'Natural resource management and development discourses in the Caribbean: reflections on the Guyanese and Jamaican experience', *Third World Quarterly*, 30 (3): 969–89.

Mistry, J., Berardi, A. and Simpson, M. (2008) 'Birds as indicators of wetland status and change in the North Rupununi, Guyana', *Biodiversity and Conservation*, 17: 2383–409.

Mistry, J., Berardi, A. and Simpson, M. (2009b) 'Critical reflections on practice: the changing roles of three physical geographers carrying out research in a developing country', *Area*, 41 (1): 82–93.

Mistry, J., Berardi, A., Simpson, M., Davis, O. and Haynes, L. (2010a) 'Using a systems viability approach to evaluate integrated conservation and development projects: assessing the impact of the North Rupununi Adaptive Management Process, Guyana', *Geographical Journal*, 176: 241–52.

Mistry, J., Berardi, A., Haynes, L., Davis, D., Xavier, R. and Andries, J. (2014) 'The role of social memory in natural resource management: insights from the North Rupununi, Guyana', *Transactions of the Institute of British Geographers*, http://onlinelibrary.wiley.com/doi/10.1111/tran.12010/abstract

Mistry, J., Berardi, A., Roopsind, I., Davis, O., Haynes, L., Davis, O. and Simpson, M. (2010b) 'Capacity building for adaptive management: a problem-based learning approach', *Development in Practice*, 21(2): 190–204.

Mistry, J., Berardi, A., Tschirhart, C., Bignante, E., Haynes, L., Benjamin, R., Albert, G., Xavier, R., Robertson, B., Davis, O., Jafferally, D. and de Ville, G. (2016) 'Community owned solutions: identifying local best practices for social-ecological sustainability', *Ecology and Society*, 21 (2): 1–17, doi: 10.5751/ES-08496-210242

Mistry, J., Simpson, M., Berardi, A. and Sandy, Y. (2004) 'Exploring the links between natural resource use and biophysical status in the waterways of the North Rupununi, Guyana', *Journal of Environmental Management*, 72: 117–31.

Nietschmann, B (1995) 'Defending the Misiko Reefs with Maps and GIS: Mapping with Sail, Scuba and Satellite', *Cultural Survival Quarterly*, 18 (4): 34–37.

Peluso, N.L (1995) 'Whose Woods are These? Counter-Mapping Forest Territories in Kalimantan, Indonesia', *Antipode*, 4 (27): 383–406. doi:10.1111/j.1467-8330.1995.tb00286.x.

Pickles, R.S.A., McCann, N.P. and Holland, A.P. (2011) 'Mammalian and avian diversity of the Rewa Head, Rupununi, Southern Guyana', *Biota Neotropica*, 11 (3): 237–51.

Read, J.M., Fragoso, J.M., Silvius, K.M., Luzar, J., Overman, H., Cummings, A. and de Oliveira, L.F. (2010) 'Space, place, and hunting patterns among indigenous peoples of the Guyanese Rupununi region', *Journal of Latin American Geography*, 9(3): 213-243.

Reynolds, M. (2011) 'Critical Thinking and Systems Thinking', in C.P. Horvath and J.M. Forte (eds), *Critical Thinking*, New York: Nova Science Publishers, pp 37–68.

Reynolds, M., Berardi, A., Bachler, M., Buckingham-Shum, S., Bernard, C., Mistry, J. and Ulrich, W. (2007) 'ECOSENSUS: developing collaborative learning systems for stakeholding development in environmental planning', OU Conference Curriculum, Teaching & Student Support Conference, The Open University, 2 May

Taylor, J.J. (2008) 'Naming the Land: San Countermapping in Namibia's West Caprivi', *Geoforum*, 39 (5): 1766–775.

Taylor, P., Li, F., Holland, A., Martin, M. and Rosenblatt, A. E. (2016) 'Growth rates of black caiman (Melanosuchus niger) in the Rupununi region of Guyana', *Amphibia-Reptilia*, 37 (1): 9–14.

Tschirhart, C., Mistry, J., Berardi, A., Bignante, E., Simpson, M., Haynes, L., Benjamin, R., Albert, G., Xavier, R., Robertson, B., Davis, O., Verwer, C., de Ville, G. and Jafferally, D. (2016) 'Learning from one another: evaluating the impact of horizontal knowledge exchange for environmental management and governance', *Ecology and Society*, 21 (2): 1–14, 10.5751/ES-08495-210241

ter Welle, B.J.H., Jansen-Jacobs, M.J. and Sipman, H.J.M. (1993) 'Botanical exploration in Guyana. Rupununi District and Kuyuwini River', Internal Report, Herbarium Division, Utrecht University.

Ulrich, W. (2005) 'A Brief Introduction to Critical Systems Heuristics', originally published on the ECOSENSUS website on 14 October 2005; updated on 31 August 2006.

Wetlands Partnership (2008a) *North Rupununi Tourist Handbook*. Georgetown, Guyana.

Wetlands Partnership (2008b) *Tourist Maps of North Rupununi*. Georgetown, Guyana.

SIX

Mapping muck: stakeholders' views on organic waste

Andy Lane, Rachel Slater and Sue Oreszczyn

Editors' introduction

In this chapter the authors explore stakeholders' understanding of what to do with organic waste within the United Kingdom. They discuss two projects that were both commissioned and funded under the same government research programme specifically to support policymaking. Although looking at the same broad environmental sustainability issue of how to treat organic waste as a resource to be exploited rather than a waste product to be disposed of, the two projects use mapping and involve participants in different ways. Both projects also highlight how the use of quantitative survey data is informed by, and in turn informs, the use of diagrams within the overall methodology. The authors also look at these projects through the different ways diagrams can be used that were discussed in Chapter Two.

Introduction

Throughout the 20th century, particularly in developed countries, the use of organic waste, either from food production, processing and consumption, or of green waste from gardening and horticulture was dominated by either very local reuse (for example, household composting, spreading of cow manure on farm land); burning (incineration) or disposal into landfill sites; or feeding to animals, particularly pigs. While very local reuse still continues to some degree today, there has been concern from scientists, environmentalists and policymakers over the contribution of both burning and landfill to emissions of green house gases and leachates. This, among other issues, has led in the past 20 years to a growing range of statutory requirements, notably within the European Union (EU), to reuse and recycle more organic waste rather than send it to landfill.[1] Further, livestock diseases, such as foot and mouth outbreaks caused by poorly treated/contaminated foodstuffs, have led to tighter regulations on the treatment and disposal of animal by-products within the EU. Similarly, significant changes in the practices and habits of food production, processing and consumption have influenced the public's and politicians' perspectives on what to do about food waste, with policy and practice on reducing and recycling waste in a more sustainable manner occurring at household, community, regional, national and international levels.

This chapter draws on our experiences in two projects of contrasting scope and scale but both focused on organic wastes and where the use of mapping techniques was a central or key part of the research process and the research outcomes. Both projects were commissioned by the UK's Department for Environment, Food and Rural Affairs (Defra) and funded under the second phase of its Waste and Resources Evidence Programme.[2] The Open University was the core research organisation for both projects, each of which was led by a different principal investigator and had three different sets of research partners.

The purpose of the first project (Thomas et al, 2009a) was to study attitudes and perceptions towards the spreading of organic waste-derived resources on land (hereafter called the organic wastes project). Essentially, organic waste is being processed in various ways, part of which is to limit its potential to cause environmental (pollution) or health (disease transmission) incidents, but equally such processed waste may provide some environmental benefits to land. Against a background of a paucity of research on attitudes to organic waste, we (the organics wastes project team) brought together for the first time perspectives and attitudes of stakeholders (producers, processors, users) from all parts of the organic resources use cycle – our system of interest (see Chapter Two) – in an interactive and iterative research process. The capacity to spread treated waste to land is determined by various factors – by technology, markets and regulation as well as passive acceptance and active support of these practices. Understanding the attitudes of the public and farmers and the whole chain of stakeholders, from waste producers, to waste processors, to land managers, to food buyers and consumers, therefore, should help inform and establish confidence in policymaking. The project undertook a telephone survey of around 500 farmers and over 1,000 members of the public as well as telephone interviews with key informants and a number of workshops that involved over 50 people from different parts of the organic resources use cycle. Diagramming was used first by us, as the researchers, to frame the methodology and the conception of the organic resources use cycle and to help identify themes from the telephone interviews; and used second with the project's advisory panel and the participants in the workshops. Although we used a large scale quantitative survey for ascertaining the general views of farmers and members of the public, we considered diagramming to be a more appropriate way of involving and ascertaining more detailed views of other groups involved in the organic resources use cycle than quantitative surveys. Not only are the numbers of people in such groups much smaller than for farmers and the public but, also, while the quantitative survey provides a systematic picture of the key issues and information on potential components of the system and a breadth of views on the questions posed by the researchers, it does not provide a systemic understanding of how these are seen to interrelate (see Chapter Two).

In the second, contrasting project (Slater et al, 2010), the aim was to explore the potential of community composting through civil society organisations (CSOs) in contributing to government waste targets and wider social objectives (hereafter called the community composting project). Community composting relates to small scale activities usually carried out by not-for-profit community based organisations or individuals engaging communally to produce compost from garden and food waste, usually for use in locally-based horticulture. Community composters often have wider social and environmental objectives that composting helps them to achieve (Slater and Aiken, 2015). For example, some may be part of broader reuse and recycling projects, local food growing and healthy eating schemes, or city farms and community gardens. Many provide opportunities for individuals to develop personal and work based skills. Although individual groups would be locally known, there was a lack of understanding among policymakers and practitioners of the nature, scale and diversity of community composting activities and impacts across the UK. After completing the first ever survey to profile the sector, this project brought together over 50 community composting groups and used mapping techniques to explore success factors and challenges. We (the community composting project team) then worked individually with five groups and a range of their stakeholders, including workers, volunteers, users, local authorities and support agencies, using a storyboard technique to explore composting activity and its effects from different stakeholder perspectives. Understanding these effects is essential for composters to articulate the value of their activities. This is vital if groups are seeking external support and is important in developing stakeholders' and policymakers' understanding of the sector.

In both cases we (the chapter authors) now reflect on the ways in which we have used mapping in the projects, the reactions and responses of the participants to the use of such methods, and whether the use of mapping led to a more holistic and robust understanding of the context and systems that were being explored. The project reports noted above are both lengthy documents supplemented by several annexes that already provide in-depth insights into the processes as well as the products of the two projects, including the use of diagrams. Our task here is to summarise some key details from these reports and annexes, to compare and contrast the use of diagrams in the two projects and to show how they were integral to them. We start with some common issues before looking at each project in more detail.

Diagrams and research design

It is important that we highlight the complex administrative and organisational context of these two projects because they are important factors in how we variously used diagrams within the projects and also in reflecting on their impact, or not, on actual policymaking. The two projects were commissioned work done under the auspices of a major, long term programme run by a UK government department – Defra. The programme consisted of four phases (each phase largely beginning in 2004, 2007, 2011 and 2013) and involved over 200 individual projects aimed at gathering evidence to inform and support policy and practice around waste and resources. Defra drew up a broad specification and budget for each project, then research teams submitted their proposed fully costed approach. Defra evaluated the various proposals and selected the team and proposal that it felt best met the programme objectives at that time. The projects within the programme ranged from literature reviews, through scientific and technical investigations to social and economic studies (the two projects discussed here fall in the latter category). Lastly, each project had a Defra nominated project manager that project teams liaised with during the project and in many cases projects had an advisory panel. The organic wastes project had such an advisory panel that met four times during the project to act as both a sounding board and for structured discussions to ensure that a cross section of views was considered by the project team, since we were looking at a diverse range of actors and stakeholders involved in organic waste production, processing, management and use. In contrast the community composting project had a more informal advisory group that had a formal meeting at the outset to help inform the research design, followed by ad-hoc input through individual conversations and correspondence throughout the project.

For the organic wastes projects, in particular, the team proposed a methodology where each phase of the project was related to and then informed subsequent phases of the project and that also had both quantitative and qualitative elements in different phases. We felt it important to be able to easily summarise and explain the methodology among the research team, to the (potential) funders of the project proposal and, once the funding was secured, to the advisory panel and to other stakeholders, many of whom were from scientific and technical backgrounds and so less used to a social science led investigation. We therefore spent much time and effort in creating and refining the project diagram (see Figure 6.1) that was our guide throughout the project. The thinking behind this diagram was informed by previous research projects (such as that involving farmers and GM crops in Chapter Four), and we felt that it captured our intentions far more effectively than a more tabular form of representation. It also went through several iterations as the research team discussed and tested their thinking on how to frame the proposal.

The community composting project team did not have a project design diagram but did use a 'design' overview diagram when developing a toolkit for practitioners (Slater et al, 2010: 44). The diagram gave a schematic outline used to communicate intended layout and content as we developed and piloted the toolkit through consultation with practitioner participants and the client. The toolkit was a rich source of information and we felt it important to be able to easily summarise and visualise the intended content among the research team and those consulted on its development.

The framework used in the project provides a structure for a conversation between community composters and their stakeholders, and uses a storyboard as the diagramming tool (which is described in the next section). This storyboarding tool itself was a major part of the participatory research activities for the community composting project and highlights a further aspect – that of providing detailed written/visual instructions on how to create a diagram using the template. It also brings in a tension. Using a very structured diagramming technique with detailed instructions that contains the participants thinking to some degree allows for easier comparisons. However, using a less structured diagramming technique with fewer rules that permits much more free thinking can then become more difficult to analyse and interpret, as we discuss in the next section.

Diagrams and data elicitation

One significant use of diagramming is for data elicitation or gathering of 'evidence' from research participants as noted in Chapter Two. This

Figure 6.1: (Final) Project diagram for the organic wastes project showing the interrelationships between the different phases and elements of the investigation

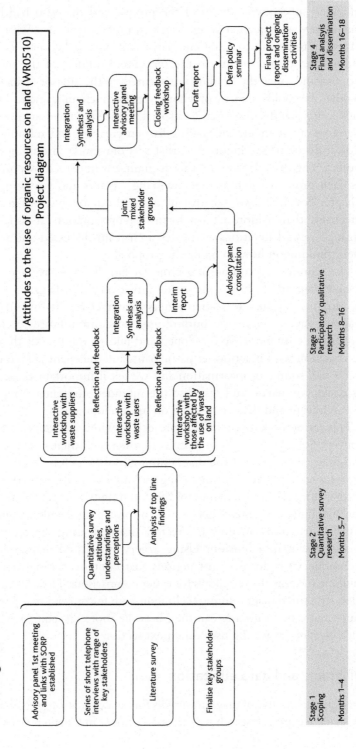

Attitudes to the use of organic resources on land (WR0510)
Project diagram

Source: Thomas et al (2009a)

was central to our two projects, where there were multiple sets of actors or stakeholders (in terms of interested formal groups or organisations) and multiple participants in the various events where diagrams were used. These participants were acting as representatives of their groups or organisations. Inevitably those participants may at times provide more of a personal perspective than an organisational one, although it is to be hoped that if acting as a representative the two are well aligned. However, by involving some of the same people in different workshops or having different representatives at different workshops and by producing photo and other reports back to participants and forward from one event/phase to the next, we believe it is possible to robustly elicit, capture and validate a wide range of perspectives, as we now exemplify from the two Defra projects.

Organic wastes project: research approach

As noted earlier, a series of in-depth workshops involving interactive mapping techniques to help structure and record activities were used to explore the range of different attitudes and perceptions held about the use of organic resources on land by different stakeholder groups and key opinion formers. They were also designed to build on the scoping study and the findings of the quantitative surveys, particularly on contentious aspects around health, safety and environmental impacts. We saw this feed-forward of findings as invaluable in helping to shape the discussions and diagramming exercises in the workshops but equally we had to be careful that these findings did not unnecessarily constrain what participants might say or draw.

To allow members of the research team the time and space to participate in activities and/or observe participant groups as they worked, all the workshops were professionally facilitated (as also seen in Chapters Three and Four). And, as with the feeding in of prior findings we, as the research team, had to be careful that we did not direct or constrain the discussions in the groups we participated in and how the participants constructed their diagrams.

We also informed participants that these events were being conducted under the Chatham House Rule (see Chapter Two) and that all material provided and generated in the workshops would not be attributed to any individual stakeholder. This had the advantage of generating some forthright and sometimes heated discussions. But it also had the disadvantages of groups sometimes focusing too much on the discussion compared to capturing their collective thinking in the diagram and this distracted from the fact that it is a collective or mixed stakeholder perspective rather than a single stakeholder perspective. In some cases we were able to have groups with only representatives from one part of the organic resources use cycle but more often the groups were mixed, as described next.

Organic wastes project: 1st phase individual stakeholder group workshops

Three participatory workshops were planned, in the first phase (see Figure 6.1). They were based around three categories of stakeholder groups:

- Organic waste processors
- Those who do or could use organic waste-derived resources on land
- Those affected by the use of these resources on land

In the end two events were held, the first event involving the first group listed and with the second event including both the latter two groups thus allowing a combination of whole group activity and a split into two parallel workshops for more group specific activities. In total 46 persons attended the workshops. Workshops two and three were combined into one event due to the poor response from two stakeholder groups in particular. This was disappointing but can often be a feature of invitation workshops. We discuss the impact of this in the section on representativeness below. Both workshops used two types of mapping exercise to focus discussions: issues mapping and force field analysis.

Issues mapping

In order to provide a wider perspective initially, we followed a similar approach to the mapping of key issues that we had done earlier in the project at an advisory panel meeting. This activity involved participants individually writing issues of concern to them around organic material on land on sticky notes. These were then collected by members of the project team and participants were given the opportunity to clarify their meaning as they were grouped on flip chart paper by the facilitator. This enabled themes to become evident and these were given labels and clustered in agreement with the participants. The reason we chose this approach is that it ensured we gathered views from all participants before they were influenced by any detailed group discussion, while clustering their individual perception collectively in open discussion provided a structured way to gain a wider perspective and have it agreed to and affirmed by the participants. A potential disadvantage of the open discussion is that, while it provides a 'crowd-based' view of the themes, it does not provide different sets of clustering that might have occurred if this had been done in smaller groups and the results compared and contrasted. In order to mitigate against such group think, we took photographic records or made transcriptions of all the diagrams produced in all the workshops and a photographic record was provided to all participants after the workshop for them to challenge or make new comments.

Figure 6.2 gives an example of one segment of the flip chart based issues map generated at one of the workshops. These maps were then

Figure 6.2: Example issues map drawn for the organic waste project

Source: Thomas et al (2009a)

transcribed to provide the official record noted above and for us as the research team to discern any different or higher level groupings of issues to reflect the balance of concerns lies for different stakeholder groups.

Force field analysis

Force field analysis (Lewin, 1951; Start and Hovland, 2004)[3] is a method used to highlight power structures helping or hindering change and was also used for one of the projects described in Chapter Three. To stimulate discussion around the force field analysis, preliminary findings from the scoping phase and the quantitative survey were reported to the participants. This prompted comments and started a very open discussion within and among the stakeholders. The first step of the analysis involved the participants, in groups of similar stakeholders, listing all relevant forces driving or restraining change either side of a box containing the issue under consideration (see Figure 6.3 for an example). The issue chosen for this exercise was: *How can we recycle more organic waste to land and close the loop* (closing the loop refers to our conception of an organic resources use cycle). Participants were then asked to give a weighting to the strength of each force ranging between one and five, with one being extremely weak and five particularly strong. After finishing these tasks the different groups were asked to present their discussions and findings to the other workshop groups.

Organic wastes project: Phase 2 mixed stakeholder group workshops

In order to explore the diversity of views of stakeholders and highlight areas where there may be agreement and/or disagreement, a workshop was held to bring together stakeholders from different groups (see Figure 6.1). This workshop attracted 29 stakeholders, 16 of which had participated in one of the earlier workshops, thus providing a reasonable degree of continuity.

Building on our previous use of scenarios to structure discussions in other projects (see Chapters Three and Four), three different scenarios were used. These concerned the future of organic resource application to land in the UK and were used as a tool for generating discussions among the participants and to highlight aspects that were felt to be important. Participants were divided into three groups and each asked to initially consider the potential causes (or drivers) and consequences (or effects) of one of the scenarios. The scenarios were chosen by

Figure 6.3: Example of a force field map drawn by participants in the organic wastes project

Source: Thomas et al (2009a)

us and endorsed by the advisory panel to represent potential short to medium term consequences of current developments (and are described in Section 5.2 of the main report by Thomas et al, 2009a). All three groups were provided with an opportunity to contribute to each of the scenarios by the sharing and presenting of each separate discussion and consequent map to the whole group (see Figure 6.4 for an example map.

Recording and feedback: the role of diagrams

As before, the maps were photographed and used to produce a photo report for the participants. These records have become a feature of

Figure 6.4: Example of a complete cause and consequence scenario map

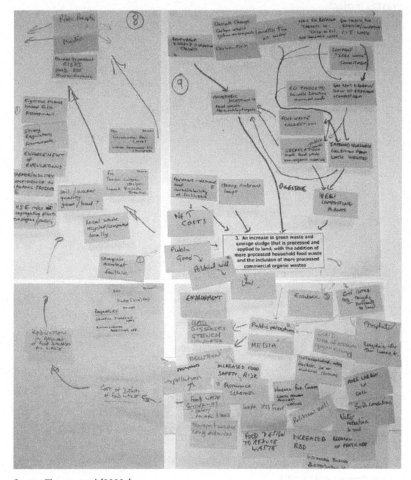

Source: Thomas et al (2009a)

our way of working as our experience has shown how important they are as both a record of the event for all the participants involved, and not just the researchers, but also as a way to provide immediate feedback following an event. This helps with enabling greater involvement of the participants, shows our appreciation for their time and helps to build relationships with them. Indeed we had many participants, and advisory panel members, comment positively on both the mapping methods we used and the photo records we provided. However while few provided any additional comments we cannot fully know if this was through agreement or indifference to the outcomes.

Representativeness in the mapping outputs

A big issue we faced in the workshops and thus the mapping exercises was ensuring that the maps and any analysis of them was representative of stakeholder views and provided a comprehensive picture of views of the organic resources use cycle as our system of interest if it is to inform and support policymaking. The individual stakeholders attending the workshops represented organisations or companies that belonged to a wide range of different stakeholder sectors or groups associated with the organic resource use cycle. However, the individuals or the organisations that they represented were not a representative sample of their stakeholder sectors, as the numbers involved were small for each sector. Consequently it was not possible to attribute the views of these individuals as being representative of the sectors of which they were a part; rather they were considered to reflect views from that sector. However, in the first phase workshops the different graphical presentations were marked to allow the outputs to be traced back to their specific stakeholder group. By doing so, like-minded stakeholders could be identified (although kept anonymous throughout the report). For instance, farmer groups and their outputs can be distinguished from other stakeholder groups.

A total of 240 stakeholders were invited to attend our workshops, which included over 1,000 separate approaches by letter, email and telephone. In approaching the stakeholders, the team experienced a high willingness to participate by the waste management industry, organic waste contractors, compost industry, water companies, regulators from the devolved regions, professional bodies, horticulture, forestry, and (in particular) farmers and farming associations.

Despite significant and ongoing efforts, over several months, to attract food retailers they were disinclined to attend although repeated efforts had been made to convince them of the importance of their participation. We approached the major supermarket chains but none were able to attend. One representative of a major supermarket chain was interviewed during the scoping phase. However, several food industry businesses and representatives (such as the British Retail Consortium) did attend the workshops.

It was also difficult to motivate many non-governmental organisations to attend. We approached many organisations representing interests around the application of organic material on land concerning either potential health/ food or environmental concerns. However, only a few were responsive; some commented that as a small organisation they were not able to commit to events outside their main campaign areas and that this was not one of them. Further, although the workshops attracted participants from England, Scotland and Wales, they did not attract participants from Northern Ireland.

The lack of involvement of these two stakeholder groups meant that the workshops did not include contributions from people from all possible stakeholder groups but, as noted above, no participants could be considered representative of their group, rather they represented likely views from that group. In addition, the findings are the combined outcomes from the specific activities undertaken in each workshop, findings that were checked with all participants to ensure they fairly represented the views expressed during that particular workshop by those participating. And by feeding findings from one workshop into the next there was further opportunity for participants to comment on and add to those findings. While contributions from these two groups would have extended participation in the mapping activities, the iterative processes described here mean that we believe the combined outcomes from the whole process are unlikely to be different to those were they to have participated.

Community composting project: research approach

As with the organic wastes project, the community composting project adopted a participatory approach (see Chapter One). Two project partners were network organisations for practitioners and in consultation with some of their members, they played an important role in helping to develop the initial proposal, design the processes and deliver the project.

The main aim of the project was to evaluate the contribution the community composting sector could make towards Defra's waste related targets and to the government's more broad based environmental and social objectives. This evaluation process necessitated both quantitative and qualitative methodologies. Phase 1 comprised a self-administered questionnaire of community composters across the UK to estimate the number and type of groups involved, and the scale and nature of activities. Questions focused on the direct, tangible and often easily quantifiable variables, such as tonnes of waste collected and composted, participation rates and numbers of volunteers involved. It represents the largest survey of community composters undertaken in the UK to date (n=243) and achieved a high response rate of 61% (n=149). Results from this quantitative approach had the advantage of providing a comprehensive snapshot of collective community composting activity across the UK, but was limited in helping to understand the effects of this activity.

Phase 2 comprised nine one-day participatory workshops with more than 150 stakeholders. The workshops employed mapping techniques for a more in-depth exploration of composting activity. Conversations and group working were focused on the effects of activities from different stakeholder perspectives and how these could be articulated, evaluated and demonstrated.

As with the organic wastes project, all the workshops were professionally facilitated and conducted under the Chatham House Rule (see Chapter Two) and participants knew that individual contributions would not be attributed. This was important to encourage participants to speak freely. There are many challenging and potentially sensitive aspects to CSO waste projects including funding and income generation, working with private and/or public sector actors, and often negotiating complicated regulations.

The nine workshops were carried out over a six-month period between autumn 2007 and spring 2008, and were structured into four workshops in Round 1 and five in Round 2.

Round 1 workshops: issues mapping and storytelling

The first workshop was a pilot carried out at an annual conference to develop the issues and questions for subsequent workshops. Then three workshops were held to bring together a large number of community composting groups representing the spread of activities and types of groups identified in Phase 1. These workshops were held in Exeter, London and Sheffield to give a wide geographical spread, and were attended by 55 participants representing 46 different groups. This represented a large proportion (over 50%) of groups active in composting household waste identified in Phase 1.

Each workshop had a similar structure; participants were provided with a workbook outlining the activities for the day together with discussion prompts. Starting with an issues mapping activity and initially working in small groups, participants undertook a storytelling exercise about their project, noting success factors and challenges. Working in plenary, these success factors and challenges were clustered and common themes identified by participants. Then, in larger groups, each with a facilitator, participants worked through the storyboard (impact mapping) outlined below.

Round 2 workshops: storyboarding

Using data from Phase 1 and Round 1 workshops, five models were developed by the research team to characterise the most common community composting activities (see Slater et al, 2010: 31, for examples of the models). Five groups were purposively selected in Round 2, each one an example of one of the five models, with the aim of capturing some of the diversity across the sector and exploring whether effects were common across the groups or specific to an individual group. Five one-day workshops were carried out, each with a different community composting group and a range of their stakeholders for example, workers from the project, volunteers, users (householders), local authorities, housing association, support agencies, and so on. The workshops focused on mapping the social and environmental impacts of the community composters' work from different stakeholder perspectives, and collectively exploring what is important to measure, and how to go about measuring it in a meaningful way.

Impact mapping using a storyboard

The storyboard for impact mapping is a diagram based tool developed by one of our project partners (New Economic Foundation, 2000). It is relatively linear and underpinned by structured and sequenced questions (for an example of the storyboard template and full set of questions see Slater et al, 2010; see Chapter Five for another use of storyboarding as a visual technique). At the heart of the storyboard are five questions on composting 'activities', 'outputs', 'outcomes' and 'ways of knowing', summarised below:

- *Activities* – what is it you do to effect some sort of change in people, the community, or environment? (For example, a composting service, a programme for volunteers.)

- *Outputs* – what are easily observable, countable, direct results? Who/what are the beneficiaries? (For example, tonnes of organic waste diverted from landfill, quantity of compost produced for local horticulture, number of volunteers, number of trainees.)

- *Outcomes* – why are the outputs important in terms of longer-term change, for a local environment or group of people? (For example, reducing methane emissions from landfill, improving health and wellbeing, engaging in meaningful activity, community cohesion, improved local environment.)

- *Ways of knowing* – how do you know if a particular outcome is achieved? (For example, can the methane emissions, health and wellbeing, new skills be demonstrated or measured?)

The storyboard also tries to make explicit the assumptions that mean outputs give rise to outcomes; for example, does volunteer involvement lead to a more cohesive community or are other activities important? It also considers barriers or challenges faced by composting groups that may limit their activities and its effects.

As an ice-breaking exercise the storyboard began with participants working in pairs and sharing a success, benefit or something about the project they were proud of, which was then recounted by their partner to the rest of the group. The aim of this was to help participants feel comfortable, to settle into their day and to promote initial dialogue. In Round 1 (with representatives from multiple projects) it proved an efficient way for participants to learn about other projects. It did run the risk of influencing some of the subsequent responses; however, the research team felt that the participatory approach through the rest of the day, together with the post-workshop opportunity to comment on data collected, limited this risk.

To discuss the storyboard questions in Round 1 participants worked in small groups, then discussed their storyboards in plenary; the Round 2 participants worked in one group. They used sticky notes, which enabled iteration in moving comments around the storyboard. Figure 6.5 shows the iterative process of a storyboard being completed. Each storyboard was transcribed by the research team and sent to participants to agree it represented their input.

Participant and researcher reflections on completing the storyboard

Feedback from participants indicated that the completion of the storyboard was a valuable exercise, illustrated by the quotes from research participants below. For Round 1 this value was embodied in composters reviewing their purpose, priorities and resultant activities, together with learning about and from other community projects. This was similar in Round 2 but the storyboard also proved a useful mechanism for composters to engage in meaningful conversation with their stakeholders, particularly around 'ways of knowing' or potential indicators to demonstrate the effects of their activities identified in the storyboard:

Figure 6.5: Participants completing a storyboard

'I thought the workshop was excellent and I learnt a good deal from it ... the way the flow diagrams worked made us really analyse what we've been doing and what more could be done.'

'Breaking down all that we do into the storyboard template was extremely useful and a real eye opener in terms of how we can work more effectively with the local community.' 'I really enjoyed Friday's workshop ... the methods used for measuring and discussion were excellent.'

From the researchers' observations, composters' completion of the first part of the storyboard and making explicit activities and identifying outputs proved engaging and relatively straightforward, and there were lively discussions about barriers and challenges.

What was much more difficult was considering longer-term effects (or outcomes) and ways to demonstrate these. For example, an inner city project claimed it had helped reduce problems with vermin and improve local green spaces but it had difficulty evidencing this to its activities. In part this is likely to reflect real world difficulties where effects are the result of multiple variables. In part it is likely to reflect the small scale and often precarious nature of many community groups frequently reliant on teams of volunteers, key individuals and grant funding that prioritises short term viability rather than long term vision.

Using the storyboard technique with its associated structured questions enabled some consistency in systematically reflecting on a range of different projects, which was important to better understand the diversity identified in Phase 1. As mentioned previously this has the potential for relatively straightforward comparisons compared to more unstructured approaches, but is likely to have influenced participants' input compared to more open and free thinking techniques such as those used in the organic waste project. We (the community composting project team) were aware of this and encouraged discussion and probed areas that participants raised beyond the elements of the storyboard. As with the organic waste project, participants were given the opportunity to comment on photo reports of data elicited in the workshops as well as the transcribed storyboards.

The storyboard proved a valuable mechanism for facilitating a conversation between composters and their stakeholders. However on reflection, the one-way linear flow of the storyboard could be adapted to consider two-way influences. For example, to consider how activities might need to change if they do not give rise to the desired effects.

Using diagrams for data analysis and presenting findings

Chapter Two discussed the issues of producing 'tidy' versions of participant generated maps to help with analysis and/or presenting findings. An example of tidying up a diagram from the organic wastes project is the force field diagram where the type of map produced in the workshop (Figure 6.3) has been reworked into a more understandable format as shown in Figure 6.6, which in turn was also used in the project report and in presentations to the funders. The community composting project produced a synthesis diagram that proved a useful top-level summary for dissemination (see Slater et al, 2010). However inferences from this top-level summary should be made with caution as they only tell part of the story.

Chapter Two also discussed presenting findings as diagrams. As we have seen both projects had iterative steps in their design such that the findings of an earlier step, both the participant generated maps and the research team's analysis and synthesis of them, were presented back not only to the actual participants of that workshop but also sometimes to

Figure 6.6: A post hoc cleaned up version of a force field diagram produced in a workshop like the one shown in Figure 6.3

Workshop 1: Organic waste processors

G 1: Regulators, professional institutions and regional authorities

+
5-fertiliser prices
5-end of waste
5-landfill targets
4-LATS
4-quality standards
3-protocols
3-local authorities' targets
3-regulations (environment protection, confidence)
3-waste strategy
2-public sector (green procurement)
2-climate change
2-feel good factor/green credentials
1-anaerobic digestion (treatment and energy recovery)
1-perceptions/acceptability
2-NVZ
3-recycling targets have effects
3-economics of production (regulation)
3-perceptions
4-regulatory barriers
5-how we produce value
5-supermarkets supply chain – loop not closed
5-waste vs. resource
5-individual agendas rather than joined up supply chain
—

Source: Thomas et al (2009a)

participants of future workshops (and in the case of the organic wastes project the advisory panel).

The final stage of the organic wastes project involved an interactive advisory panel meeting and a final interactive stakeholder workshop to provide feedback on our main findings, both of which involved the presentation of diagrams and more mapping exercises. It also involved a seminar hosted by Defra to discuss the projects outcomes with a range of policy representatives.

Lastly, we also talked about communicating the issue around this topic in a conference publication (Thomas et al, 2009b) where we discussed stakeholders' knowledge of the organic resources use cycle, uncertainty over impacts and benefits, impact of knowledge on attitudes, the need for research and better knowledge and public understanding and communications. But next we want to consider the impact of our work on some of those stakeholders before making some concluding observations.

Impacts on policymakers and practitioners

Evaluating the impact of the diagramming as one (significant) part of our research projects on subsequent policy and practice is not straightforward. In one sense the methods we used for collecting, analysing and presenting the evidence could be said to be much less important for policymakers and practitioners than the actual findings and recommendations. Attitudes to, and willingness to participate in, the organic wastes mapping exercises was generally very positive among both the advisory panel members and the workshop participants. The greatest scepticism about diagramming (and qualitative methods in general) came from natural scientists who were more interested in the quantitative elements of the project. From our broader experience we attribute this scepticism to scientists' greater reliance on statistical evaluations to ensure findings are robust and have difficulties in accepting the robustness of findings based on qualitative evidence. This is why, from the outset, we designed a detailed, iterative and participatory methodology for the organic wastes project as set out in Figure 6.1. We also think that as mapping in various forms is being increasingly used in businesses and consultation workshops such that practitioners are more familiar with it as a tool or technique in general, if not within a research project. Having said all that, we also have extensive experience in our teaching and research with people who dislike diagrams, do not see themselves as 'visual thinkers' and where mapping possibly hinders the data elicitation and capture process.

A similar form of scepticism can be found around systems thinking and presenting findings within that paradigm rather than a scientific paradigm. However, we have increasingly found that policymakers in general, and Defra staff in particular, are aware of, and using, systems thinking, including diagramming in their own work. A clear example is that one of the other funded projects within the same Waste Resources Evidence Programme was on systems thinking and system dynamics modelling to support policy development using waste prevention and recycling as case studies (Freeman et al, 2014), while one of us has personal experience of attending meetings and events at Defra where the training or professional development of Defra staff in systems thinking and diagramming has been a key theme.

Assessing the exact impact on policy and policymaking of the two projects discussed in this chapter is easier for one (community composting) than the other (organic wastes). In part this is because, as already noted, these were but two of a large number of projects looking at different aspects of waste. In part, the project briefs Defra set out were designed more to do with providing findings to inform policy rather than to generate clear policy recommendations. And in part it was down to the scope of the commissioned project itself.

Thus with the organic wastes project a policy seminar was held at Defra with a range of policymakers from Defra – from departments concerned with waste strategy and waste policy; farming and food; and water quality. Also attending were representatives from other policy bodies. The aims and objectives of the seminar were to disseminate the main findings of the research to a particular policy audience and discuss policy implications of the project outcomes (these are fully set out in the project report) grouped under:

- attitudes to policy arrangements, for example, a perception that regulation and 'standards' were too weak and lacked appropriate enforcement;
- attitudes driving behaviours, for example, public opinion can have a strong impact on whether more organic waste-derived resources will be used on land;
- attitudes and understanding, for example it is the use of recycled food waste on agricultural land – part of the food chain cycle – that gives rise to most concerns; and
- attitudes affecting motivation respectively, for example, it is vital to gain the support of food retailers for the use of organics waste-derived resources on land used to grow food as presently they were perceived by stakeholders as a barrier to increased application.

However, Defra also had (and still has at the time of writing) significant strands of work around organic wastes and in particular anaerobic digestion as a means both to safely process organic waste but also to generate energy from the waste (as methane). Indeed it is fair to say that recently in the UK more policymaking effort has been put into dealing with the organic wastes stream through anaerobic digestion than with composting.[4] Although it is notable that the UK government published comprehensive guidance on managing waste on land for land managers in 2014[5] and at the time of writing is consulting on proposed changes to land spreading and waste storage standard rules.[6]

Similarly it is difficult to assess whether either project has had significant impacts on the practitioners who participated. Many participants commented on how useful they found the workshops in gaining a better understanding of all parts of the organic resources use cycle (organic waste project) or analysing their project motivations and activities (community composting) and the thinking of other stakeholders. But it was not part of the projects to follow up with the participants after the projects themselves has finished. Indeed this can be a significant weakness in that while attention and enthusiasm of participants can be sustained during the projects this will almost inevitably fall away afterwards unless there are definite policy or practice changes that flow from the research itself.

There is a much clearer influence on actual policy from the survey work in Phase 1 of the community composting project but not from the storyboard. Organisations dealing with waste are subject to strict regulations and licensing via permits, from the largest commercial companies through to small community recyclers or composters. There are some exemptions to this licensing requirement and, as part of a UK government review, a new criteria for exemptions was proposed. The exemption is vital for many community composting groups because they operate at such a small scale and the costly licensing process, designed primarily for commercial waste companies, is prohibitive and not fit for purpose. Using the data from the survey the community composting network were able to demonstrate how many small scale operators would be affected and made a case for a more scale and risk based approach. Defra accepted this case and thus amended the criteria.

The project helped to raise the profile of community composting and some of the findings were reported in the waste management press (Letsrecycle, 2007). Findings showed that composting projects aimed at developing environmental sustainability (such as diverting organic waste from landfill and using compost to develop community gardens) can have wider benefits for the individuals and communities involved, such as helping to create a sense of belonging and wellbeing, learning new skills, developing community green spaces (Slater et al, 2010; Frederickson et al, 2013). This adds to accumulating evidence of a relationship between environmentally responsible behaviour and subjective wellbeing (Brown and Kasser, 2005; Jacob et al, 2009). Following the project, a review of waste policy by Defra (2011) highlighted the potential of community composting for delivering local environmental, economic and social benefits.

Conclusions

From our experiences in this and other projects, we hope it is clear how diagramming has played a role in all stages and processes of our research, although this has admittedly been more significant at some stages than others. We have discussed various advantages and disadvantages of the diagramming throughout the chapter but here we want to add to those reflections.

As with other projects in this book, continuous reflection on our methods and or findings was an important part of the research process and was therefore ongoing throughout the research. This included long discussions as to the exact diagram to use at which event. So our first conclusion is that the use of mapping methods within research projects has to be clearly designed in from the outset and that all or part of that design also needs clearly communicating to both the funders (the clients), any advisory panel and all the workshop participants, and that diagrams can help do this.

A second, related conclusion is that using a professional facilitator to reduce any bias that may be caused by forceful or reluctant individuals helps groups to arrive at a reasonable and robust collective (plural not singular) view alongside the diagramming technique. However, as discussed earlier, some participants may be antagonistic to the use of diagrams for a variety of reasons. We did not, however, experience this in our two projects. This may be because all the diagramming work was done in groups rather than with individuals and so any antagonism may have been hidden or compensated for by others in the group.

Our third conclusion also relates to the importance of building and maintaining good relationships with all our projects' participants. Providing records of the diagrams produced (and any notes or recordings of conversations about them) is also important in making the participants' contributions feel valued and acknowledged, and for inviting further input. There can be a downside to this in that a non-response to such an invitation may be because they are happy with these records and summaries but may also be down to an indifference or unwillingness to respond even though they had something more to say. Again, by seeking input from as many people as feasible and having some participants attending more than one phase of the project we tried to mitigate against any such non-response bias.

Our final conclusion is also about good relationships but in this case with the funders. As these were commissioned projects, unlike others in this book, there were particular constraints placed on the projects' initial design and who could be involved in it. This direct interaction with the project funder throughout the research was not a problem in itself but did take up more time than has been the case for projects where we have not been so constrained.

Acknowledgements

The authors would like to thank Defra for funding the research projects discussed in the chapter as part of the Waste and Resources Evidence Programme. Views expressed herein are those of the authors and are not necessarily those of Defra. The authors would also like to acknowledge the contributions to this research by our project partners and the many participants.

Notes

[1] The European Environment Agency – www.eea.europa.eu – details these alongside other environmental sectors, including producing an annual state of the environment report.

[2] The most recent Defra plan can be found at https://www.gov.uk/government/publications/collaborative-waste-resources-and-sustainable-consumption-evidence-programme

[3] See also www.mindtools.com/pages/article/newTED_06.htm and www.valuebasedmanagement.net/methods_lewin_force_field_analysis.html

[4] See www.gov.uk/government/uploads/system/uploads/attachment_data/file/406928/pb14019-anaerobic-digestion-annual-report-2013-14.pdf

[5] See www.gov.uk/guidance/manage-waste-on-land-guidance-for-land-managers

[6] See www.gov.uk/government/consultations/proposed-changes-to-landspreading-and-waste-storage-standard-rules

References

Brown, K.W. and Kasser, T. (2005) 'Are psychological and ecological well-being compatible? The role of values, mindfulness, and lifestyle', *Social Indicators Research*, 74(2): 349–68.

Defra (2011) 'Government Review of Waste Policy in England 2011', London: Department for Environment, Food and Rural Affairs (Defra), www.gov.uk/government/uploads/system/uploads/attachment_data/file/69401/pb13540-waste-policy-review110614.pdf

Frederickson, N., Frederickson, J. and Slater, R. (2013) 'Psychological outcomes of community composting projects', in Proceedings: American Psychological Association Annual Convention, Hawaii.

Freeman, R., Jones, L., Yearworth, M. and Cherruault, J-Y. (2014) 'Systems Thinking and System Dynamics to Support Policy Making in Defra', Project Final Report, http://randd.defra.gov.uk/Default. aspx?Menu=Menu&Module=More&Location=None&Project ID=18386&FromSearch=Y&Status=3&Publisher=1&SearchText= systems thinking&SortString=ProjectCode&SortOrder=Asc& Paging=10#Description

Jacob, J., Jovic, E. and Brinkerhoff, M.B. (2009) 'Personal and planetary well-being: Mindfulness meditation, pro-environmental behavior and personal quality of life in a survey from the social justice and ecological sustainability movement', *Social Indicators Research*, 93(2): 275–94.

Lewin, K. (1951) *Field Theory in Social Science*, New York: Harper.

Letsrecycle (2007) 'Community composting limited by lack of space', Letsrecycle.com, www.letsrecycle.com/news/latest-news/ community-composting-limited-by-lack-of-space/

New Economics Foundation (2000) *'Prove it'!* London: New Economics Foundation, http://b.3cdn.net/nefoundation/ c5034927ec5d18d5c6_11m6ba5sc.pdf

Slater, R., Frederickson, J. and Yoxon, M. (2010) 'Unlocking the potential of community composting: Annex 3 Workshop Findings', full peer reviewed project report to Defra, http://randd.defra.gov. uk/Default.aspx?Menu=Menu&Module=More&Location=None &ProjectID=14759&FromSearch=Y&Publisher=1&SearchText= WR0211&SortString=ProjectCode&SortOrder=Asc&Paging=10 #Description

Slater, R. and Aiken, M. (2015) 'Can't you count? Public service delivery and standardized measurement challenges – the case of community composting', *Public Management Review*, 17 (8): 1085–102.

Thomas, C., Lane, A., Oreszczyn, S., Schiller, F. and Yoxon, M. (2009a) 'Attitudes to the Use of Organic Waste Resources on Land', full peer reviewed project report to Defra, http://randd.defra.gov.uk/Default. aspx?Menu=Menu&Module=More&Location=None&ProjectID =15241&FromSearch=Y&Publisher=1&SearchText=WR0510& SortString=ProjectCode&SortOrder=Asc&Paging=10#Description

Thomas, C., Lane, A., Oreszczyn, S., Schiller, F. and Yoxon, M. (2009b) 'Recycling organic waste resources to land – communicating the issues', in proceedings of The International Solid Wastes Association World Congress 2009, 12–15 October, Lisbon, Portugal, http://oro. open.ac.uk/22896/

Start, D. and Hovland, I. (2004) *Tools for Policy Impact: A Handbook for Researchers*, London: Overseas Development Institute.

SEVEN

Understanding and developing communities of practice through diagramming

Chris Blackmore, Natalie Foster,
Kevin Collins and Ray Ison

Editors' introduction

In this chapter the authors draw on their experiences over many years of research into social learning systems. They focus particularly on communities of practice *as* social learning systems and reflect on their experiences of using diagramming to map and share understandings and develop knowledge in such systems, mainly in the context of water governance and climate change. The authors have used diagramming techniques as a core part of their research, building on a range of systemic and participatory traditions that are a prime focus of this book. They explain and reflect on how their experiences with diagrams have been an essential part of various action-oriented research processes that have been designed to take a systemic approach to understanding the institutional, biophysical, social and economic dynamics associated with managing water resources, climate adaptation and the related issues of governance.

Introduction

Communities of practice (CoPs) have become well known and popular among academics and other practitioners (see also Chapter Four). Both the concept of a CoP and its enactment appear to provide explanatory power and create value for many when used for social learning activities such as creating knowledge together, and stimulating change (Wenger et al, 2011). CoPs reached encyclopaedia status in the context of information and knowledge management over a decade ago (Coakes and Clarke, 2006) and a quick internet search provides evidence that they remain relevant to large numbers of practitioners.

In this chapter we are concerned with practices of relevance to environmental sustainability in the context of water and with those who are engaging in them or facilitating these practices. The process and role of making visual representations, specifically diagramming, is explored here as a part of these engagement or facilitation processes. We argue that diagramming can be used in the context of CoPs as tools for communication and for exploring ideas and meanings both collectively and individually. The use of appropriate tools for communication and negotiating meanings associated with practice has long been recognised as an essential part of the shared repertoire of any community of practice (Wenger, 1998).

Communities of practice

As previously noted in Chapter Four, the term community of practice was coined by Jean Lave and Etienne Wenger and appeared in a range of literature from around 1991 (for example, Barab and Duffy, 2000; Brown and Duguid, 1991; Chaiklin and Lave, 1993; Kimble et al, 2000; Lave and Wenger, 1991; McDermott, 1999; Wenger, 1998, 2010; Wenger and Snyder, 2000; Wenger et al, 2002). Wenger et al (2002: 4) define CoPs as 'groups of people who share a concern, a set of problems or a passion about a topic and who deepen their knowledge and expertise in this area by interacting on an ongoing basis'. This kind of interaction suggests a need for communication and conversation skills and techniques. The recognition of groupings of people who interact around their practices, with the aim of improving them, goes far back in history. Wenger et al (2002: 5) suggest that CoPs were humankind's first knowledge-based social structures, exemplified by cave people working together on their hunting strategies, the 'corporations' of craftsmen of ancient Rome, and the guilds of artisans of the European Middle Ages. We know from cave drawings and other artwork relating to these times, from many parts of the world, that visual representations of practice-based interactions have been made throughout human history.

Examples of contemporary CoPs and the use of the theories that have developed around them can be found in different sectors ranging from health (Stephens, 2007; le May, 2009), to police services (de Laat, 2006), to farming (Oreszczyn and Lane, 2006; Bailey, 2013) to education (Kimble et al, 2008) to water and environmental regulation, risk and management (Jørgensen and Lauridsen, 2005; Attwater and Derry, 2005; Allen et al, 2011; Collins and Ison, 2010; Dieperink et al, 2012; Madsen and Noe, 2012). Practices of relevance to environmental sustainability and those who are engaging in them or facilitating them cross many of these sectors. In recent years there has been a growing interest in the practices of sustainability (Collins and Ison, 2009; Barth and Michelsen, 2013; Shove and Spurling, 2013; Strengers and Maller, 2014; Colvin et al, 2014; Westberg and Polk, 2016). This increased interest is particularly evident in the context of consumption and climate change which are areas where discourses underpinned by behaviourist theories of learning have tended to dominate, rather than more systemic views of changing practices.

Wenger et al (2002: 27–8) present a structural model of a CoP with three fundamental elements:

- a *domain* of knowledge, which defines a set of issues,
- a *community* of people who care about this domain and
- the shared *practice* that they are developing to be effective in their domain.

Snyder and Wenger (2004) observed that a community's effectiveness as a social learning system depends on its strength in these structural dimensions of 'domain', 'community' and 'practice'. 'The art of community development is to use the synergy between domain, community and practice to help a community evolve and fulfil its potential' (Wenger et al, 2002: 47).

Communities of practice and sustainability

The notion of a community of practice has particular resonance among those who are trying to learn their way together towards concerted action for the purpose of managing or bringing about systemic change in the context of sustainability (for example, Collins and Ison, 2009; Colvin et al, 2014). Concerted action means that the overall performance is significant. As in a concert individuals need to make their contributions together but in relation to others. In terms of domain these groups are usually associated with an area of specialist knowledge rather than with a whole sector, for instance practitioners involved in developing and promoting renewable energy, growing and supplying local food, or managing water catchments.

By way of examples of where we have found diagramming useful we consider mainly domains associated with water. In these cases elements of CoPs may be described as follows.

Domains of knowledge

Knowledge and knowing about water covers a huge range as water is fundamental to all life. Examples of domains of knowledge that define sets of issues include meteorological, hydrological, chemical and biophysical domains. Floods, droughts, groundwater, rivers, wetlands, drinking water and wastewater services also provide examples of such domains, framed less academically.

Communities of people

Many groups focus on the water sector. These groups take different forms, ranging from professional groups to project teams to informal networks. Some groups either see themselves or could be considered as communities in the sense that they identify with the group and interact on a regular basis. Depending on whether their focus is purely their mutual interests or improving their practices they could be conceptualised as communities of interest or CoPs.

Shared practices

Among the many communities involved in practices of sustainability are those who share a concern about managing and governing water both systemically and sustainably and who are also committed to learning with others about how this can best be done for example, at the International Water Centre (IWC) based in Australia.[1] As such groups are usually involved in developing knowledge concerning practice, rather than just passing on information, they can be thought of as CoPs rather than networks, at least for the purpose of drawing on insights into learning.

Design for learning in communities of practice

CoPs usually serve the purpose of creating, expanding and exchanging knowledge in order to develop individual capabilities within that context. They tend to emerge, and to evolve and end organically, lasting as long as there is interest in learning together (Wenger et al, 2002: 42). As such and unlike other structures such as project teams, CoPs focus on learning and improving practice, not on project-based outcomes.

Wenger (1998: 225) argued that learning cannot be designed but is something that happens irrespective of design. He focused instead on designing social infrastructure that fosters learning, claiming that there are few more urgent tasks.

Wenger and his colleagues went on to consider a community of practice as a simple social system and to view complex social systems as interrelated CoPs (Wenger, 2010). They developed and demonstrated a wide range of conceptual tools for understanding CoPs as social learning systems (Wenger, 2010) such as boundaries, identity, trajectories and participation. All these tools also have applied aspects. According to Wenger – boundaries connect different communities and as such provide learning opportunities; identity focuses on negotiating being and becoming part of a community; trajectories connect past, present and future pathways. Using the notion of participation in relation to identity, through recognising who participates in what and how, helps to distinguish an individual's relations to CoPs. Elements that also play a vital part in CoPs include: (i) the roles and responsibilities of members, (ii) events – where things of significance to a community happen, whether synchronous or asynchronous, face-to-face or online, and (iii) actual or virtual places to 'meet' whether geographical locations or web-based platforms. Interactions and communication are an essential part of developing both understandings and practices. In our experience, diagramming has an important role in this development process often contextualised in an event or discussion that is part of a learning and/or inquiry process (Furniss and Blackmore, 2009). In our research, we have used diagramming for the purpose of exploring and sharing perspectives and developing some sort of shared vision or idea. Diagrams can be particularly useful in exploring and communicating CoPs concepts such as boundaries and trajectories, as we discuss later in the chapter.

Wenger developed a social theory of learning that contributes to an extensive academic discourse on social learning (for example, Blackmore, 2007, 2010; Steyaert and Jiggins, 2007; van Bommel et al, 2009; Reed et al, 2010; Lotz-Sisitka, 2012; Ison et al, 2015). As a part of this discourse, de Laat and Simons (2002) plotted learning processes against learning outcomes at both individual and collective levels and distinguished four kinds of learning as a result: (i) individual learning; (ii) individual learning processes with collective outcomes; (iii) learning in social interaction; and (iv) collective learning. All these different kinds of learning are relevant to CoPs and diagramming has a potential role in all of them which we elaborate in the discussion below.

Next we provide two examples of diagramming processes that formed part of our research.

Example 1: Diagramming to start a group inquiry process

As researchers we have often used two particular diagramming techniques to start off a group inquiry process – trajectory diagrams and conversation maps.

The first of these diagrams relates to Wenger's (1998) notion of a trajectory as a past, present and future pathway, used to understand identities in relation to CoPs:

> [Trajectories] give significance to events in relation to time construed as an extension of the self. They provide a context in which to determine what, among all the things that are potentially significant, actually becomes significant learning. A sense of trajectory gives us ways of sorting out what matters and what does not, what contributes to our identity and what remains marginal. (Wenger, 1998: 155)

We developed the technique of drawing a diagram to show relevant aspects of an individual's past, present and planned (future) experiences as a way of individuals exploring and communicating their starting points and perspectives for an inquiry process. This kind of diagram has some similarities with influence diagrams, comprising blobs and arrows (see Chapter Two).

Since 2012 two of the authors of this chapter (Blackmore and Ison), along with Nadarajah Sriskandarajah of the Swedish Agricultural University, have run systemic inquiry processes of relevance to sustainability, alongside major international symposia of the International Farming Systems Association (IFSA) and the International Systems Sciences Society (ISSS). A systemic inquiry in this case was an *inquiry* in the sense of finding out through a learning process how to improve a situation experienced as problematic. It was a *systemic* inquiry in that it set out to recognise interconnections among issues and to contextualise practices, drawing on inquiry-based practice that has been a concern within different systems practice lineages for many years (Ison, 2010). This includes Dewey's ideas of inquiry as thought intertwined with action and beginning with 'problem situations' (Dewey, 1933); inquiry based on Vickers' idea of appreciative systems (Vickers, 1965) and Churchman's 'inquiring systems' (Churchman, 1971), particularly in the sense of recognising that there are many worldviews and perspectives (Blackmore, 2009). These particular systemic inquiries were run as a systems training course for research students. (The extent to which a conference community can be considered a community of practice is discussed below.)

In several workshops where we have conducted systemic inquiries an additional or alternative starting point has been to split participants into small groups (typically between five and seven participants) and use *conversation maps* (see Figures 7.1a and 7.1b) to facilitate conversation and encourage participation of all stakeholders. For example in a water governance project-based workshop in 2014 attended by around 30 people and in a pre-conference workshop in 2015 attended by around 70 people. (Again we discuss how these groupings relate to CoPs below.)

Work conducted by McKenzie (2005) and other systems practitioners has shown that using conversation mapping is a productive way to start a group-based inquiry into a complex situation (Collins et al, 2005). Conversation maps typically include two parts: a conversation topic, often in the form of a question and used as a 'trigger', written in the centre of a large piece of paper; and participants' responses, which are written down and linked together as the conversation progresses with each participant using a different coloured pen. The trigger question is usually identified beforehand in the workshop as a whole. Ideally the process continues until all of the participants' responses have been

Figure 7.1a: Example conversation map

Source: Photograph by Chris Blackmore, relating to Ison and Collins (2016)

Figure 7.1b: Example of a re-drawn conversation map

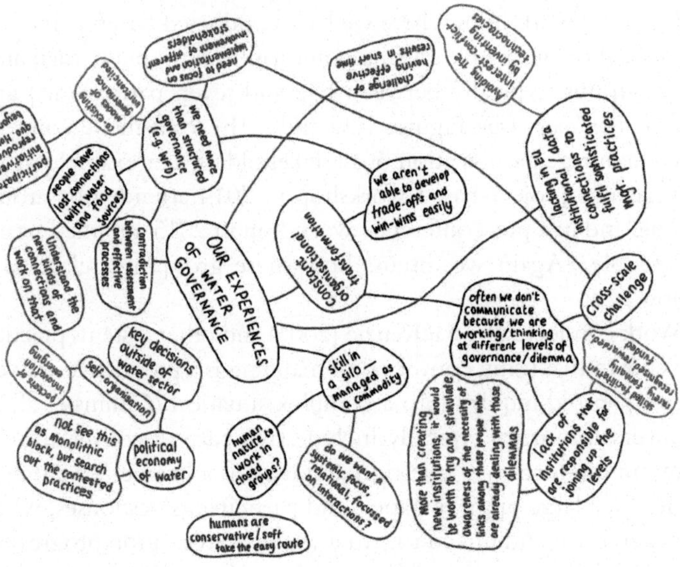

Source: Foster et al (2014: 11)

discussed and recorded on the conversation map (see Open University, 2006a, for further details).

In our examples, in one case five groups of up to six participants created five conversation maps (one per group) about their experiences of water governance, and in the other case ten groups of seven mapped their conversations about cybersystemic possibilities for governing the Anthropocene. They wrote down the main topics of their conversation and showed the relationships between them. The aim here was to initiate dialogue among the participants, to capture their perspectives on a situation of interest to them and to communicate it to others. This activity was also intended to start a process of thinking systemically about a problem situation, in particular to recognise interconnected issues and to view a 'whole' situation from multiple perspectives.

At the end of around half an hour for the smaller groups and three quarters of an hour for the larger groups, each group had produced a colourful 'mess' which resembled a complex spray diagram (see Chapter Two) that represented the complexity of the original idea from their perspectives and showed interconnections. From this conversation map the group looked for emergent insights and issues that seem to be the basis of the main sections of the map and initially recorded these on sticky notes then recorded their themes and issues on a large sheet of paper for sharing with all workshop participants.

For example, two overall themes that emerged from the conversations about water governance were: (i) breaking-out of silos and governance structures; and (ii) a mismatch between expectations of new processes and the outcomes. Two themes from the other workshop were: (i) re-politicising science; and (ii) limits to participation.

Further to conversation mapping these groups each continued a process whereby they identified systems of mutual interest and considered how improvements could be made, using both diagramming and non-diagramming techniques. These processes were similar to those described in Example 2, although they were not the same workshops.

Example 2: Diagramming as part of a co-inquiry into improving water governance

This example comes from the context of inquiring into water governance but uses systems maps, rich pictures and conceptual models. Some of the key sustainability challenges of this domain for practitioners lie in the way that water catchments are characterised by connectedness, complexity, uncertainty, conflict and multiple stakeholders (Ison et al, 2007a). Governments have a role in governance but, increasingly, in responding for example to extreme weather events or issues of water consumption, other actors from communities, NGOs and those with particular skills or knowledge come to the fore to work alongside government actors. There has been a process of renegotiating the political, social, economic and administrative systems that are needed to develop and manage water resources and the delivery of water services at different levels of society. This particular view of water governance as systems comes from Rogers and Hall (2003) and sits well with our focus on systemic approaches to water governance as researchers. The way in which governance arrangements have been changing can be seen from reviewing how multiple actors and stakeholders have dealt with flooding for example, in 2014 and 2015 in Somerset, York and Cumbria in the UK, in Brisbane, Australia in 2011 and in Sardinia in 2013. Communities have in effect helped themselves and each other to adapt and respond to flooding with varying degrees of support from government (FLAG, 2015; Roggero, 2014; CADWAGO, 2013). Water governance has begun to evolve through such events.

One example of where diagramming was used to explore questions about water governance was in a systemic co-inquiry aimed at understanding and improving water governance practices in England, designed and facilitated by the authors, as researchers, as part of the international project CADWAGO (Climate change adaptation and water governance – reconciling food security, renewable energy and the provision of multiple ecosystem services).[2] This project aimed to improve water governance by developing a more robust knowledge base and enhancing capacity to adapt to climate change. The co-inquiry was collaborative among the researchers and various practitioners with a mutual interest in learning with and from each other about how to improve water governance in England for the long term. There were 20 people involved overall. The co-inquiry process involved two workshops held in London in 2015, one focused on current water governance and one on the future. Diagramming was an essential part of the process as sub-groups in the workshops shared experiences, developed their ideas and reported back to all participants in the workshop in plenary sessions.

The context of the diagramming in this example includes working with a range of practitioners from national and local governments, NGOs, consultants, academics and local communities who have experienced issues of water governance for many years from a range of different perspectives. They have recognised the recent evolution of governance arrangements along with the need for continued evolution of water governance practices. But an unsustainable 'business as usual' pattern to water governance has tended to prevail in parts of England for many years, as evident for instance from widespread failure to meet legislative targets set by the Water Framework Directive and failure of service providers to achieve a good balance between providing water for people and water for their environment (Foster et al, 2016). There is also a cultural tendency for those experiencing floods and droughts and the 'wrong sort of weather' to blame the UK government (Blackmore, 2014) rather than feeling empowered to take responsibility for water governance. Against this backdrop, many of the practitioners we work with in our research highlight examples of good practice (Foster et al, 2015) but also recognise the need for more systemic and adaptive responses to climate change. How to affect such responses and get away from 'business as usual' approaches to water governance were key questions for all participants.

First workshop

The first workshop comprised an informal introduction, a series of three interactive participatory sessions, and five short presentations. The participatory sessions are discussed next and the presentations enabled the participants to contribute different perspectives of the current water governance situation. There were 16 participants, who worked together in plenary sessions and divided into three small groups for the participatory sessions which were designed to actively engage participants in systems thinking, modelling, negotiating and evaluating in order to explore water governance, to formulate problems and opportunities, and to begin to identify feasible and desirable changes. This design of the event was influenced by the researchers' previous use of systems approaches (Open University, 2006a, 2006b; Collins et al, 2007; Ison et al, 2007a, 2007b; Colvin et al, 2014).

The first participatory session focused on developing systemic awareness of the current water governance situation by exploring the participants' experiences using diagrams. Systemic awareness is an awareness of a situation as a whole that pays particular attention to interconnections. It comes from understanding cycles, counter-intuitive effects and unintended consequences. The process of developing systemic awareness begins with 'standing back' in order to explore (or re-explore) the wider context of a situation. This process is encouraged by using tools and techniques (Open University, 2006a, 2006b) such as rich pictures, as also described in Chapters Two, Three and Eight.

As noted in Chapter Two, rich pictures were originally developed as part of soft systems methodology (Checkland, 1981, 2000; Checkland and Scholes, 1990). They are pictorial representations of everything that is perceived to be relevant to a given situation by the person (or people) who drew them. Creating a rich picture as a group involves both drawing and explaining what is being drawn and why to the rest of the group. Participants also explicitly make apparent their own perspectives by including themselves within the diagram. The process of developing the rich picture (described below) should ideally continue until all of the participants' responses have been discussed and represented on the diagram (see Open University, 2006a, for further details). In practice, whether or not this happens depends on how well the group manages the time available.

In the workshop, the diagramming process was introduced in a simple manner. Each small group table (with six or seven participants) was asked to draw a rich picture of the current water governance situation.

- Use a flipchart and large pens
- Use pictorial symbols
- Allow free thinking

- Include everything that you think might be relevant
- Avoid wordiness
- Avoid overstructuring

Some general points were also made around diagramming, namely:

- Value of drawing is well recognised in problem investigation/ creative thinking methods
- Can both evoke and record insights into a situation
- Does not impose a structure
- Can represent experiences of complexity, uncertainty and diverse views
- Can show emotions and reactions as well as things happening
- Can show all insights together
- Shows actors' perspectives

Several participants had taken part in previous workshops in which diagrams had been used, some with the researchers.

Figures 7.2a and 7.2b shows two rich pictures: (a) was developed by one of three small groups in the first workshop; (b) was developed in a second workshop that focused on future and ideal water governance rather than the current situation.

Figures 7.2a and 7.2b were redrawn from the original, for legibility. They were drawn partly for the purpose of exploring a situation and partly for communication. Redrawing here may have the disadvantage of making the diagram appear as if it is the work of one person rather than many, though the different colours used by the different contributors has been maintained.

In these figures elements of the pictures include actors, artefacts and processes. The interplay among these elements as perceived by the drawers is shown by how they are placed. Figure 7.2a showed the current water governance situation as dynamic, complex and messy. The diagram shows different stakeholder positions and in some cases conflicting interests within and between different groups. For instance, water users are shown as divided from others in the 'business of managing water' by a brick wall. The picture also shows cycles of activities triggered by water crises such as pollution, floods and droughts, as well as governance mechanisms and institutional factors such as EU and national standards on water governance practices, drawn on this occasion as a big black cloud!

Subsequently, the groups collectively identified themes emerging from their rich pictures and reported them back to a plenary discussion

Figure 7.2a: A rich picture of the current water governance situation in England drawn by one of the three small groups of workshop participants (redrawn from the version created at the workshop)

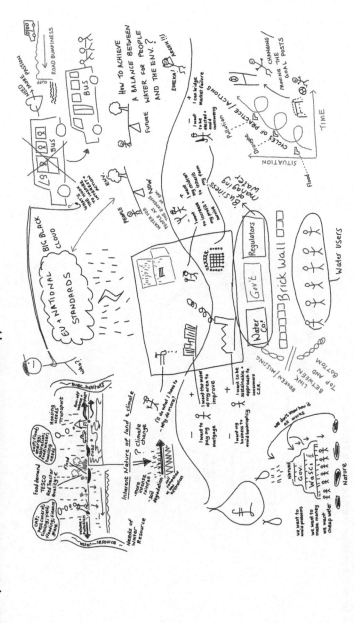

Source: Foster et al (2015: 10)

Figure 7.2b: A rich picture of an 'ideal' water governance situation in England drawn by one of three small groups of workshop participants (redrawn from the version created at the workshop)

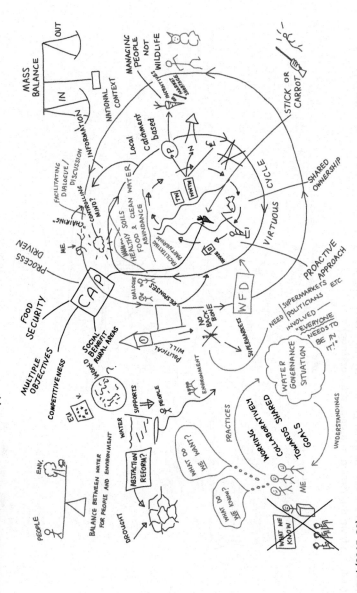

Source: Foster et al (2015: 20)

of the whole group, each group using their rich picture as a visual aid. The following themes corresponded to Figure 7.2a, although in total there were 15 emergent themes from the three groups (from Foster et al, 2015):

- uncertainty regarding accountability (ownership) of water governance;
- lack of incentives for water/sewerage companies to consider the whole environment;
- principal aim/goal of water governance to achieve EU and national standards;
- need for a call to action;
- disconnect between water 'managers' and water 'users'.

The aim of the reporting back was to capture the small group's perspectives on the situation and to communicate them to others. This process was also intended to start the process of thinking systemically about the situation — viewing it from multiple perspectives — and to further the dialogue among the participants.

The second participatory session in the first workshop started a process of convergence by defining the participants' systems of interest (that is the most relevant or interesting parts of a situation from their points of view). This process used a systems map (see Chapter Two) which identified boundaries and subsystems. It also identified the key parts of a system using the mnemonic BATWOVE (Beneficiaries, Actors, Transformation, Worldview, Owners, Victims, Environmental constraints). 'Root definitions' – short systems descriptions that incorporated all the BATWOVE elements – were then formulated. At this stage in the process these 'systems' descriptions were renditions of what the complex situation of water governance was perceived to be by participants, rather than representations of an ideal.

Systems maps, which were developed by The Open University for teaching purposes, are snapshots of situations at one moment in time. They have proved to be a useful modelling technique for the purpose of identifying boundaries, both of a system of interest and of its subsystems, and classifying components of the system (Open University, 2006a, 2006b). Workshop participants created three systems maps (one per group) identifying elements within their system of interest and where boundaries lay. The example in Figure 7.3 was produced by the same group who produced the rich picture in Figure 7.2a. Again the diagram has been redrawn for legibility. The aim of this diagramming activity was for the group to choose what to

Figure 7.3: A systems map constructed by the workshop participants (redrawn from the versions created at the workshop)

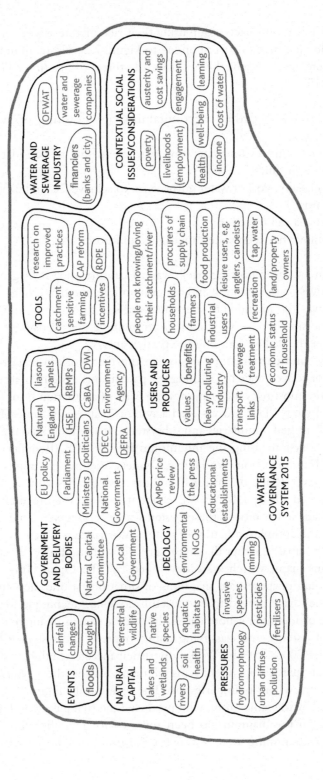

Source: Foster et al (2015: 12)

focus on and how they would structure the situation. It was intended both to further develop participants' systemic awareness and to help to bring together understandings about what was perceived as important. Drawn at another time both the elements and boundaries shown in Figure 7.3 could be different, depending not just on what is going on at the time and who is involved and how but the perception of the people drawing the diagram.

The systems maps enabled participants to identify and structure the actors and elements in the water governance situation they perceived to be important. In drawing both the rich pictures and the system maps, participants were very engaged. They took a little time to get started, possibly in engaging with the technique as much as the situation and in trying to work out how to represent and bring together the points made. There was generally a lot of conversation and energy around the process. By completing the systems maps, participants were able to appreciate that the group as a whole tended to have a better overall understanding of the elements in their system of interest than any one individual. They did not always agree on where boundaries should be placed but the process of negotiating the boundaries provided an opportunity for discussion and building further understanding. The groups varied in terms of whether they reached a final agreement on what should be represented. There was someone in each group taking the role of facilitator, sometimes through helping the drawing process along, either through drawing or urging others to draw and sometimes focusing more on making sure each individual was able to participate. The task surfaced issues such as participants' familiarity with many acronyms and, for some, being prepared to ask for explanations. Participants commented that they found the task challenging because it was difficult to decide what was relevant, but that it helped them to unravel the complex 'mess' represented in the rich pictures. Participants recognised that systems maps are a simplified representation of the water governance situation but found the task of constructing them helped to understand different perspectives and to develop shared understandings of the situation. Systems maps also informed subsequent tasks in the workshop, for instance in the case of the sub-groups that developed Figures 7.2a, 7.2b and 7.3, in working out how to focus on what 'is' and what 'ought to be' regarding natural capital and measures of performance of water governance (Foster et al, 2015).

Second workshop

The second workshop had a similar design, also with three participatory sessions. There were 13 participants this time. Nine participants had attended the first workshop and there were four people there for the first time. Rich pictures were again used in the first participatory session but this time not in relation to a current water governance situation but as a means of exploring and representing the participants' perspectives of what the water governance situation *ought* to be in an ideal world, based on their own understandings, knowledge and experiences. To some extent this activity followed on from identifying what 'is' and what 'ought to be' in the final session of the first workshop but as some were new to the process the outputs from the first workshop tended to just trigger and remind participants of what might be an ideal. Participants were asked to self-organise into small groups to allow both for those who wanted to work with the same people as before and those who wanted a change. In both the workshops, in our roles as facilitators of the overall process, we were not aware of any participants who were averse to working together.

The aims of this second workshop were to articulate, represent, understand and communicate participants' perspectives and ideas about water governance in an ideal world. It was also intended to further dialogue among the participants in order to create the conditions to 'design' as opposed to simply 'analyse' a situation. The rich pictures (exemplified by Figure 7.2b) recognised that the 'ideal' water governance situation was likely to be just as dynamic, complex and messy as the depictions from the current situation, portrayed in the first workshop. One key difference from the rich pictures of the first workshop was that these rich pictures showed water governance more as virtuous than vicious circles. The various actors and other elements in the situation were shown as working together towards shared goals, as can be seen from Figure 7.2b, for example, there is a distinct focus on communities working collaboratively, sharing ownership and responsibility, and facilitating dialogue and partnerships. There were also fewer obstacles and discontinuities represented (no brick wall this time!). More emphasis was given to finding balances – between water for people and environment and between inputs and outputs. There was also recognition of multiple benefits of water governance, including to human health, in addition to improved water quality and other legislative standards.

Themes this time included:

- interactions between people and/about the environment;
- many goals, achieving multiple benefits;
- 'one vision' realised through subsidiarity principle (local governance);
- motivation — stick and/or carrot?
- collaboration rather than competition; and
- culture change – planning for the long term.

(Foster et al, 2015: 21)

Systems maps were not used in the second participatory session this time as more idealised systems of interest were explored using soft systems methodology (SSM) type root definitions, that is, narrative expositions of relevant systems in terms of what they do, how they do it, and why they do it. For the group whose diagrams are shown the root definition was:

> An iterative learning system operated by a 'system operator' on behalf of everyone and within a set framework, to optimise the management of water in all its forms by engaging and empowering society to make equitable decisions and take collective/concerted actions, in order to deliver human health and well-being (with recognition that health and well-being depends upon a healthy, functioning natural environment) within the constraints of social, environmental and economic capital. (Foster et al, 2015: 22)

Diagramming was then used in the final small group session when, also in keeping with SSM, participants developed conceptual models to show how to enact part of the ideal systems of interest that they had described in their root definitions. The process involved writing down a series of actions suggested by the root definition, ensuring that verbs were used to describe actions. Working out whether all necessary actions had been identified appropriately and their sequence was an iterative process. A focus on human health and wellbeing came up in all three conceptual models in the workshop in different configurations. However, all three diagrams recognised that 'delivering human health and wellbeing' is not something that can just be enacted, rather that it can be seen as an emergent outcome of a system as a whole. The models also all showed water governance as a learning system with iteration – as something that is ongoing and adaptive to the changing (improving) water governance situation. The three small groups worked separately but the plenary discussions that were interspersed between participatory sessions meant that participants were not entirely working independently towards this finding but it was a recurring theme.

Further to the conceptual modelling, workshop participants identified actions to improve water governance using the models as a visual and mental aid. These actions fell broadly into four categories:

- Stakes and stakeholding
- Facilitation
- Institutions and policies
- Knowing and learning about water governance

A full report of the co-inquiry events is available on the CADWAGO website (see Foster et al, 2015).

Discussion

Diagramming had an important place in our examples in helping to develop understandings of thinking and practices among the groups who took part. Whether these groups saw themselves as one community of practice or more, or a different sort of grouping, varied with perspective. The conference-based communities where trajectory diagramming and conversation mapping took place certainly saw themselves as communities. However, those communities are quite dynamic and diverse, with a core of people who have aligned their interests with the conferences for a long time and who identify with the conference community, and a significant proportion of newcomers to each conference who identify with their own CoPs but who do not necessarily see themselves as part of an IFSA or ISSS community. In Wenger-Trayner and Wenger-Trayner's (2015: 13) terms these conference communities could well be seen more as 'a "landscape of practice", consisting of a complex system of CoPs and the boundaries between them'. It is in understanding and negotiating some of the roles, boundaries and dynamics of these landscapes of practice that diagramming has a useful role. For these purposes different diagramming types are required, including some of those included in this chapter as examples – for example, trajectory diagrams and systems maps. But these particular diagram types are snapshots at a particular moment in time. Although there are systems diagramming types that represent relationships, influences, multiple causes, and so on (see Chapter Two), some are limited in showing temporal aspects. For that reason in our research we tend to conceptualise what we are doing as a learning system paying particular attention to interconnections and dynamics, keeping context in mind and watching out for unintended consequences. We have also used further diagrams and models to contextualise our inquiry processes (for example, timelines of events and various learning system conceptual frameworks). We feel that part of our skill as systems practitioners is in knowing which diagrams and other techniques to use when.

The project-based examples come from contexts of multiple CoPs working in the domain of water in practices relating to governance. In this case diagrams were found particularly helpful in illuminating issues associated with organisational and institutional complexity and for exploring, developing and sharing ideas on how to make improvements in situations.

Both the conference-based and project-based communities are international communities and we have found that diagramming has helped to bridge language and culture differences in these contexts. Participants associated with both communities also work at different levels of organisation, ranging from local to global. We have found that diagrams are useful to make explicit key focuses of activity and how the levels relate to each other.

For some participants our workshops were a one-off exploration, others have continued on with their inquiries and in developing actions identified. The purpose of creating, expanding and exchanging knowledge and developing individual capabilities within that context was certainly evident. The lens of a community of practice puts a focus on community as well as practice. It is apparent from the examples included in this chapter that the process of diagramming illuminated much about both these elements. The meta-level focus was water governance but the diagramming enabled people not only to explain their own perspectives but to contextualise that perspective among others and, in so doing, led not just to individual learning but also to collective learning.

Diagrams can certainly be developed and used individually with individual learning processes and individual outcomes but, as is shown in this chapter, the learning process and outcomes can also be collective. Using de Laat and Simon's matrix mentioned earlier (de Laat and Simons, 2002) can highlight the nature of diagramming in relation to individual and collective learning processes and outcomes. Box A in Table 7.1 makes a statement about the individual outcomes of an individual diagramming process, B the collective outcomes of individual process, C the individual outcomes of a collective process and D the collective outcomes of a collective process.

Table 7.1: Characteristics of individual and collective diagramming processes and related outcomes

Diagramming process	Outcomes	
	Individual	Collective
Individual	A. Exploring, visualising, recording, encouraging individual systemic thinking	B. Recognising a contribution, provoking others, appreciating, communicating
Collective	C. Gaining inspiration, developing diagramming skills, contextualising own perspective, stimulating ideas	D. Pooling perspectives, creating rich situation descriptions and visions, negotiating boundaries, communication, building understanding, developing trust, empathy and mutual respect, collaborative inquiry

Another purpose of CoPs besides creating and sharing knowledge is to develop capabilities, both individual and collective. Time will tell whether these events succeeded in this respect but one particular challenge that did arise from the process were some difficulties individuals reported after trying to conduct their own systemic inquiries away from this particular group setting.

Conclusion

A community of practice in a practical sense potentially provides a sounding board for wrestling with difficulties and further developing skills, which in the cases described in this chapter were in conducting a systemic inquiry that included diagramming. Diagramming is one technique among many used in understanding and developing CoPs. However, there is evidence from the examples supplied here that diagramming does have the potential to support the sharing of perspectives on both communities and practices and can help develop a sense of individual and group identity.

In the context of water governance, with the complex and interconnected institutional, biophysical, social and economic dynamics that are associated with managing water resources, collective action and also concerted action are required. Each contribution needs to be harmonised with others in a timely manner for maximum effect. Our most significant change in our understandings and practices from our research in relation to diagramming is probably also related to concerted action. We have come to recognise which technique to use when and how to bring different elements of our design for learning together in a dynamic way, as a choreographed performance rather than just seeing ourselves as producing outputs.

Our advice to early career researchers (and practitioners) would be to develop not just your own diagramming skills so you can explore issues in relation to your research questions but to develop your skills in using diagrams as a part of an inquiry process and methodology, including facilitating others to develop diagrams as part of collective as well as individual processes. This means developing diagrams that are suitable for communication as well as exploration. In our view it is important to remember that diagrams and other models do not stand alone. We need to understand the processes they are a part of, recognise their strengths and limitations, and incorporate them appropriately as part of the design for overall processes of learning.

Notes

[1] See www.watercentre.org/services/communities-of-practice

[2] See www.cadwago.net for more details on this project.

References

Allen, W., Fenemor, A., Kilvington, M., Harmsworth, G., Young, R.G., Deans, N., Horn, C., Phillips, C., de Oca, O.M., Ataria, J. and Smith, R. (2011) 'Building collaboration and learning in integrated catchment management: the importance of social process and multiple engagement approaches', *New Zealand Journal of Marine and Freshwater Research*, 45: 525–39.

Attwater, R. and Derry, C. (2005) 'Engaging communities of practice for risk communication in the Hawkesbury Water Recycling Scheme', *Action Research*, 3: 193–209.

Bailey, A. (2013) 'Once the Capacity Development Initiative is Over: Using Communities of Practice Theory to Transform Individual into Social Learning', *The Journal of Agricultural Education and Extension: Competence for Rural Innovation and Transformation*, 20 (4): 429–448.

Barab, S.A. and Duffy, T. (2000) 'From practice fields to communities of practice', in D. Jonassen and S.M. Land (eds), *Theoretical Foundations of Learning Environments*, Mahwah, NJ: Lawrence Erlbaum Associates, pp 25–56.

Barth, M. and Michelsen, G. (2013) 'Learning for change: an educational contribution to sustainability science', *Sustainability Science*, 8: 103–19.

Blackmore, C. (2007) 'What kinds of knowledge, knowing and learning are required for addressing resource dilemmas? – a theoretical overview', *Environmental Science and Policy*, 10 (6): 512–25.

Blackmore, C. (ed) (2010) *Social Learning Systems and Communities of Practice*, London: Springer.

Blackmore, C. (2014) 'Learning to change farming and water management practices in response to the challenges of climate change and sustainability', *Outlook on Agriculture*, 43(3): 173–78.

Blackmore, C.P. (2009) 'Learning systems and communities of practice for environmental decision making', PhD thesis, The Open University, Milton Keynes.

Brown, J.S. and Duguid, P. (1991) 'Organizational learning and communities-of-practice: toward a unified view of working, learning, and innovation', *Organization Science*, 2 (1): 40–57.

CADWAGO (2013) 'Response Capacity in Extreme Flooding Events: The South East Queensland Floods – a case study', 2 July, www.cadwago.net/?p=113

Chaiklin, S. and Lave, J. (1993) *Understanding Practice Perspectives on Activity and Context*, Cambridge: Cambridge University Press.

Checkland, P. (1981) *Systems thinking, systems practice*, Chichester: Wiley

Checkland, P. (2000) 'Soft systems methodology: a thirty year retrospective', *Systems Research and Behavioural Science*, S1: S11–S58.

Checkland, P. and Scholes, J. (1990) *Soft systems methodology in action*, Chichester: Wiley.

Churchman, C.W. (1971) *The Design of Inquiring Systems: Some Basic Concepts of Systems and Organization*, New York, London: Basic Books.

Coakes, E. and Clarke, S. (2006) *Encyclopedia of Communities of Practice in Information and Knowledge Management*, Hershey, PA: Idea Group.

Collins, K. and Ison, R. (2009) 'Jumping off Arnstein's Ladder: Social learning as a new policy paradigm for climate change adaptation', *Environmental Policy and Governance*, 19 (6): 358–73.

Collins, K., Ison, R. and Blackmore, C. (2005) River basin planning project: social learning, Science Report SC050037/SR1., Bristol: Environment Agency.

Collins, K., Blackmore, C., Morris, R. and Watson, D. (2007) 'A systemic approach to managing multiple perspectives and stakeholding in water catchments: some findings from three UK case studies', *Environmental Science and Policy*, 10 (6): 564–74.

Collins, K.B. and Ison, R.L. (2010) 'Trusting emergence: some experiences of learning about integrated catchment science with the Environment Agency of England and Wales', *Water Resources Management*, 24 (4): 669–88.

Colvin, J., Blackmore, C., Chimbuya, S., Collins, K., Dent, M., Goss, J., Ison, R., Roggero, P.P. and Seddaiu, G. (2014) 'In search of systemic innovation for sustainable development: a design praxis emerging from a decade of social learning inquiry', *Research Policy*, 43: 760–71.

de Laat, M. (2006) 'Networked Learning', PhD thesis, Utrecht, IVLOS, Universiteit Utrecht, http://eprints.soton.ac.uk/20358

de Laat, M.F. and Simons, P.R.J. (2002), 'Collective learning: theoretical perspectives and ways to support networked learning', *European Journal for Vocational Training*, 27: 13–24.

Dewey, J. (1933) *How we think: A restatement of the relation of reflective thinking to the educative process*, Boston: D.C. Heath and Company.

Dieperink, C., Raadgever, G.T., Driessen, P.P.J., Smit, A.A.H. and van Rijswick, H.F.M.W. (2012) 'Ecological ambitions and complications in the regional implementation of the Water Framework Directive in the Netherlands', *Water Policy*, 14: 160.

FLAG (2015) 'Flooding on the Levels Action Group', www. flagsomerset.org.uk

Foster, N., Blackmore, C., Ison, R. and Collins, K. (2016) 'Renegotiating boundaries for systemic water governance: some experiences from the implementation of the Water Framework Directive in England', paper presented at the 12th European International Farming Systems Association Symposium, Harper Adams University, 12–15 July.

Foster, N., Collins, K., Blackmore, C. and Ison, R. (2014) on behalf of the CADWAGO project team, CADWAGO Governance Learning Workshop Report, London, 24 June, www.cadwago.net/wp-content/uploads/2015/01/Governance-learning-workshop-report-London-2014.pdf

Foster, N., Collins, K., Blackmore, C. and Ison, R. (2015) *Water governance in England: Improving understandings and practices through systemic co-inquiry*, Workshop report, Milton Keynes: The Open University, https://mcs.open.ac.uk/cadwago/full_report.pdf

Furniss, P. and Blackmore, C. (2009) 'Tools and techniques for environmental decision making', in G. Wilson, P. Furniss and R. Kimbowa (eds) *Environment, Development, and Sustainability: Perspectives and cases from around the world*, Oxford, UK: Oxford University Press, pp 250–58.

Ison, R. (2010) *Systems Practice: How to Act in a Climate-Change World*, London: Springer.

Ison, R. and Collins, K. (2016) 'Governing the Anthropocene. Cybersystemic Possibilities?' Draft report of systemic inquiry, Herrenhausen Palace, Hanover, 30–31 July. (Available from the authors.)

Ison, R.L., Collins, K.B. and Wallis, P.J. (2015) 'Institutionalising social learning: towards systemic and adaptive governance', *Environmental Science & Policy*, 53 (Part B): 105–17.

Ison, R., Röling, N. and Watson, D. (2007a) 'Challenges to science and society in the sustainable management and use of water: investigating the role of social learning', *Environmental Science and Policy*, 10 (6):499–511.

Ison, R., Blackmore, C., Collins, K. and Furniss, P. (2007b) 'Systemic environmental decision making: designing learning systems', *Kybernetes*, 36 (9-10): 1340–61.

Jørgensen, U. and Lauridsen, E.H. (2005) 'Environmental professional competences: the role of communities of practice and spaces for reflexive learning', *Greener Management International*, 49 (Spring): 57–67.

Kimble, C., Hildreth, P. and Bourdon, I. (2008) (eds) *Communities of Practice – Creating Learning Environments for Educators, Volumes 1 and 2*, Charlotte, NC: Information Age Publishing.

Kimble, C., Hildreth, P. and Wright, P. (2000) 'Communities of Practice: Going Virtual' in Y. Malhotra (ed) *Knowledge Management and Business Model Innovation*, Hershey, PA: Idea Group Publishing, pp 220–34.

Lave, J. and Wenger, E. (1991) *Situated Learning: Legitimate Peripheral Participation*, Cambridge: Cambridge University Press.

le May, A. (ed) (2009) *Communities of Practice in Health and Social Care*, Oxford: Blackwell Publishing.

Lotz-Sisitka, H.B. (ed) (2012) *(Re) Views on Social Learning Literature: A monograph for social learning researchers in natural resources management and environmental education*, Grahamstown/Howick: Environmental Learning Research Centre, Rhodes University/EEASA/SADC REEP.

Madsen, M.L. and Noe, E. (2012) 'Communities of practice in participatory approaches to environmental regulation. Prerequisites for implementation of environmental knowledge in agricultural context'. *Environmental Science & Policy*, 18: 25–33.

McDermott, R. (1999) 'Learning across teams; how to build communities of practice in team-based organisations', *Knowledge Management Review*, 8 (May/June): 32–6.

McKenzie, B. (2005) 'Conversation mapping. Cognitive Edge', Systemic Development Institute, Vincentia, Australia, http://old.cognitive-edge.com/wp-content/uploads/2005/06/29-Conversation-Mapping-BMcK-0605.pdf

Open University (2006a) *Techniques for environmental decision making*, T863 Environmental decision making: a systems approach, Milton Keynes: The Open University.

Open University (2006b) *Starting off systemically in environmental decision making*, Book 2 T863 Environmental decision making: a systems approach, Milton Keynes: The Open University.

Oreszczyn, S. and Lane, A. (2006) 'Farmer communities of practice and high tech futures' in 'The Rural Citizen: Governance, Culture and Wellbeing in the 21st Century', compilation from University of Plymouth Rural Futures Conference, 5–7 April, Plymouth, UK.

Reed, M.S., Evely, A.C., Cundill, G., Fazey, I., Glass, J., Laing, A., Newig, J., Parrish, B., Prell, C., Raymond, C. and Stringer, L.C. (2010) 'What is social learning?' *Ecology and Society* 15 (4): r1, www.ecologyandsociety.org/vol15/iss4/resp1/main.html

Rogers, P. and Hall, A.W. (2003) *Effective Water Governance*, TEC Background Papers No. 7, Global Water Partnership Technical Committee, Stockholm, Sweden, www.gwp.org/global/toolbox/publications/background%20papers/07%20effective%20water%20governance%20(2003)%20english.pdf

Roggero, P.P. (2014) 'Finding their own way towards sustainable water governance', CADWAGO blog, 21 January, www.cadwago.net/?p=412

Shove, E. and Spurling, N. (eds) (2013) *Sustainable Practices: Social Theory and Climate Change*, Abingdon, UK: Routledge.

Snyder, W.M and Wenger, E. (2004) 'Our world as a learning system: a communities of practice approach', in M.L. Connor and J.G. Clawson (eds), *Creating a learning culture: strategy, technology and practice*, Cambridge: Cambridge University Press, pp 35–58.

Stephens, C. (2007) 'Community as practice: social representations of community and their implications for health promotion', *Journal of Community and Applied Social Psychology*, 17: 103–14.

Steyaert, P. and Jiggins, J. (2007) 'Governance of complex environmental situations through social learning: a synthesis of SLIM's lesson for research, policy and practice', *Environmental Science and Policy*, 10 (6): 575–86.

Strengers, Y. and Maller, C. (eds) (2014) *Social Practices, Intervention and Sustainability: Beyond behaviour change*, Abingdon, UK: Routledge.

Vickers, G. (1965) *The Art of Judgment: a study of policy making*, London: Chapman and Hall.

van Bommel, S.V., Röling, N., Aarts, N. and Turnhout, E. (2009) 'Social learning for solving complex problems', *Environmental Policy and Governance*, 19 (6): 400–12.

Wenger, E. (1998) *Communities of Practice: Learning, Meaning and Identity*, Cambridge: Cambridge University Press.

Wenger, E. and Snyder, W. (2000) 'Communities of practice? The organizational frontier', *Harvard Business Review*, Jan–Feb: 139–45.

Wenger, E., McDermott, R. and Snyder, W.M. (2002) *Cultivating Communities of Practice: a Guide to Managing Knowledge*, Boston, MA: Harvard Business School Press.

Wenger, E. (2010) 'Communities of Practice and Social Learning Systems: the career of a concept', in C. Blackmore (ed), *Social Learning Systems and Communities of Practice*, London: Springer, pp 179–98.

Wenger, E., Trayner, B. and de Laat, M. (2011) 'Promoting and assessing value creation in communities and networks: a conceptual framework', Rapport 18, Ruud de Moor Centrum, Open University of the Netherlands.

Wenger-Trayner, E. and Wenger-Trayner, B. (2015) 'Learning in a Landscape of practice – a framework', in E. Wenger-Trayner, M. Fenton-O'Creevy, S. Hutchinson, C. Kubiak and B. Wenger-Trayner (eds), *Learning in Landscapes of Practice: boundaries, identity and knowledgeability in practice-based learning*, London and New York: Routledge, pp 13–29.

Westberg, L. and Polk, M. (2016) 'The role of learning in transdisciplinary research: moving from a normative concept to an analytical tool through a practice-based approach', *Sustain Sci*, 11: 385.

EIGHT

'Imagine': mapping sustainability indicators

Simon Bell

Editors' introduction

Collaborating with others is central to participatory methods, as we have seen in previous chapters. However, the nature of the collaboration and the role that diagrams play in the methods used also depends in part on the topic being addressed. This chapter tells the story of how a systems method for sharing perspectives on and then agreeing sustainability indicators, which makes extensive use of two forms of diagram, was conceived and then applied in a wide variety of places. Central to this method's evolution were the intentions of its initial creators and the contributions of the different project collaborators and participants in the related workshops. Central to the method's effectiveness are the way two diagram types are used to visualise, and make more relevant to specified communities, indicators of environmental sustainability. This chapter is also another example of the interplay between method and visualisation, both of the method and within the method, and that it can be difficult to say which is the chicken and which is the egg. They are complementary parts of an holistic and ongoing process, particularly where the main objective is action to improve people's lives rather than research on people's lived experiences.

Beginning at the beginning

The story begins in 1999. Professor Steve Morse and I had met at the University of East Anglia (UEA) in Norwich, UK, and found compatibility in our worldviews despite working in different fields. I was exploring the use of systems analysis specifically relating to ICT. Steve was focused on the human impacts of agricultural innovation. We both worked in West Africa and were painfully aware of the regular mis-steps made by international aid agencies in their often clumsy interfaces with local people (see Sumberg et al, 2012). Where aid and development projects came face to face with local people there was often/usually a communication chasm – well-intended scientists non-communicating with local populations in what was often experienced as a complex non-iterative process (see, for example, Chambers, 1997; Fisher and Green, 2004; Cooke and Kothari, 2001). Why was this important to us at this time? First, we both saw that a key issue for us was communities and engaging with them. Second, we had, again separately, been working on metrics and measurement. We were concerned with indicators in our diverse fields and we were aware that metrics and indicators in particular 'turn off' the most likely users and beneficiaries of the indicators (for a discussion around the issues, see Rosenstrom, 2009). Most metrics are used only by their creators or the specialists who are the main detractors of their use (a useful conversation on this can be found in Harnard, 2008).

With my background in systems analysis and Steve's rich and diverse interests in the biological and geographical sciences we agreed to collaborate on an adventurous writing project. Steve and I began working on what we hoped would prove to be *the* book on sustainability indicators. Our presumption was that the world needed our book and that when it was published we would find ourselves in demand. Our conceit was in fact realised by the environmental agency Plan Bleu (as shall be shown) but maybe not quite as we had assumed it would be.

The 1999 book was *Sustainability indicators: measuring the immeasurable*. As academics we thought that the best way to understand a difficult thing is to evidence it. To show how it has moved and changed in space and time. So, in our view at that time, the best way to really understand sustainability was to measure it. But this raises issues of what is being measured by whom and for whom? If local communities in particular and the public at large are not consulted or interested in this measurement, then the indicators may well be ignored and the sustainability discussion will be an oubliette – a thing to be forgotten. Our new concern was not, therefore, the concern of most academics of that time. We were not concerned too much by precision and maths. We did not worry too much about computer processing power and data – rather we were concerned that communities did not understand the thinking and values of the experts and the experts did not value indicators produced by communities.

Our 1999 book contained the seeds of our resolution to this issue, this non-meeting of minds – a method to engage communities of stakeholders in the consideration of their own sustainability. The remainder of this chapter is a narrative account of the mapping of sustainability indicators through the evolution of systems-based and community orientated methods.

Starting somewhere: inelegant names and methodology evolution

In our work on sustainability indicators Steve Morse and I used the word methodology a lot – and we made sure that we used the word correctly. Our approach was to create a method that was intended to develop and grow, to be reflexive of practice and to be adaptable – it was a method which also involved 'ology' or 'a subject of study; a branch of knowledge' (Oxford Dictionary of English). We never intended our method to be fixed or finalised. Rather we saw it as a means to map out and visualise sustainability indicators with the input of a wide range of stakeholders. It can also be noted that in early conversations with esteemed colleagues at UEA we were told that our project was mad, 'off the wall' because of our focus on visualisation techniques and citizen participation in sustainability indicator use – a focus that ran contrary to much of the 'expert driven' legacy of sustainability indicator practice.

We assumed that the stakeholders would help to inspire changes in the method – we were not intending to impose it as a straight-jacket or as a tyranny – we had some experience of that and deliberately did what we could to avoid it (Bell, 1994). Our methodology had a holding name/title: Systemic Sustainability Analysis (SSA). SSA was clearly not intended to be a snappy title. It was more about being an accurate description of what it was rather than a memorable term. SSA was our methodological means to set out what we felt was needed to allow stakeholders, including local communities and 'experts' (scientists and politicians) to collaborate in mapping out and visualising mutually agreed values of sustainability.

What did SSA look like?

When setting out the basics of the Systemic Sustainability Analysis we made these points as our rubrics for the development and application of the methodology:

The premises for the development of hypothetical SSA are:

- sustainability can provide a qualitative measure of the integrality and wholeness of any given system;

- subjectivity on the part of the stakeholders in any given system (including researchers) is unavoidable;
- subjectively derived measures of sustainability are useful if the subjectivity is explicitly accepted and declared at the outset and if the method for deriving the measures are available to a range of stakeholders;
- measures of sustainability can be valuable aids to planning, forecasting and awareness building [...];
- rapidly employed and participatory tools for developing our thinking and our modelling concerning measures of sustainability are of value to a wide range of stakeholders within development policy.'

(Bell and Morse, 1999: 103).

In this list/statement of intent Steve and I were recognising that we needed to orientate sustainability measurement towards the needs of different stakeholders and not just the scientific and policy establishment; and we needed a structure and means that included the perspectives of this diverse groups of stakeholders and that this is best represented in diagrams.

Prior to any real world application, the preliminary form of SSA is shown in the cyclical diagram in Figure 8.1.

In essence, the method consisted of five stages for variously identifying and mapping the sustainability context and potential sustainability indicators. The different stages make use of two key diagramming techniques – the rich picture (which is the fundamental tool used in stages 2 and 5 in Figure 8.1, and is also used and explained in Chapters Two, Three and Seven) and the Amoeba diagram (set up, analysed and reviewed respectively in stages 3, 4 and 5).

To explain the rationale behind the untested method in brief, at stage 1 the stakeholders in the context under study would be brought together. As recognised in the diagram, we understood that the stakeholders would be very likely to have discrete interests and contrasting/conflicting views. They would have coalitions of interest and these coalitions would vary depending on the issue under discussion. A very fluid situation. At stage 2 rich pictures would be used as a means to collect information about issues of interest. Both authors were keen on systems approaches and regularly used rich pictures in their research and teaching. Rich pictures (as also noted in Chapters Two, Three and Seven) provide a symbolic visual representation of a complex situation. They are very powerful in allowing mixed stakeholder groups to engage with a difficult context

Figure 8.1: The five steps to producing the SSA

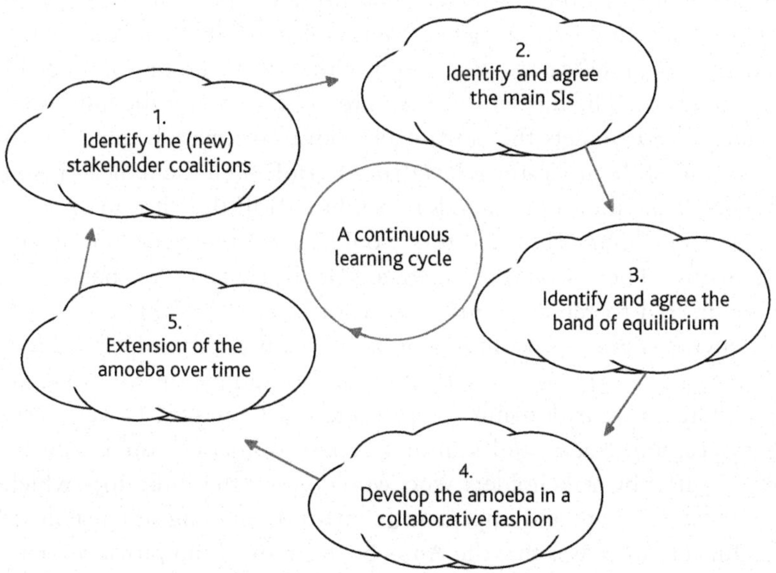

Source: Bell and Morse (1999: 121)

and provide the opportunity for new insights and ideas to emerge in a context of optimal indiscretion and for stakeholders to often draw things that they found it hard to talk about or write about.[1] The rich pictures would lead on to and inspire the development of the Amoeba diagram at stage 3 of the method. In drawing the rich pictures stakeholders would identify sustainability issues of concern to them and these issues would be translated by the SSA process into indicators. For each indicator the stakeholders would develop what became known as a 'Band of Equilibrium' (BoE). The BoE would be what the various stakeholders in their diverse coalitions of interest agreed to be the 'sustainable' range for each indicator. This meant that the stakeholders needed to speculate and agree on what sustainability would look like as an indicator value of the issues which they had identified at stage 2. The BoE was a recognition by all stakeholders that any sustainability factor and related measure will have a 'sustainable' value which most stakeholders can agree to.[2] SSA encouraged stakeholders to agree a BoE for every indicator agreed. This would act as a reference position for all future mapping in the Amoeba diagram. Following the agreement on the BoE an 'Amoeba' diagram could be drawn. The Amoeba diagram is rather like the more familiar 'kite' or 'radar' diagram but also subtly different. An example of an Amoeba is shown in Figure 8.2. The Amoeba is an irregular shape or a 'blot' which represents the combined values of a range of indicators for a range of stakeholders for a given context. Essentially each 'arm' of the Amoeba is an indicator – the length of the arm indicates the value of the indicator. The further the arm extends, the greater the indicator's value. The BoE sets the 'sustainable' position for each indicator. If the value of the indicator is less than the BoE then the indicator is in deficit. If the indicator extends beyond the BoE then it is in excess.

As part of SSA the indicators would be clustered into groups or 'domains'. These would be suggested by the stakeholders but would be expected to represent major areas of interest or concern – such as 'environment' or 'economy' or whatever the stakeholders decide. There can be many or few domains. In the example shown in Figure 8.2 there are four domains – represented as Economy, Governance, Services, and Social and Cultural. These domains would each be represented by stakeholders who would agree the indicators which are most pertinent and important in terms of ongoing sustainability.

Our intention was that the Amoeba diagram would provide a stark and instant impression of sustainability but would also represent the considered evaluation of the gathered stakeholders of the system in question. If the system/area under analysis was sustainable then all the 'arms' would be within the BoE. In Figure 8.2 the only domain that looks to be vaguely sustainable is Economy, and in that case two of

Figure 8.2: A hand-drawn amoeba diagram

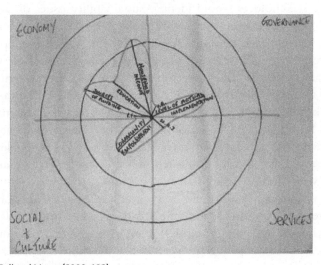

Source: Bell and Morse (2008: 183)

the three indicators or 'arms' of the Amoeba are just in the BoE. This example looks unsustainable.

The final stage (5) of SSA was intended to project the Amoeba and the related indicators backwards and forwards in time. In this exercise the stakeholders would be encouraged to draw an historic Amoeba of how things had been and a fantasy Amoeba of how things could be in 10 or 20 years' time. By engaging in this process the community could gain a sense of trajectory and evolution of factors, and then could try to avoid negative futures and encourage the features of positive futures.

The next two sections of this chapter deal with the manner in which the SSA method was applied, learned from, adapted and changed (and therefore evolved as a methodology) following its use in a variety of contexts.

Plan Bleu: SPSA and Imagine

In 2000 I was called by Elisabeth Coudert – a Project/Programme Officer with the agency 'Plan Bleu'.[3] Plan Bleu is a French based Regional Activity Centre (RAC), one of a number of such RACs mandated to engage with aspects of environmental management in marine and littoral contexts in the Mediterranean basin. Elisabeth had read our book and wondered if it would help her with a conundrum that she was dealing with. She needed to organise a series of workshops for stakeholders on the Mediterranean island of Malta. The project that Elisabeth had in mind was a Coastal Area Management Programme (CAMP). The CAMP projects that Plan Bleu was involved with would take in most of the countries with Mediterranean sea-boards. Each CAMP would involve Integrated Coastal Zone Management (ICZM), and each of these would require stakeholder engagement and participation. CAMP and ICZM are both complex and highly political protocols – of necessity as they involve a wide range of countries from all around the Mediterranean basin in collaborating and sharing data and information. The lead RAC in ICZM matters is the Priority Action Programme (PAPRAC) based in Split in Croatia.[4] PAPRAC had an overarching interest in all matters relating to the CAMP projects as we shall see shortly. In the early stages of the initial use of SSA it was Elisabeth who was central to its development. Elisabeth simply thought that SSA might just be a useful method for engaging local population in the CAMP project and for developing the sustainability indicators that the project would need as part of the ICZM process. SSA was about engagement with local communities and the development of indicators and that is exactly what she was looking for. Here are Elisabeth's memories on the matter.[5]

> 'Reading the Bell and Morse's book, I felt completely familiar with the tools and concepts they wrote about. Both their approaches and mine seemed very complementary. I thought that combining the two approaches would produced a very relevant tool for this project and probably for many others. I was particularly interested by the participative approach Simon described and by the Amoeba graphic with its strong pedagogical power.' (Elisabeth Coudert, February 2016)

So the first application of SSA was in CAMP Malta from 2000 to 2002. The project is the subject of a book and is fully written up there (Bell and Morse, 2003). For the purposes of this chapter it is necessary to make a number of points.

First of all, the SSA approach evolved with the use-plan of Plan Bleu. Plan Bleu was very interested in the future sustainability of the CAMP project locations and as a consequence had included a scenario planning or 'prospective' approach in its methods toolbox, more specifically, the prospective method of Michelle Godet (Godet et al, 1999; Godet 2001). In order to accommodate a prospective element, SSA was evolved to SPSA (where P = 'prospective' and developed in a visual manner through a nuanced application of rich pictures; participants in rich picture workshops are encouraged to draw the diagrams basing content on agreed sets of trends and surprises drawn for the current context). Further, the overall method was adjusted from the previous circle to a more pleasing and internally consistent infinity symbol. Part of the evolution of SPSA was the recognition of the learning process which was such a large part of the method. To make this learning more explicit the revised presentation of SPSA also included a learning cycle of Reflecting, Connecting, Modelling and Doing, based on the Kolb cycle (Kolb, 1984). The explicit inclusion of the learning cycle provided for the SPSA process to be orientated more to learning than to evaluation and more to a cyclic learning process rather than a single, unreflective analysis.

Second, SPSA was rolled out for local Maltese colleagues from agencies to apply and learn with local communities. Participation was organised by local project members but the overall format revolved around direct invitations being sent to local community representatives (for example, representatives of farming co-ops, tourist industry, Non-

Governmental Agencies, residents groups, among others) to attend workshops. The workshops were originally planned to be four half-day events (incorporating the five stages of SSA noted in Figure 8.1) over a 12-month period. At each workshop event the stakeholders would be shuffled into heterogeneous groups of eight or so individuals and taken through the various stages of SPSA. The participants would draw the initial rich picture in the first workshop, develop indicators from issues in the second, draw an Amoeba diagram based on data provided by the project team and stakeholders in the third, and consider a rich picture of the future situation in the fourth.

The SPSA process suffered from the range of issues which all action-orientated research participatory processes experience (for a more in depth discussion, see Stirling, 2006). Challenges for the method included gaining trust for the research team to work 'with' the community stakeholders, getting a representative range of stakeholders to attend, maintaining interest over a lengthy period of engagement, keeping on track with the process, and encouraging consensus from highly opposed positions. However, over the project period the workshops took place the number and range of participants was generally adequate or good. A quote from a member of the SPSA Maltese team at the time is informative of the outreach which SPSA provided:

> 'The first time I got involved in the SSA exercise, now called the SPSA, I could not imagine the involvement and commitment this would entail. The matter of Sustainability Indicators was familiar to me and from experience the identification of such indicators has always been an exercise carried out by experts. The SPSA has brought *in a wider participation in this exercise through the involvement of stakeholders* and hence brings into the picture a wider understanding of the concept of sustainable development and how this relates to the requirements and perception of the different stakeholders.' (Bell and Morse, 2003: 94, emphasis added).

This was a critical part of our learning. The use of participatory methods is still often 'experimental' in the experience of stakeholders. It would seem that SPSA was helping local people to engage with sustainability beyond the usual 'experts' but the methodologies like SPSA are not trivial in learning or application.

Another comment from a stakeholder at an SPSA workshop sets out some of the benefits of this kind of work:

'I must admit that the most interesting part of the whole CAMP activity was in fact the SPSA activity. Workshops were fun, highly interactive and more than any other workshop, managed to keep us away from those occasional snoozes, so common during long presentations. The whole process through which the indicators were developed was innovative for me, and my team and definitely gave us all a sense of ownership and responsibility about what we were actually trying to do. The innovative way of tackling problems etc through diagrams made the issues so much easier to visualise and definitely brought out the best in us. Team work was at its best, something that is very lacking here in Malta due to our small size and a culture of 'protecting one's turf' and by the end of your first seminar, we all felt that we were rowing the same boat in the same direction'. (Bell and Morse, 2003: 101–02)

Reactions of this kind were often repeated. It seemed to us that people were not used to being included, having their view self-represented and being listened to.

However, SPSA was no panacea. The project went on for almost two years with up to six rather than three months between each of the five, rather than four, SPSA workshops. The end product of the process was to provide an input to a report on the development of the north west of the island. But as the process dragged, some momentum was lost at times and some of the enthusiasm for the process declined as witnessed by the following quote from a member of the CAMP team in Malta:

'I did feel a little lost when it came to the final stages. For me (once again I say that it may have been only my impression!), it seemed as if suddenly when we got close to the finishing line, the momentum slowed down and that we never actually finalised the end product to perfection. At the last seminar we were informed what to do and how to do it, but never actually worked our way right up to the polished end product ... a bit of a frustrating experience after all the interest that your activity had built up. ...'(Bell and Morse, 2003: 132).

This was a good lesson. SPSA was focused on a rational method for engagement and visualisation. There were also issues of momentum, inclusion and delivery of some important deliverable – beyond a dry report to be consistently committed to. It was around this time that SPSA found its final label or form – it was decided between Elisabeth and me that it was too much of a mouthful and we needed a process name which was more elegant, intuitively obvious concerning meaning and readily understandable in English and French – we struck on the name: *Imagine*, which summed up the creative and visual focus of the method. Shortly afterwards we produced a manual for the inclusion of Imagine in future CAMP projects (Bell and Coudert, 2005). The importance of the manual cannot be overstated as the object of the exercise was to produce a generic method that could be applied by non-specialists who were not in the original research team and in numerous contexts. I talk about this next.

Mapping perspectives through Imagine: Lebanon, Algeria, Slovenia, Cyprus and Spain

Imagine as a revised and refined version of SPSA was used in a number of the CAMP projects that followed Malta: Lebanon (2002–03), Algiers (2003–05), Slovenia (2003–05), Cyprus (2006) and Spain (2011–12).

To provide a sense of the progress made with the methodology as it evolved from location to location, I want to bring in voices of some of those who were locally engaged with the work undertaken in Slovenia and Spain. These tell us how Imagine was experienced, how it was applied and what was learned in each case about the method and its value in dealing with the environmental sustainability issues under consideration.

We found that Imagine could result in some valuable insights and reflections on encouraging sustaining engagement and participation:

> 'In the beginning I was very sceptical, concerned and focused on the goal to get enough representatives of different stakeholders on five two-days workshops in following 6 months. It is not an easy job to get people on so many full days to participation on voluntary basis apart from their work. During five workshops the biggest challenge for us was how to keep a core group of desired 7 to 10 participants on all meetings to keep the desired flow of Imagine process and to build each phase on the previous results. In reality we had a lot of problems with

the fluctuation of the participants from one workshop to the other causing some disagreements and modifications of the results from previous workshops. On the other hand, we managed to get at least several important stakeholders on each workshop (mayors, municipal employees, CEO's of regional companies and agencies, some leaders of civilian initiatives ...) which was very helpful with strengthening the results from each workshop to the end of the process ... The success of the Imagine was not based only on very good results with proposed indicators, scenarios and collected data, but also on some long term relationships between several stakeholders worked together in Imagine in future development projects in coastal region many years after Imagine finished.' (Igor Maher – the CAMP SPSA/Imagine lead in Slovenia, January 2016)

The themes which appeared in Malta – of the engagement in process being based on diagrams and group work, of being 'fun' (particularly in the drawing of the rich pictures), enjoyable and focused on issues of real, local concern in order to encourage participation of stakeholders – were carried forward. Indeed, the process appears to achieve two of the main objectives Steve Morse and I had been intent on in the first instance – to attract stakeholders and retain them in a process of visual indicator development.

This relative success from two CAMPs was possibly assisted by the way in which Imagine was incorporated into the larger CAMP process. This suggests that the Imagine method can be seen to fit, as a participatory and visual-based approach, into wider and more expert/policy orientated frameworks:

'The Protocol on Integrated Coastal Zone Management in the Mediterranean (the ICZM Protocol) is the most comprehensive international legal instrument dealing with sustainable development of the Mediterranean coastal region. ... The success of any ICZM initiative depends on a dialog among the stakeholders and experts. And the Imagine method is the one to enable building consensus, creating trust among the stakeholders and making ownership of the initiatives, all being essential elements for a positive change.' (Marco Prem – the Deputy Director of PAPRAC and instigator of Imagine in CAMP Spain, January 2016)

ICZM is expert driven and remote from the experiences of local people. Imagine seems to offer a means to encourage both more engagement and more persistent engagement:

> 'CAMP Levante de Almería was very challenging from the beginning. … stakeholder involvement had to be gained in order to drive all projects activities.
>
> … We couldn't convince as many organizations as we hoped but we did bring together 44 participants for the first Imagine workshop. Its success was fundamental for the next project phases. We needed active people in order to achieve the project aims. So, there was nervousness and big expectations in the Imagine process.
>
> 'The first workshop was a crucial milestone and it allowed us to maintain the number of participants during the rest of the project, attract more participants, and avoid "losses" during the process. Of course there was a lot of hard work for the team but, Imagine was a positive additional factor that helped us. Following the second Imagine workshop real motivation emerged in the participants.
>
> 'Three years after the CAMP implementation, the feeling of closeness remains between the team, and between the stakeholders and technicians of the administration. Even now I sometimes receive calls asking me about the project from research groups; from technicians from other administrations that are looking for possibilities to revive the CAMP process or use the project results. I also hear from stakeholders that would like to continue the process.'(Ana Correa Pena – CAMP Imagine lead in Spain, January 2016)

Ana's reflections provide evidence of the problems of attracting attendance (after all these are voluntary workshops – inducement to attend is often hard to provide) but that momentum once achieved seemed to help with the persistence of the Imagine process beyond the initial workshop and indeed beyond the life time of the project, and a key Imagine element for supporting this is the visual diagramming.

The importance of visual mapping for identifying and capturing perspectives

In Malta, Lebanon, Algeria, Slovenia, Cyprus and Spain, the Imagine approach was applied and developed – from the initial and theoretic

SSA, an idea about how indicators could be gathered and shared in a systemic and participatory way, via SPSA – with the vital development of the method supplied by Plan Bleu and the explicit inclusion of a futures assessment.

Key to the success of Imagine was the application of rich pictures within the method, closely followed by the Amoeba diagrams.

As already noted in this book and in this chapter, the rich picture is a deceptively simple diagramming device that allows groups, teams and communities to share perspectives in complex contexts (for example, see Bronte-Stewart, 1999). Rich pictures are frequently used in change and conflict environments but have a real process value in gaining early interest in issues of shared interest (for example, see Carrizosa, 2002). In Imagine the rich picture was used as an initial device to 'collect' and share thinking as has been seen previously by users of the Soft Systems Methodology (Lewis, 1992). They were also used as means to map out the future.

Figure 8.3 is a rich picture from the early stages of CAMP Lebanon. Figure 8.5 is from the later scenario planning stage of CAMP Almería.

Rich picture content analysis is an analysis process that is in its infancy at the time of writing (see Bell et al, 2016: 172–3) and is inherently difficult given the intensely subjective nature of the picture in the first place. Generally interpretation is a combination of an assessment of the diagram itself linked to the narrative of the authors of the diagram. Focus can also be applied to the use of colour, metaphor and degree of integration (the amount the picture holds together as one picture or, in contrast, the degree to which it is a fractured bricolage of diverse elements from the various authors working in isolation from each other). The picture shown in Figure 8.3 is rich with colour, energy and meaning and to some extent holds together as one story – parts linking to parts. There are strong visual metaphors of the issues that face the regions –increasing temperatures, frustrations around renewable energy, farming and fishing concerns, marine pollution, and civic inertia and complacency. Each of these could be seen as an issue for sustainability and could result in the development of indicators for monitoring and displaying in an Amoeba diagram – one such emerging diagram is shown in Figure 8.4.

Keeping in mind that a 'sustainable' Amoeba would show all points in the BoE (the yellow area in this diagram), the Amoeba shown in Figure 8.4 maps out in a single domain six key indicators. The diagram shows in a very clear and stark manner how three indicators (to the left of the diagram) are in deficit of the BoE almost to vanishing point whereas of the remaining three indicators, two are in excess. A

Figure 8.3: Rich picture from CAMP Lebanon

Figure 8.4: Amoeba diagram from CAMP Lebanon

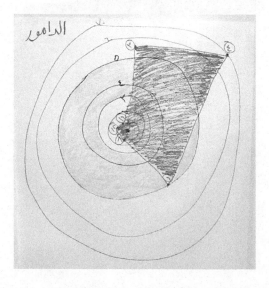

very unbalanced and clearly unsustainable visual with most indicators outside the BoE. Importantly, the lack of sustainability demonstrated in the rich picture is picked up and modelled with indicators in the Amoeba.

Figure 8.5, by contrast to Figures 8.3 and 8.4, is a future scenario-plan rich picture taken from Almería.

The picture is geographic in format and demonstrates suggestions for meaningful change (in terms of water use, energy production and new civics as well as many other items).

Although rich picture assessment is not the main subject of this chapter (for a fuller discussion see Bell et al, 2016) it is particularly interesting to consider the use of geography in the rich picture 'map'. In this case the more conventional visualisation technique of space has been adopted in order to allow the stakeholders in the workshop to explore regional variations and differing responses to potential sustainability measurement. Issues of education, alternative forms of renewable energy, tourism and coastal urbanisation have a clear geographic relevance to the region and they are shown in a substantial manner. Of course the use of a literal map also acts as an integrating device. It allows all members to find their 'place' in the picture and input the elements that are of specific interest to them but at the same time recognising the wide variety of other views for other areas.

Figure 8.5: Rich picture from the Scenario planning stage of CAMP Almeria

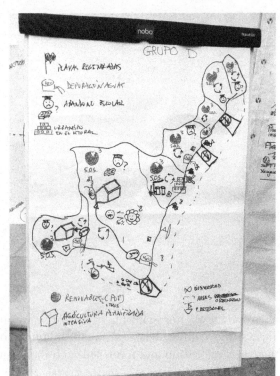

Interpretation of the specific meaning of the rich picture is again a challenge. It involves interpretation of the explicit and implicit narrative contained in the visual metaphors of the picture (Krippendorff, 2012). Such a content analysis of rich pictures is a subject in the very early stages of development but from a cursory analysis of the rich pictures produced at the end of CAMP Almería – and combining this with the verbal 'story' told by each group concerning the meaning of the images, these later, tidier and less cluttered diagrams describe the issues seen in the first set of rich pictures as being addressed – there is a strong sense of improved clarity around the core issues. The feedback from stakeholders in the final meetings often pointed to a need and determination to take up issues displayed in the final rich pictures and progress them beyond the lifetime of the specific CAMP project. In the case of Almería this was made manifest in the establishment of a number of strategic goals of which the fourth noted:

> Strategic goal 4: consolidate a transparent, participatory governance: social participation and institutional coordination (CAMP Almería 2012: 4).

Although Imagine and its various tools and techniques may appear evolutionary and therefore somewhat 'free form' and even chaotic (especially the rich pictures) the outcomes can, nevertheless, be concrete and highly practical. On the other hand analysis of this kind will be productive of its own critique. Such critiques include issues of inclusion, specificity and rigour, all of which can seriously impact on the Imagine process, potentially leading to misleadingly plausible results.

Inclusion

All Imagine workshops can be accused of misrepresentation or underrepresentation of stakeholder view as those who do not attend have no say. However, five diagrams drawn by five different groups may well be substantially different from each other even if depicting the same context and so represent diversity of perspective. Inclusion is therefore obviously key to the resulting meaning of the exercise and this means that representation is a major concern for the validity of the exercise.

Specificity

Amoeba diagrams in particular are entirely dependent upon the specifics demonstrated in the rich picture that preceded it. Simply put, the specifics of indicators, their label, format, content and calculation are dependent upon those included in the process. This imposes a demand on the process to be as clear, consensus driven and 'agreed' as is possible. The specifications of the Amoeba may be interpreted as 'fact' and this will of necessity be a partial case.

Rigour

This leads to the question of rigour. Despite taking six to twelve months to complete, the Imagine process operates in bursts of workshop activity. It is in the inter-workshop periods that the project team do what they can to impose rigour on the various outputs from the workshops. Expert driven analysis with stakeholder consultation face fewer challenges in this regard. More formal workshops employing listing of features and requests for information rather than contribution to design are less prone to the bias of specific, stakeholder groups. Rigour is always an issue for participatory processes which attempt to pass the baton of responsibility of analysis and synthesis to the local communities.

The need for Imagine to be based within a supporting and monitoring research structure is one means to respond to these points.

Conclusions so far: the social life of methods

The story of SSA, SPSA and Imagine is one of a learning method shift (and therefore methodology) in terms of social and institutional need. At one level the story of this chapter is of a participatory mapping technique – the rich picture developed as part of the theory of SSA and the resulting practice of SPSA leading to Imagine. The rich picture provides an adequate and sufficient basis for further mapping in the evolving methodology and is the basis for the Amoeba diagrams. Rich pictures and Amoeba diagrams are social and cultural constructs which to some extent emerge out of and in response to perceived need for some kind of assessment of environmental sustainability. Action research and methodological innovation run side by side as the original theory is modified in practice (particularly in the refinement of the workshops and the more direct inclusion of scenario planning). In this process it is argued that indicators are not just technical means to capture data – they represent a power relationship between social agencies. Indicators are customarily owned and presented from the perspective of experts. In the Imagine process the indicators emerge from workshops and are owned and presented from the perspective of the workshop participants. In this manner SSA/SPSA and Imagine – in attempting to include the views of local and formally unrepresented people in the development of indicators – represent a response to existing forces that create social form. As Savage puts it when referring to a variety of social methods:

> Social networking sites, audit processes, devices to secure 'transparency', algorithms for financial transactions, surveys, maps, interviews, databases and classifications can be seen as modes of instantiating social relationships and identified as modes of 'making up' society. (Savage, 2013: 5).

This 'social life of method' has been extended to encompass the double social life of methods:

> First, methods are social because they are constituted by the social world of which they are a part. This step is relatively easy. ... But we also take a second step: they are social because they also help to constitute that social world. (Law et al, 2011: 4)

It would be presumptuous to suggest that SSA, SPSA and Imagine and the associated rich pictures which they make use of constitute the social world but, and this essay bears witness to this process, the social world of practical project management has certainly been highly influential in the initial formulation of the approach (evidence: the frustration of Bell and Morse at the lack of social inclusion in indicator development), the re-formulation of methods under new circumstances (evidence: the evolution of SSA into SPSA in the context of the input and agenda of Plan Bleu, the value of scenario making and the first context of Malta) and the subsequent development of Imagine (evidence: the further requirement for a package of processes to use in CAMPs in a generic manner during and after CAMP Lebanon).

In practice, I have found visual methods both innovating and enervating in social contexts. The development of a visual representation of a complex reality – be it the current world as experienced by a group and represented in a rich picture or the semi-quantitative assessment of that complexity in an Amoeba diagram – allows a group to think innovatively about its situation and what this may mean in terms of wider sustainable criteria. Set against this is the observation that any picture, no matter how creatively arrived at or accurately drawn, requires substantial and exhaustive follow-up work in terms of assessment, verification and comparative analysis against other sources of information. In this sense the picture is not the end but rather the beginning of a process of critical assessment. Thus the rich picture or Amoeba diagram may be a magnificent means to engage and enthuse contrary and conflicting views in exchange but the image will still require thoughtful and coherent content analysis. This process of content analysis is still in its infancy.

Notes

[1] The rich picture is described in much more detail in other places – Campbell Williams (1999), Bronte-Stewart (1999) and Bell et al (2016) – and other examples of them being used are shown in Chapters Three and Seven.

[2] This may not be universally approved of but it can be generally agreed to. For example, if we were looking at global warming today (the end of 2015 just following the COP21 meeting in Paris) then the BoE for global warming might be argued to be between 1.5°C and 2°C. The range between these points would be the range of the BoE.

[3] See http://planbleu.org/en/activites/littoral

[4] See www.pap-thecoastcentre.org/about.php?blob_id=13&lang=en

[5] I have left this entry in Elisabeth's own words. Her English is not perfect but the meaning is I think very clear, and clearer than it would be if I moulded it into a false but grammatical English.

Acknowledgements

As well as those who commented on this text and provided their thoughts within it, particular thanks are due to Guillaume Benoit, the Director General (DG) of Plan Bleu when I became involved with it and a supporter of the SSA/SPSA/Imagine process when it was struggling to find its feet; Ivica Trumbric, the DG of PAPRAC who also supported Imagine in various situations over the years; Tony Ellul, who worked tirelessly for SPSA in Malta; and Pila Villegas Campos, who was a wonderful colleague in CAMP Spain.

References

Bell, S. (1994) 'Methods and mindsets: Towards an understanding of the tyranny of methodology', *Public Administration and Development*, 14(4): 323–38.

Bell, S. and Coudert, E. 2005. 'A Practitioner's Guide to "IMAGINE": the Systemic and Prospective Sustainability Analysis' [Guide d'Utilisation pour «IMAGINE»: l'Analyse de Durabilité Systémique et Prospective]. Blue Plan for the Mediterranean, Paper No. 3. Sophia Antipolis, 51 pages. France. ISBN 2-912081-15-7

Bell, S. and Morse, S. (1999) *Sustainability Indicators: Measuring the immeasurable*, London: Earthscan.

Bell, S. and Morse, S. (2003) *Measuring sustainability: learning by doing*, London and Sterling, VA: Earthscan Publications.

Bell, S. and Morse, S. (2008) *Sustainability Indicators: Measuring the immeasurable*, 2nd edition, London: Earthscan.

Bell, S., Berg, T. and Morse, S. (2016) *Rich Pictures: encouraging resilient communities*, London and New York: Routledge.

Bronte-Stewart, M. (1999) 'Regarding rich pictures as tools for communication in information systems development', *Computing and Information Systems*, 6(2): 85–104.

CAMP Almería (2012) 'Sustainable Development Reference Framework', Almería. Previously available at http://www.camplevantedealmeria.com/en/content/reference-framework-sustainable-development-and-portfolio-urgent-investments.

Campbell Williams, M. (1999) 'Rich pictures on the path towards systemic being', *Systems Research and Behavioural Science*, 16 (4): 369.

Carrizosa, A. (2002) 'Rich pictures, metaphors and stories as mechanisms to improve collective actions', in G. Castell, A.M. Gregory, A.J. Hindle, G.A. James, and M.E. Ragsdell (eds), *Synergy Matters: working with systems in the 21st Century*, New York: Kluwer Academic Publishers, pp 43–8.

Chambers, R. (1997) *Whose Reality Counts? Putting the first last*, London: Intermediate Technology Publications.

Cooke, B. and Kothari, U. (eds) (2001) *Participation the New Tyranny*, London: Zed Books.

Fisher, D.R. and Green, J.F. (2004) 'Understanding disenfranchisement: civil society and developing countries' influence and participation in global governance for sustainable development', *Global Environmental Politics*, 4 (3): 65–84.

Godet, M. (2001) *Creating Futures: Scenario planning as a strategic management tool*, London and Paris: Economica.

Godet, M., Monti, R., Meunier, F. and Roubelat, F. (1999) 'Scenarios and strategies: a toolbox for scenario planning', Working paper of the Laboratoire d'Investigation en Prospective, Stratégie et Organisation CNAM, Paris.

Harnard, S. (2008) 'Validating Research Performance Metrics Against Peer Rankings', *Ethics in Science and Environmental Politics*, 8: 1–6.

Kolb, D. (1984) *Experiential Learning: experience as the source of learning and development*, London: Prentice-Hall.

Krippendorff, K.H. (2012) *Content Analysis: An introduction to its methodology*, 3rd edition, London: Sage Publications.

Law, J., Ruppert, E. and Savage, M. (2011) 'The double social life of methods', Centre for Research on Socio-cultural Change, Working Paper no. 95, Milton Keynes: The Open University.

Lewis, P.J. (1992) 'Rich picture building in the soft systems methodology', *European Journal of Information Systems*, 1 (5): 351–60.

Rosenstrom, U. (2009) 'Sustainable Development Indicators: Much wanted, less used?', *Boreal Environment Research*, Helsinki Monograph no. 33.

Savage, M. (2013) 'The "Social Life of Methods": A Critical Introduction', *Theory, Culture and Society*, 30 (4): 3–21.

Stirling, A. (2006) 'From science and society to science in society: Towards a framework for "co-operative research"', Report of a European Commission workshop, 'GoverScience', 24–25 November, http://eurosfaire.prd.fr/7pc/bibliotheque/consulter.php?id=308

Sumberg, J., Thompson, J. and Woodhouse, P. (2012) 'Why agronomy in the developing world has become contentious', *Agriculture and Human Values*, 30 (1): 71–83.

NINE

Evaluating diagramming as praxis

Martin Reynolds

Editors' introduction

This chapter provides a stark contrast to the previous chapters dealing with the practice of using diagrams in participatory research. The author steps back to look at his development over many years of some diagrammatic representations of core systems principles and ideas discussed in Chapter Two; diagrammatic representations that can be used for evaluating diagramming as praxis in environmental sustainability. This braiding of theory and practice, including braiding between systems ideas and diagramming, is aimed at providing a robust and comprehensive approach to evaluation, which is an increasingly important part of all funded projects and programmes. We have seen in other chapters how funders and stakeholders are looking for 'measurable' outcomes or impacts from many of the projects being described in terms of changes to policy and/or practice. However, in this chapter the author examines what types of 'conversation' are needed in different situations in order to evaluate diagramming used in environmental sustainability projects and programmes.

Introduction

Since the beginning of the millennium, increasing concern has been expressed among researchers, wanting to influence policymakers, programme commissioners, commissioners of evaluations, and evaluators, about failures with interventions addressing complex environmental issues (Fukasaku, 2000) and about sustainable development issues more widely (Ramalingam, 2013). While many helpful discussions have emerged on the relevance of systems based and complexity-based approaches towards evaluation (Williams and Imam, 2007; Forss et al, 2011; Reynolds et al, 2012), commissioners and evaluators alike have expressed concern about the lack of uptake of new ideas (Stern et al, 2012; Befani et al, 2015). Relevant stakeholders appear to be talking past each other. Prevailing evidence-based approaches and contingency approaches to planning and evaluation appear not to be providing the way for valuing systems thinking generally, and visual based techniques specifically. The urgency of developing alternative ways of using research for planning and evaluating using different tools and ideas have increased markedly with the publication of The 2030 Agenda for Sustainable Development (United Nations, 2015) and associated implementation of the sustainable development goals (SDGs) in succession to the 2000–15 millennium development goals (MDGs).

Researching into systemic failure associated with complex situations of environmental sustainability involves many different interactions among many different entities (human and non-human). For example, the trigger of climate change (caused primarily by use of fossil fuels in developed countries) has encouraged the rapid development of biofuel agriculture through grants from rich countries in the global North to Brazil and other tropical countries in the global South. This has generated what Sawyer (2008) calls an eco-social collapse: involving both ecological problems (deforestation, pesticide pollution, and so on) and socioeconomic problems (particularly with concentration of land tenure, very poor working conditions for those forced to provide cheap labour for biofuel plantations, and increasing food prices for the population). To what extent might such a situation arise from breakdowns in the quality of communications? Apart from researching the importance of inter-human communication, there might also be important factors associated with the quality of our 'communication' with the natural world.

As evidenced in the case study chapters (Three to Eight), diagramming can be a powerful tool for expressing the complicatedness of inter-relationships, the complexity of multiple perspectives, and the conflicts of contrasting boundary judgements on issues of environmental sustainability. So how might it be possible to better evaluate such attributes? This chapter is about using diagramming both as a means of praxis generally, and more specifically, as a means for evaluating environmental sustainability as praxis. Praxis is understood here as the braiding together of theory (thinking) and action (practice). Praxis encompasses all forms of research into environmental sustainability. Good environmental praxis can thus be summarised as thinking in practice for supporting a flourishing sustainable natural (including human) environment.

In this chapter I use the metaphor of 'conversation' for describing praxis. The chapter weaves together three stories about diagramming as a means of developing sustainability through praxis. The first story provides some context. It is about evaluation in the field of sustainable development, and particularly the conversation between what might be called big 'E' evaluation – institutionalised demands for evidence-based guarantors or assurances for successful interventions as expected, for example, by funders of research – and small 'e' evaluation – the multitude of practices including visual based tools that may contribute towards developing value in, for example, a funded research project. The story tracks the growing importance of what has been called 'developmental evaluation' (Patton, 2011) – a tradition involving research evaluation – as a means of conversing between big 'E' and small 'e'.

The second and third stories track the history of a particular diagram developed by the author; a representation of praxis that has been shaken up, messed about with, and adapted for different uses during the past 15 years. The first of these two stories relates to representing the praxis of environmental responsibility (as a core constituent of developing environmental sustainability), and the second relates to making visual representations of developmental evaluation. Both stories narrate the changing form of the diagramming to suit particular needs. The purpose here is to demonstrate how a diagrammatic representation might allow space for 'conversation' at different levels of practice, including disciplinary (among specialist experts), interdisciplinary (between different experts) and transdisciplinary (between experts and civil society) practices.

Weaving the stories together, a mapping tool – the heuristic of systemic triangulation – is presented as a systems based influence diagram. The tool can be used for evaluating interventions at different levels, including the intervention of using visual techniques.

Diagramming and 'conversing' with sustainability

As noted earlier, I use the metaphor of 'conversation' to capture the notion of research praxis as thinking in practice. In line with other contributing authors to this compilation, I further invoke the use of 'diagramming' as a core language tool for enacting the conversation. The 'conversation' between thinking and practice has a number of manifestations in relation to researching environmental sustainability. Talbott (2004) identifies communication as a key problem in promoting sustainability – both communication *with* the natural world and communication among humans *about* the natural world. In making the case for a different type of relationship with nature, Talbott explores 'conversation' as a means of revealing what might constitute a more constructive and respectful relationship.

Chapter One highlighted the multiple definitions of environmental sustainability which in part arise from the meanings placed on these words by different disciplinary traditions. However, these meanings also reflect different worldviews in terms of how people within those traditions act towards the natural (ecological) environment. The idea of conversing with nature is not particularly new, though more often it is associated with endeavours of the 'arts' (poetry, prose, music, performance arts) than with scientific pursuits, where the notion is traditionally seen as being 'irrational'. Talbott brings out the tensions between two perspectives on ecological issues: the more eco-centric 'radical preservationist' tradition, and the more anthropocentric 'scientific management' tradition. His essay explores what it means to undertake an ecological conversation, using this as a metaphor to overcome the sometimes intransigent positioning of each tradition.

Here, I want to focus on conversation working at two levels, and to further focus on the value of diagramming as a mediating tool for enabling both conversations. The first level of conversation is that between human agents and the messy (complicated, complex, and conflictual) real world of human and non-human nature. The second level is the more conventional conversation among human agents about the real world. As referred to in Chapter Two, researching into environmental sustainability involves making clear the distinction between ontological real world issues of sustainability (*situations* of interest) to which humans will always have inevitably limited knowledge, and the more codified epistemological constructs (*systems* of interest) that we may use for understanding through research into such situations. The distinction is sometimes signalled by the use of upper-case initials for situations (Situations) and lower-case initials and/or inverted commas for codified constructs (such as systems of interest); for example, Nature versus 'nature' (Soper, 1995) or Environment versus environment (Cooper, 1992). Kate Soper makes a distinction between 'nature' as a codified construction that is often contested in its meaning (and hence sometimes put in inverted commas) and Nature as an extra-discursive reality, something that we acknowledge as existing outside conceptual construction or any attachment to human meaning. David Cooper criticised the conventional view of Environment as too vague – 'just one big ... biosphere, the order of things' (Cooper, 1992: 167) – as used in conventional institutionalised discourse about global warming and climate change among scientists and policymakers. He suggested

Environment was too unwieldy, and essentially lacking any sense of significance or purposefulness.

To what extent can we make sense of the idea of a conversation with nature and environment, as described by Soper and Cooper respectively, in order to support purposeful evaluation of research into environmental sustainability? And to what extent can we avoid what Talbott (2004) describes as an inadequate conversation with what he calls the 'Other':

> There is no such thing as a nature wholly independent of our various acts to preserve (or destroy) it. You cannot define any ecological context over against one of its creatures – least of all over against the human being. If it is true that the creature becomes what it is only by virtue of the context, it is also true that the context becomes what it is only by virtue of the creature.
>
> This can be a hard truth for environmental activists to accept, campaigning as we usually are to save 'it', whatever 'it' may be. In conversational terms, the Other does not exist independently of the conversation. We cannot seek to preserve 'it', because there is no 'it' there; we can only seek to preserve the integrity and coherence of the conversation through which both it and we are continually transforming ourselves. (Talbott, 2004: 43–4)

The challenge set by Talbott is how to converse meaningfully with the environment. In fleshing out what 'conversation' on sustainability might look like, it is perhaps as well to remind ourselves as *Homo sapiens* (people, folk, citizens, communities, cities, economies, private corporations, nations, regions and intergovernmental bodies) of three important issues:

1. While environmental praxis involves some understanding of the natural world, there are essential limits to our understanding of the (upper-case) natural world to which we belong, whether this is understood as the extra-discursive realm of integral relationships (including humans) that Soper (1995) calls Nature, or more scientifically as some globalised conception of what Cooper (1992) refers to as Environment.
2. Ideas of 'nature' and 'environment' (using quotation marks) are often contested depending on the practical situation and personal perspective taken. In any particular instance, for example, one

person's idea of nature might be more inclusive of, say, humans than another person's perspective; similarly, an environmental issue might be regarded by some people as being more local than global, whereas for others it is the other way round.

3. Given the idea that natures and environments are partial (both in the sense of being incomplete and in the sense of being subject to perspective/bias), it is helpful to have some appreciation of the human purpose behind the use of these terms. For example, the different purposes associated with evaluating an intervention based on sustainability may invite particular and contrasting use of terms such as nature and environment respectively.

Talbott's distinction between 'radical preservationist' and 'scientific management' signals what he describes as 'two very different conversations' (Talbott, 2004: 55). Figure 9.1 gives my impression of this conversation through a simple mental model.

The two orders of conversation depicted in Figure 9.1 itself provides a formalised expression of environmental praxis – thinking in practice – which is used for both depicting the reality of praxis from my perspective, and for conveying this understanding (my 'reality') to you as a reader.

First and second order conversations concur respectively with two aspects of using diagrams for research discussed in Chapter Two – working alone and working with others. The six case study illustrations in this book can be regarded as examples of using diagramming and mapping as mediating devices – conceptual expressions – for conversing both with reality and with others about that reality, in order to not only improve the reality but improve the understandings of that reality (through improved research).

The two ensuing stories exemplify separate though related sets of conversations. Both stories encompass both orders of conversation. The second story describes the evolution of a mental model for evaluating issues of sustainability; an account principally focusing on 1st order conversation. The first story is more focused on a 2nd order conversation among practitioners about the use of tools for evaluating sustainability. I start with this story as a means of providing the context for the ongoing development of diagramming for environmental praxis, and diagramming for evaluating environmental praxis.

Figure 9.1: Mental model or visualisation of environmental conversation showing (a) 1st order 'conversation' between practitioners and reality of environmental issues, and (b) 2nd order conversation among practitioners about the reality of environmental issues; both mediated through formalised expressions of systems, including diagramming

(a) 1st order conversation

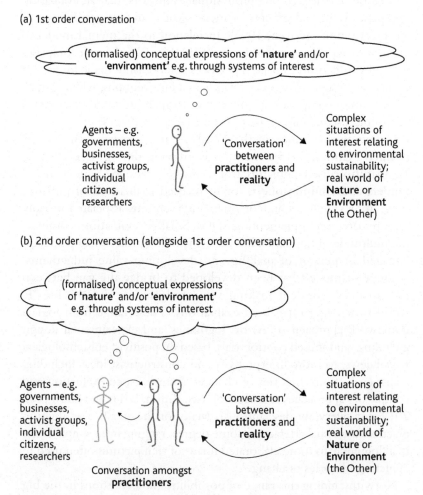

(b) 2nd order conversation (alongside 1st order conversation)

Source: Adapted from Reynolds and Howell (2010: 7) and Reynolds (2014a)

Story 1: Evaluating environmental praxis

A common conceptual understanding of evaluation suggests a practice comprising three elements: an *evaluand* – the real world situation being evaluated, usually an intervention of some kind (project, programme, or policy); *evaluators* – human agents either professionally commissioned and/or intervention personnel responsible for providing some kind of feedback on the value of the intervention; and the actual formalised notions of *evaluations* – that is, value judgements on the intervention. There is a general consensus in the formalised field of evaluation practice, among professional evaluators, that an evaluation comprises value judgements of merit, worth and/or significance of an intervention (Scriven, 1995). In relation to the mental model of environmental conversation (Figure 9.1b), big 'E' evaluation comprises the real world institutionalised practices and demands made for formal evaluations associated with environmental interventions, whereas small 'e' evaluation comprise various ways of formalising value judgements regarding sustainability as part of the evaluation process.

Following the launch of the 17 SDGs and associated 169 targets (United Nations, 2015), attention is growing on big 'E' evaluation – institutionalised demands from, and services to, policymakers, funders and commissioners, for formalised evaluations of projects, programmes, policies and/or other interventions associated broadly with research on implementing SDGs. Small 'e' evaluations comprise the multitude of human endeavours (including professional practices) engaged in pursuit of making and developing value judgements. A range of models has been developed to bridge the gap between the small 'e' world of making value judgements and the big 'E' world of needing formalised evaluations. These range from logical framework approach (LFA) or 'logframes' and experimental design including randomised control trials, based on positivist epistemological worldviews, to more interpretivist and constructivist ideas including realist evaluation, 'theories of change', systems based evaluation and complexity approaches to evaluation (see Patton, 2011, and Stern et al, 2012, for overview descriptions). Many of the small 'e' evaluation practices use visual artefacts to some degree, ranging from simple tables in a 'logframe' to more elaborated forms of rich pictures often used in depicting 'theories of change'.[1]

Notwithstanding this range of possibilities, interventions in the big 'E' world – both in planning and evaluating – remain more rooted in the positivist mode of experimental design based on simple causal attribution. Such attribution is conventionally regarded using a simple linear mental model: moving seamlessly from 'planned work' (inputs to activities) towards 'intended results' (outputs to outcomes to impacts).[2]

From a small 'e' world perspective of systems thinking, three problems arise with this simple 'mental mapping' in conversing between the reality of evaluands and evaluators' evaluations (Reynolds et al, 2016). First, the reality of sustainability issues being evaluated – the evaluand

– never conforms to linearity. Sustainability issues in particular are always non-linear – comprising multiple feedback connections and loops. Second, given the infinite inter-connectedness of the 'reality' being evaluated, an 'evaluator' (professional or otherwise), as with any research practitioner, has an inevitably partial position as an attributor in attributing causality. In complex situations with many actors as well as many factors, such attribution can be very problematic (Forss et al, 2011). Other attributes and attributions may be valid from other perspectives. Third, an intervention – whether an intervention being evaluated or an evaluation itself – is a real world activity subject to ongoing change. Reality does not stand still. Rigid input-output models for evaluation are by definition likely to be poorly adaptive to changes in the evaluand.

Securing the implementation of SDGs provides a real world evaluand of interdependent issues. Patton (2016) has responded to the challenge of evaluating SDGs in rethinking the evaluand in terms of 'the Blue Marble' – the famous photographic image of planet Earth taken in 1972, by the crew of Apollo 17.[3] As Patton describes it, the Blue Marble perspective means thinking globally, holistically and systemically: in essence, thinking of the world and its peoples as the evaluand. Blue Marble is a powerful image that more closely depicts Nature or the Environment than formalised conceptual notions of 'nature' or 'environment' as described respectively by Soper (1995) and Cooper (1992). To use the long-serving systems adage, Blue Marble represents the *territory* not the *map* (Korzybski, 1941). As with using the metaphor of conversation more generically (see Chapter Two), systemic evaluation involves three orders of conversation: (i) speaking to the real world of Environment in gaining factual judgements; (ii) speaking to other stakeholders in order to develop value judgements; and (iii) 'speaking' to, and reflecting on, the boundaries that are used for formulating both factual and value judgements.

The conventional impoverished first-order 'conversation' between the real ('factual' based) world of complicatedness, complexity and conflict, and the human (values-based) world of making evaluations, presents particular challenges among practitioners equipped in the small 'e' world of systems thinking, and the particular mobilisation of diagramming for (evaluating) environmental sustainability. The challenge for myself as someone working in the small 'e' world of evaluation from a tradition of systems thinking, has been to explore the use of diagramming to mobilise interest towards more systemic evaluation practice among practitioners in both the small 'e' world and big 'E' worlds of evaluation.

Story 2: Diagramming environmental responsibility as praxis

The source of getting a visual representation of praxis – an appropriate mapping of thinking in practice – came from Ulrich (2000) and his ideas of boundary critique and systemic triangulation which he presented as an 'eternal triangle'. The three elements of the triangle are real world 'facts', human 'values', and bounded 'systems'. Systems are understood by Ulrich as being conceptual constructs used as essentially 'thinking' devices – boundary judgements (see also Chapter Two) – for the 'practice' of mediating between making judgements of fact and value judgements. Later, boundary critique was described by Ulrich and myself in dual terms of (i) boundary reflection and (ii) boundary discourse, each illustrated with an empirical case study related to managing natural resources (Ulrich and Reynolds, 2010). The two types of boundary critique conform respectively with 1st order and 2nd order conversations, in turn, correlating with diagramming for working alone and working with others (see Chapter Two).

Figure 9.2 presents an evolutionary storyboard of the development of a diagrammatic learning device (heuristic) for understanding environmental responsibility (Reynolds and Blackmore, 2013) based on principles of systemic triangulation. The heuristic was developed with colleagues for teaching a postgraduate module entitled 'Environmental Responsibility: ethics, policy and action' for mature-age, part-time students, many of whom were professionally engaged with environmental management (Reynolds et al, 2009).

The notes below draw on the captions in Figure 9.2 in narrating the evolution of the heuristic for environmental responsibility.

Figure 9.2a, Systemic triangulation, depicts how real world judgements of fact (regarding, say, Nature or Environment) relate to value judgements (human agency) through the medium of boundary judgements:

> Thinking through the triangle means to consider each of its corners in the light of the other two. For example, what new facts become relevant if we expand the boundaries of the reference system or modify our value judgments? How do our valuations look if we consider new facts that refer to a modified reference system? In what way may our reference system fail to do justice to the perspective of different stakeholder groups? Any claim that does not reflect on the underpinning 'triangle' of boundary judgments, judgments

Figure 9.2: Evolutionary storyboard of an environmental responsibility heuristic

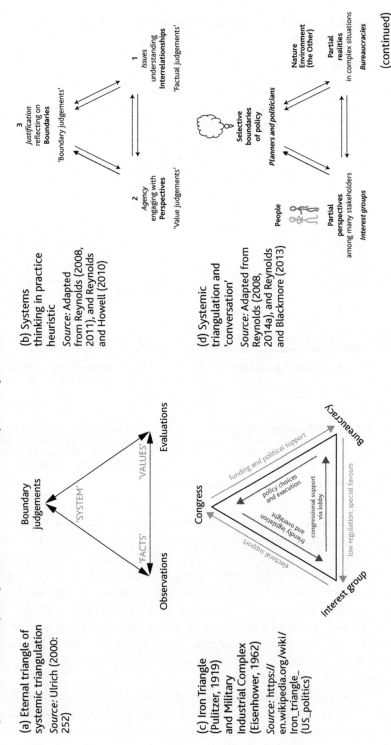

(a) Eternal triangle of systemic triangulation

Source: Ulrich (2000: 252)

(b) Systems thinking in practice heuristic

Source: Adapted from Reynolds (2008, 2011), and Reynolds and Howell (2010)

(c) Iron Triangle (Pulitzer, 1919) and Military Industrial Complex (Eisenhower, 1962)

Source: https://en.wikipedia.org/wiki/Iron_triangle_(US_politics)

(d) Systemic triangulation and 'conversation'

Source: Adapted from Reynolds (2008, 2014a), and Reynolds and Blackmore (2013)

(continued)

Figure 9.2: Evolutionary storyboard of an environmental responsibility heuristic (continued)

(e) Environmental responsibility heuristic

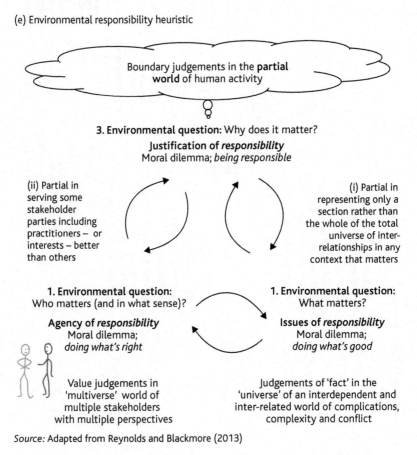

Source: Adapted from Reynolds and Blackmore (2013)

of facts, and value judgments, risks claiming too much, by not disclosing its built-in selectivity. (Ulrich 2003: 334)

The important thing about systemic triangulation is the essential partiality involved with the 'practice' of making judgements. All boundary judgements (associated with the 'thinking' world) are inevitably partial in the sense of being selective. They are (in the 'practical' world) selective of facts deemed relevant to the task at hand, and selective of values and norms associated with practitioners' own views.

The systems thinking in practice heuristic (or systemic triangulator) – (Figure 9.2b) – arose from wanting to develop a model of understanding and teaching 'systems thinking in practice' as part of a postgraduate programme of that name. A simple understanding was initially developed based on the idea of systems thinking in practice serving three purposes: (i) understanding inter-relationships; (ii) engaging with multiple perspectives; and (iii) reflecting on boundary judgements (Reynolds and Holwell, 2010; Reynolds, 2011). The systemic triangulator was developed building on Ulrich's original figurative triangle of facts, values and boundary judgements. In my rendition: 'facts' relate to real world situations of change, or issues, associated with all entities in infinite *inter-relationships*; 'values' relate to practitioners – human agents involved with managing change – having varied and unique *perspectives*; and 'boundaries' relate to the conceptual realm of ideas/tools/models used by practitioners for decision making about managing change, and justifying such decisions by reflecting on *boundary* judgements.[4]

Aside from embellishing Ulrich's eternal triangle with slightly different terminology, I made two changes to Ulrich's original diagram. First, I numerically sequenced the three component parts and exchanged the sides on which 'facts' and 'values' were situated. My reason for this is to make the triangulator more workable for practitioners to systematically engage with the heuristic. The postgraduate module for which the triangulator was developed was structured so as to deal sequentially with understanding inter-relationships, engaging with perspectives, and reflecting on boundaries. Inter-changing the 'facts' and 'values' enabled an initially more intuitive clockwise pass through the triangulator for heuristic purposes.

The second change involving separation of double-headed arrows into separate single headed arrows may seem minor and insignificant. The use of arrows in systems diagramming is very important in that they signal a substantive relationship – an action of some kind, or a relationship of causality or influence. In reality, the lines on the arrows going in different directions are never directly equivalent; they are always different and peculiar to the direction of the arrow. The way in which 'values' inform factual judgements, for example, is very different from the way in which value judgements might be informed by observation of 'facts'. Double-headed arrows can often mask rather than clarify relationships between entities.

Figure 9.2c, the iron triangle, provides a potential bridge between different academic disciplines and professional traditions. One of the challenges in teaching systems thinking ideas to professional practitioners involved with, say, environmental planning or international development, is over-coming the language barrier. One example relevant to this book is in the way in which the term 'system' is understood. From a scientific viewpoint (including complexity science and social science, as well as natural science) most researchers would tend to adopt a conventional 'lay' perspective of systems as real world (ontological) entities existing outside of any human perception, to be researched on. Alternatively, the authors in this compilation invite you to view systems more philosophically as conceptual (epistemological) constructs used actively for researching. Simplifying systems thinking in practice in terms of dealing with entities of interrelationships, perspectives and boundaries goes some way towards gaining a basic understanding of what the components are, but how they connect up remains a challenge. While systems thinking can remain conceptually challenging to understand, the notion of systemic failure or systemic breakdown is intuitively understood particularly in the media (both professional and social) and among politicians. However, explaining the mechanism of such processes can again be tricky. Researchers are increasingly reminded of the need to make their ideas, findings, recommendations, intelligible to policymakers. Addressing policy analysts and policymakers from a social science tradition, I have found the notion of the 'iron triangle' helpful in leveraging interest in the mechanisms of systemic triangulation (Reynolds, 2014b, 2015a).

The iron triangle metaphor provides a useful handle on which to explain systemic failure. The idea was first expressed by Ralph Pulitzer, a political journalist reporting critically on the Paris Peace Conference among victorious allied governments following the First World War in 1919 (see Pulitzer and Grasty, 1919). Pulitzer warned against the damaging confluence of interests among three exclusive sets of actors – military personnel (soldiers experiencing reality of conflict), military industry (with vested interests), and politicians making the decisions. While not using the term 'systemic failure' Pulitzer at the time warned against the longer-term success of a treaty built on limited conversations; a prophetic judgement given the events leading to the Second World War in the late 1930s. Later, the notion of the iron triangle and its visual image proved a powerful means in speaking to a wider sense of systemic failure; one popular expression being the 'military-industrial complex' used by American President Dwight Eisenhower during his 1961 presidential resignation speech. Political activists like Arundhati Roy have adapted ideas of the 'iron triangle' to surface pernicious confluences of interest regarding, for example, the building of dams in Narmada Valley in India; interventions that have had considerable ecological as well as rural socioeconomic disruptive impact (Roy, 2001).

The iron triangle metaphor is generically used to describe interaction between three entities:

> (i) some loosely defined 'bureaucratic' entity which represents the site of real world implementation of decisions (e.g. civil servants, managers and administrators), (ii) interest groups/ individuals who stand to benefit from the implementation of decisions (e.g. commercial and corporate interests of various kinds, or commissioned advisory groups whose task is to capture different interests), and (iii) decision makers themselves responsible for making and justifying decisions (e.g. Congress or Parliament, or at a lower level, commissioners of interventions). (Reynolds, 2015a).

With Figure 9.2d, Systemic triangulation and 'conversation', the triadic points on the visual representation of the iron triangle (Figure 9.2c) conforms conveniently to the systemic triangulator depicting systems thinking in practice (Figure 9.2). Pulitzer's original metaphor signalled the impoverished conversations being held drawing up the Versailles Peace Treaty, with particular reference to exclusion of important parties like representatives of civil society and representatives of the vanquished ('enemy') of Germany. In developing the visual model so that it spoke to the mental model of conversation developed earlier (Figure 9.1), ideas of partiality in systems thinking became particularly important. Figure 9.2d is an attempt to use ideas of the iron triangle to signal impoverished environmental conversations. In sequence, the three axes of the triangle can be used to represent: (i) real world Nature or Environment; (ii) inevitably partial or biased value judgements of environmental actors (stakeholders) regarding the reality; and (iii) inevitably partial or incomplete boundary judgements from environmental decision makers (planners and politicians) (Reynolds and Blackmore, 2013).

Figure 9.2e, the environmental responsibility heuristic, is a model used for understanding and teaching environmental responsibility (adapted from Reynolds and Blackmore, 2013) derived from a confluence of ideas across different disciplines and traditions including systems thinking, political economy, development management, environmental studies, business studies, and ethics. The heuristic is built on several underpinning principals.

First, the issues of environmental responsibility can be understood either as an extra-discursive reality – something that exists outside conceptual construction or any attachment to human meaning

(Nature) – or as contested ideas relating to human conceptual meanings ('nature').

Second, two views of environment can be understood in terms of a radical preservationist viewpoint and a more scientific resource-based viewpoint as depicted by Talbott (2004). The third, 'integral', view of nature constitutes a focal point for environmental responsibility and is one that might be expressed in terms of forging an ecological conversation. Using an integral view helps in understanding responsibility. It involves perceiving environment in terms of both the 'natural' and the 'human' worlds, deeply interlocked.

Third, in understanding issues of environmental responsibility ('nature' matters), three integral questions might be asked – what particular issues matter? Who matters and in what way? And why do these things matter? For instance, what matters can be associated with what is good and vice versa. If I consider clean air to be something that matters, what is good might be determined by action that contributes as little as possible to air pollution, like riding a bicycle instead of driving a car. What matters (goodness in terms of air quality) drives who matters and how (rights and duties of stakeholders). Doing what is right might similarly be related to an assessment of who matters and how; in other words, questions regarding agency in a situation invite attention to the idea of doing the right thing. Given the situation, what is the right thing to do and who should be doing it? If the situation is air quality (without making a claim about whether it is good or bad), a right course of action might be considered to be 'penalising polluters' or conversely 'educating citizens/consumers'. This in itself suggests who matters and how they matter. Finally, being responsible (or virtuous) can be related to an assessment of why it is that these matters are regarded as important, and why some agents and their particular roles matter and not others.

Fourth, systems thinking provides a practical way of framing matters that works in two ways: as a 1st order of conversation, it frames our understanding of Nature in terms of thinking about the natural world as holistic systems with interrelated and interdependent parts; and as a 2nd order of conversation, it offers opportunities for exploring different framings – framings representing multiple and often conflicting perspectives on Nature. Framing issues of environmental responsibility for policy design and action requires appropriate discursive space for dealing with our limitations on being holistic and being 'multiverse' (that is, tolerant of multiple perspectives). It requires framing that allows for new frameworks among experts of different disciplines, and between those experts and citizens.

The environmental responsibility heuristic enables conversation (being response-able) at two levels; one in understanding systemic failure and breakdown associated with interventions associated with sustainability; another at not only teaching environmental responsibility but planning for better environmental responsibility. The third story illustrates how the visual ideas of systemic triangulation can be adopted and adapted for evaluating sustainability interventions including interventions associated with implementing the SDGs.

Story 3: Diagramming evaluation as praxis for sustainable development

In a paper entitled '(Breaking) The iron triangle of evaluation' (Reynolds, 2015a), an attempt was made to understand the current situation of big 'E' evaluation as described in Story 1 above. In the paper I drew explicitly on the metaphor of the iron triangle and adapted the visual representation of the Military-Industrial Complex (M-IC) to what might be an equivalent of an Evaluation-Industrial Complex (E-IC). My primary aim as part of a 1st order conversation was to give more concise expression of misgivings regarding the big 'E' world of evaluation. In order to do this, I was keen to put a meaning on each of the six arrows as is done with the M-IC visual representation in Figure 9.2c. This addresses one of the issues raised in the preceding story about the need for (systems) diagramming to be explicit and transparent about the meaning of the arrows.

The three corners of the triangulator were re-presented in terms of: (i) evaluand, including managers/administrators implementing interventions, representing the real world of interrelated issues of complications, complexity and conflict; (ii) evaluators, with the task of representing (and inevitably) privileging different interests, in short, representing different perspectives; and (iii) evaluations, as expressions of advice to decision makers (commissioners of interventions), as representing, in short, boundary judgements.

In drafting the paper I was encouraged by the editor and other colleagues to explore an alternative form of evaluation practice – what might be referred to as small 'e' evaluation – to counter some of the more impoverished aspects of contemporary institutionalised big 'E' evaluation. In effect, I became engaged with developing an alternative model of what I called an evaluation-adaptive complex (E-AC); an expression of 2nd order conversation promoting more purposeful deliberation on improving evaluation practice among evaluation practitioners. Figure 9.3 illustrates the generic broad representation

Figure 9.3: Evaluation-in-practice – an influence diagram illustrating six activities: (a) auditing; (b) planning; (c) evaluating (understanding); (d) evaluating (practising); (e) commissioning; and (f) learning

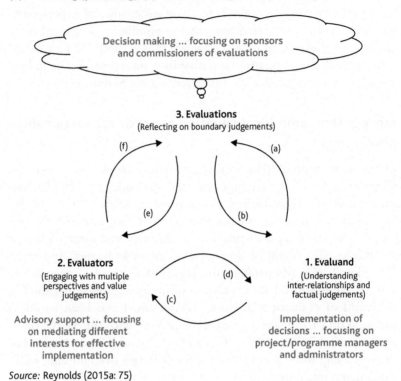

Source: Reynolds (2015a: 75)

of the triadic relationships between the three domains for what might be called 'evaluation-in-practice' or evaluation as praxis.

For a more detailed understanding of the six activities associated with evaluation–in-practice, (a)–(f), you may like to see the original source (Reynolds, 2015a), which also includes a table that represents work in progress towards moving from a model of 'evaluation-in-practice' (viewing evaluation as itself an intervention) towards a more refined model of 'evaluating practice' (evaluating an intervention).[5]

A mapping tool for evaluating environmental praxis

The evaluation-adaptive complex heuristic can be adapted for use with planning and evaluating at different levels of intervention. The E-AC might be used as a conversation device for a more focused level of developmental evaluation in the use of diagramming/mapping for sustainability.

The notes below provide some generic questions regarding the role of diagramming for researching environmental sustainability based on the six core activities of evaluating practice noted above. They might be applied to any of the diagramming case studies in the preceding chapters, or indeed to your own diagramming praxis.

- *Auditing*: To what extent might diagramming and mapping give expression to the inevitable complications (inter-relationships), complexity (multiple perspectives) and conflict (boundary judgements) arising from researching environmental sustainability? How might mapping situations support greater clarity for environmental decision makers in their endeavours to understand the contexts in which they work? Possibly helpful diagrammatic forms might be rich pictures and spray diagrams.

- *Planning*: Which entities are important and which are not in terms of being 'inclusive' with researching environmental sustainability? How might visual renditions of planning – such as logframes and project cycles – accommodate the necessary iterative (non-linear) nature of purposeful planning? Possibly helpful diagrammatic forms may include systems mapping, influence diagramming, cognitive mapping and multiple cause diagramming, among others.

- *Evaluating (1)* (summative): How may diagramming give appropriate expression to judgements of worth (impacts on most vulnerable, including non-human nature), merit ('rights' of non-human as well as human nature), and significance (behavioural change) generated through researching environmental sustainability? How may diagramming embellish a range of value judgements in a questioning provisional sense, rather than an assertive 'judgementally' didactic and dogmatic sense?

- *Evaluating (2)* (formative): How may diagramming support conversations with other stakeholders about realities of researching environmental sustainability, while developing value in the process? To what extent may diagramming support the notion of developmental evaluation (Patton, 2011) triggering new ways of seeing and thereby valuing? Here it is the value of diagramming for prompting 2nd order conversation that is of particular importance.

- *Commissioning* (provision of guarantors): How might diagramming provide more wider reaching alternative guarantor-sets for researching environmental sustainability. Funded researchers need to provide assurances of rigour based not only on conventional co-guarantor attributes of 'representation' of environmental reality (objectivity), but also attributes of 'resonance' (speaking to different disciplines and traditions) and 'relevance' (speaking to civil societal and public concerns) (Reynolds, 2015b).

• *Learning*: How can diagramming enable not just single loop learning (in making appropriate representation of activities either working or not working with interventions), but also double loop learning, in raising ethical issues around particular interventions, and triple loop learning in raising political issues of power dynamics associated with researching environmental sustainability (Flood and Romm, 1996; Reynolds, 2014a). Taking the visual representation of the iron triangle as an example, what particular diagramming techniques might foster understanding of power dynamics (1st order conversations) and triggering ideas of alternative power relationships (2nd order conversations) associated with, for example, generating better autonomy (power-within).

Each of the examples of diagramming used in this book compilation can be evaluated individually using these ideas. In this section a more generic evaluation of diagramming is presented.

Concluding thoughts

Talbott (2004) regards the quality of communication, particularly between human and non-human nature, but also between stakeholders, as being fundamental to the kinds of problems associated with eco-social collapse and systemic failure. This chapter has set out an alternative framing of complex interventions that values diagramming as a core constituent of systems thinking in practice and of researching into environmental sustainability.

The three stories briefly narrated in this chapter together weave a wider story of praxis and the use of diagramming. In narrating the story through a personal trajectory of diagramming development, much of the actual messiness – or what I prefer to call playfulness – of the practice in diagramming has been filtered out. Behind each of the diagrams presented in this chapter there is a raft of iterative and discarded drawings. Diagramming at an individual and collective level is praxis; thinking in practice. What this means is that diagramming promotes conversation between thinking and practice – conversation at the level of making sense of reality (1st order), and conversation at the level of exchanging perspectives (2nd order). When both levels of conversation are engaged with reflectively, that is, accommodating inevitable partialities in factual and value judgements, the conversation might be regarded as at 3rd level, thereby generating new senses of reality and new possibilities of change (Reynolds, 2014a). Being mindful and playful of diagramming can not only promote better conversations around sustainable development, but also may mitigate against systemic failure and systemic breakdown of interventions associated with environmental sustainability, including researching environmental sustainability.

Acknowledgements

Some of the material in this chapter is adapted from the author's own contributions to the following postgraduate modules (each with an Open University reference code): Environmental Responsibility: ethics, policy and action (TD866); Managing Beyond the Mainstream (BB847); and Thinking Strategically: systems tools for managing change (TU811).

Notes

[1] For example, see the graphic on 'A Theory of Change approach' at www.idex.org/blog/2014/01/28/idex-theory-of-change/

[2] See the simple mental model depicting this conventional linear logic of evaluation at http://impactinvesting.marsdd.com/social-impact-measurement/how-social-impact-measurement-tools-and-methods-fit-into-your-logic-model/

[3] See also www.utilization-focusedevaluation.org/blue-marble-evaluators

[4] The three triangulator nodes also align with the simple definition of 'system' introduced in Chapter Two – a collection of entities interacting together (inter-relationships), as seen by someone (perspectives) in order to do something (judgements of boundary) (Morris, 2009).

[5] Since writing this chapter, research practitioners associated with evaluation have expressed an interest in adopting and adapting E-AC model for evaluating their own areas of research practice. For example, in 2016 I was appointed member of an Advisory Panel for the United Nations Women group on developing guidance for an inclusive systemic evaluation approach called GEMs (gender equality, environments, and voices from the margins). The GEMs Framework is a systemic evaluation approach designed to support human-centred monitoring and evaluation in global development interventions – see www2.hull.ac.uk/hubs/pdf/CSS080716.pdf

References

Befani, B., Ramalingam, B. and Stern, E. (2015) 'Towards Systemic Approaches to Evaluation and Impact', *IDS Bulletin*, 46 (1): 1–6.

Cooper, D.E. (1992) 'The idea of environment' in D.E. Cooper and J.A. Palmer (eds), *The Environment in Question: Ethics and Global Issues*, London: Routledge, pp 163–78.

Flood, R.L. and N. Romm (1996) *Diversity Management: Triple Loop Learning*, Chichester: John Wiley and Sons.

Fukasaku, Y. (2000) 'Chapter 2: Innovation for environmental sustainability: a background', in Organisation for Cooperation and Development, *Innovation and the Environment*, pp 17–32.

Forss, K., Marra, M. and Schwartz, R. (eds) (2011) *Evaluating the complex: Attribution, contribution, and beyond*, Volume 1, New Brunswick, NJ: Transaction Publishers.

Korzybski, A. (1941) 'General semantics, psychiatry, psychotherapy and prevention', *American Journal of Psychiatry*, 98 (2): 203–14.

Patton, M.Q. (2011) *Developmental evaluation: Applying complexity concepts to enhance innovation and use*, New York: Guilford Press.

Patton, M.Q. (2016) 'A Transcultural Global Systems Perspective: In Search of Blue Marble Evaluators', http://dmeforpeace.org/learn/transcultural-global-systems-perspective-search-blue-marble-evaluators (originally published in *Canadian Journal of Program Evaluation*, 30 (3))

Pulitzer, R. and Grasty, C.H. (1919) 'Forces at War in Peace Conclave', *New York Times*, 18 January.

Ramalingam, B. (2013) *Aid on the edge of chaos: rethinking international cooperation in a complex world*, Oxford: Oxford University Press.

Reynolds, M. (2008) 'Getting a grip: Critical systems for corporate responsibility', *Systems Research and Behavioral Science*, 25 (3): 383–95.

Reynolds, M. (2011) 'Critical thinking and systems thinking: towards a critical literacy for systems thinking in practice', in C.P. Horvath and J.M. Forte (eds), *Critical Thinking*, New York: Nova Science Publishers, pp 37–68.

Reynolds, M. (2014a) 'Triple-loop learning and conversing with reality', *Kybernetes*, 43 (9/10): 1381–91.

Reynolds, M. (2014b) 'Systemic failure in macroeconomic modelling', *International Journal of Applied Systemic Studies*, 5(4): 311–28.

Reynolds, M. (2014c) 'Equity-focused developmental evaluation using critical systems thinking', *Evaluation – The International Journal of Theory, Research and Practice,* 20 (1): 75–95.

Reynolds, M. (2015a) '(Breaking) The iron triangle of evaluation', *IDS Bulletin*, 46 (1): 71–86.

Reynolds, M. (2015b) 'Rigour (-mortis) in evaluation', *Connections, Newsletter of the European Evaluation Society*, June: 2–4.

Reynolds, M., Gates, E., Hummelbrunner, R., Mira, M. and Williams, B. (2016) 'Towards Systemic Evaluation', *Systems Research and Behavioural Science*, 33 (5): 662–73.

Reynolds, M. and Blackmore, C. (2013) 'Two cultures? Working with moral dilemmas in environmental science', *AWERProcedia Advances in Applied Sciences*, 1: 233–40.

Reynolds, M., Blackmore, C. and Smith, M.J. (eds) (2009) *The Environmental Responsibility Reader*, London: Zed Books

Reynolds, M., Forss, K., Hummelbrunner, R., Marra, M. and Perrin, B. (2012) 'Complexity, systems thinking and evaluation – an emerging relationship?', *Evaluation Connections: Newsletter of the European Evaluation Society*: 7–9.

Reynolds, M. and Holwell, S. (eds) (2010) *Systems Approaches to Managing Change: A Practical Guide*, London: Springer.

Roy, A. (2001) *Power politics*, Cambridge, MA: South End Press.

Sawyer, D. (2008) 'Climate change, biofuels and eco-social impacts in the Brazilian Amazon and Cerrado', *Philosophical Transactions of the Royal Society B*, 363: 1747–52.

Scriven, M. (1995) The logic of evaluation and evaluation practice, in D.M. Fournier (ed), *Reasoning in Evaluation: Inferential Links and Leaps, New Developments in Evaluation*, San Francisco, CA: Jossey Bass.

Soper, K. (1995) *What is Nature?* Oxford: Blackwell.

Stern, E., Stame, N., Mayne, J., Forss, K., Davies, R. and Befani, B. (2012) 'Broadening the range of designs and methods for impact evaluations', Report of a study commissioned by the Department for International Development. London: Department for International Development (DFID).

Talbott, S. (2004) *In The Belly of the Beast: Technology, Nature, and the Human Prospect*, Ghent, NY: The Nature Institute, http://natureinstitute.org/txt/st/mqual/misc/conversation.pdf

Ulrich, W (2000) 'Reflective practice in the civil society', *Reflective Practice*, 1 (2): 247–68.

Ulrich, W. (2003) 'Beyond methodology choice: critical systems thinking as critically systemic discourse', *Journal of the Operational Research Society*, 54 (4): 325–42.

Ulrich, W. and Reynolds, M (2010) 'Critical systems heuristics', in M. Reynolds and S. Holwell (eds), *Systems Approaches to Managing Change: A Practical Guide*. London: Springer, pp 243–92.

United Nations (2015) *Transforming our World: The 2030 Agenda for Sustainable Development*, https://sustainabledevelopment.un.org/post2015/transformingourworld/publication

Williams, B. and Imam, I. (eds) (2007) *Systems concepts in evaluation: An expert anthology*, Point Reyes: American Evaluation Association/EdgePress.

TEN

Conclusions

Andy Lane and Sue Oreszczyn

In Chapter One we said that there were four inter-related themes running through this book as indicated by its title: mapping, environmental sustainability, systemic practices and participatory research. We explained what we meant by each of these and then in Chapter Two set out in more detail how mapping was a feature of systems thinking and that systems thinking influences how we view environmental sustainability and how we practice our research. That research practice includes working closely with the participants of the situations we are researching and acting within. Chapters Three to Eight then provided different case studies on the use of mapping within their research. These case studies are from people at The Open University who share a common praxis (in that we all collaborate on developing coherent teaching materials on these topics) but are free to undertake their own research in various 'niches' relating to the broad field of environmental sustainability. Chapter Nine then took a theoretical perspective on using systems thinking and mapping to help with the evaluation of research projects and programmes.

As well as reflecting on these four themes, we want to add a fifth theme in this final chapter, one that has been implicit throughout the book, that of research methods. This is important since we said in Chapter One that the idea for this book arose out of interest in our use of visual methods in research from doctoral students and research fellows at The Open University and elsewhere. They wanted to know what the benefits of using such participatory visual approaches were, but also the limitations or drawbacks. They were interested in how we had used mapping as a tool or technique as a method for engaging participants, and as a way to frame a methodology. And although the book is particularly relevant to researchers, these same issues around the methods used are also relevant to any practitioner working in complex environmental situations that necessarily involve many different people and perspectives. What follows are our concluding remarks on each of these themes, but what will also be apparent is how each theme is closely tied to the other themes. Hopefully this exposition will help you in developing your own praxis.

Mapping

Modes and means of communication are not neutral in the sense that social and cultural norms and available technologies shape how people respond to them individually and collectively. The practice of mapping or diagramming for eliciting and collecting data brings both benefits and limitations.

As our case study examples demonstrate, a major benefit is that mapping techniques can be used effectively with people of different cultures, languages and ages, making it a very accessible approach. It can also, if facilitated well, enable all participants to engage equally and equitably and bring greater depth and breadth to the situations being discussed than might be the case with interviews. In other words, they can help to provide a collective, more holistic view rather than many separate partial views. As we have noted previously, this collective view can, in turn, help to improve the accuracy and relevance of the data collected for subsequent analysis.

The limitations or weaknesses mirror these strengths. First, some participants dislike drawing and see it as childish, remembering school days when they were criticised for their artistic skills, and so they do not participate at all or as fully as is desirable. This belief or attitude is very common and one we have witnessed with many thousands of our students over the years (Lane, 2013). As has been demonstrated through this book, though there are many forms of diagram, many do not require any artistic drawing at all as they are mostly based on the spatial arrangements of words/phrases (for example, systems maps, scenario maps). So, when creating diagrams in groups it is possible for those more relaxed about 'drawing' to create the diagram based on what others have said. Inevitably this gives more power to the people who wield the pen, which is why good facilitation and the recording of discussions can help capture aspects that might otherwise be lost (not forgetting that, as noted earlier in Chapter Three, using participatory methods such as workshops requires good facilitation and communication skills which are not necessarily well developed among academics).

Second, while drawing can span social and cultural settings, the precise type of drawing and the technology used to create them has to be chosen carefully or adapted in the light of experience, otherwise they may constrain the data collected or the levels of engagement. This is particularly so where the forms and genres of visual communication that participants are used to are different to those experienced by the researchers (we saw this strongly in Chapter Five with indigenous communities in Guyana). Throughout the chapters you will have seen examples of how the uses of diagramming were developed, and/or adapted over time, to suit a particular context (such as the evolution of the Imagine approach described in Chapter Eight). In one case, Chapter Five (but also evident in Chapters Three, Four, Six and Seven), the researchers used a particular diagramming technique to fulfil a particular purpose in a particular moment in time. Having achieved that purpose, they then applied other visual techniques deemed more appropriate for the next stage in the research. In other words, they had a 'visual toolbox' approach – using what they thought was the most appropriate tool for the specific requirements of that research phase. So not all visual techniques, however facilitated and participatory, are suitable for all contexts. Rather than insisting on using the same visual technique in all cases and/or persevere after much struggling, sometimes it is best to move on. However, this also raises a methodological point – visual techniques, such as those described in this book, might be participatory, but we do not necessarily ask participants which technique they would prefer to use.

Third, another general issue raised in the examples is of people believing the map or diagram is of something real 'out there', rather than a device for thinking about, or representing what people think about, the scenario/system and so on. Related to this is whether the map also includes consequences for the participants personally or is viewed in a more abstract way as being about someone else's problems. Any representation is an abstraction but a diagram produced by people with a stake in the system of interest is likely to show greater levels of 'ownership' by them of the issues identified in that system of interest. In turn this may lead to a greater desire by themselves to take the issues raised (and possibly the mapping techniques) forward (as we saw in Chapter Eight) or to use the diagrams as records to be reviewed in later years (as seen in Chapters Three and Five).

Lastly, for researchers, visual mapping methods can be more of a challenge to analyse or synthesise compared to interview data or transcripts. That is why having recordings, or notes of conversations or plenary explanations of maps by the participants, is important as those recordings or notes provide both contextual and corroborative data which can be used to identify and validate key themes from that visual data. Similarly, providing photo reports (as in Chapters Four and Six), or sending analyses to the participants to comment on (as in Chapters Three, Four and Six), all help to ground the analysis with the research participants themselves.

In addition to these considerations, there is also the acceptability of mapping by the wider research community, not only mapping to elicit and collect data, but also the presentation of maps as primary (participant generated) or secondary (researcher synthesised) data in research reports and articles. While there has been some questioning of, and reluctance to, accept such visual methods within multidisciplinary research studies by some disciplines, this is changing as is shown by the many research articles referenced throughout this book. Even so, as we noted in Chapter One, the predominance of the written word as the main communication mode means it can still be difficult to include many diagrams to fully evidence the mapping methods and techniques that were used in reports and articles and which is partly why we have produced this book! (Although we, ironically, have used a mainly written medium in this book to deal with diagramming in research, the free Open University teaching materials referred to in Chapter Two do use visual media.)

Environmental sustainability

We noted in Chapter One that while we, as academics, can and do debate what is meant by environmental sustainability, it is just as important when researching into complex situations involving people to also be mindful of, and accept how, the funders and participants frame environmental sustainability or their environmental situation; and what outcomes they might be expecting from the project. Bracken et al (2015) have noted the shift in research agendas towards utility and addressing real world concerns with policymakers able to use the best available knowledge. Although of course this may mean privileging scientific knowledge over other types of 'knowing' from the people involved in a particular situation. This can be particularly so with environmental sustainability projects and raises further questions of the ethicality of the approaches being used and whether, as noted by Boschetti et al (2016), we need sound, empirically based guidelines for working with others within participatory and action-oriented projects. Something similar is noted by Long et al (2016), who suggest a check list of 'questions that won't go away in participatory research' to help stimulate reflection.

Equally, we always have to be mindful of how language can be inclusive or exclusive in framing the discourse of an educational philosophy or movement, as noted by Wals and Jickling (2002: 222) for a related topic:

> ... education for sustainability runs counter to prevailing conceptions of education: it breathes a kind of intellectual exclusivity and determinism that conflicts with ideas of emancipation, local knowledge, democracy and self-determination. The prepositional use of "for" prescribes that education must be in favor of some specific and undisputed product, in this case sustainability. At the same time, an emphasis on sustainability, or sustainable development, might hinder the inclusion of other emerging environmental thought such as deep ecology and ecofeminism.

We also saw in Chapter Nine that there are different ways in which we can view/converse with the natural environment and that recognising and acknowledging different perspectives is very important. To demonstrate this point, in line with the themes of this book, we reproduce a word cloud from White (2013) as a graphical demonstration of how defining sustainability can be elusive because of all the other words associated with it in various definitions (Figure 10.1).

Another view is given by Costanza and Patten (1995: 193):

> The basic idea of sustainability is quite straightforward: *a sustainable system is one which survives or persists.*
>
> But there are three additional complicating questions: (1) What system or subsystems or characteristics of systems persist? (2) For how long? (3) When do we assess whether the system of subsystem or characteristic has persisted?' (original emphases).

Figure 10.1: 'Wordle' cloud of words appearing in definitions of sustainability

Source: White, 2013

To which we can add, who does that assessment or evaluation?

These different (disciplinary) views of environmental sustainability are more than just an academic exercise within multidisciplinary or transdisciplinary projects, they are a crucial feature of transdisciplinary research (Lyall et al, 2015), which, as we noted in Chapter One, is characterised by the involvement of non-academic stakeholders, including those people affected by the research.

The research we have described in this book shows how complexity (and contestation) in environmental situations involving people and their different perspectives may be embraced and yet outcomes still achieved. The research has sought to find better ways of involving various stakeholders and, in many cases, find a better way of linking research, policy and practice. The systemic approaches we use recognise the need to look beyond formal government policymaking and towards the informal relationships and networks that constitute a wider policy process. Further, our research has an extra dimension in that in addition to our research findings or outcomes, our processes – methods and techniques – may get taken up by those we research with. Learning does not simply occur between the formal researchers, but also between those involved in the project. The results or outcomes of the projects are not simply disseminated at the end to those who may use them; rather learning occurs throughout the project and in many cases has the ability to continue. Projects such as Imagine (Chapter Eight) and Cobra (Chapter Five) particularly had the ability to continue beyond the initial funding. All those who participated in our research have gained new skills and insights that might help sustain their activities, activities that in turn may help with sustaining their environment(s).

Systemic practices

We have been up front in explaining how systems thinking has collectively influenced our own researching (and teaching) practices. This extends to how we view environmental sustainability, how we try to engage with others and how we use mapping as a means to get ourselves, and the people we work with, to view situations more holistically and so complement reductionist thinking and explanations. This bridging of perspectives and in particular academic disciplines, whether described as inter-, trans- or multidisciplinary, is central to our practices and one we would encourage you to also follow. This has advantages and disadvantages already touched upon. The advantages are about enabling conversations around the mapping exercises to ensure that we correctly and adequately portrayed peoples thinking and/or disciplinary knowledge to provide a more holistic account. Similarly, to enable participants to discuss their views and experiences in relation to others and draw out aspects that would not otherwise have necessarily been apparent. The disadvantages are that it can be more complex to record and analyse the 'data' and to represent that in a way that is acceptable to all, including journal editors and reviewers. But overall our research praxis is informed by systems thinking and systems practices, and reflection on that praxis. This means that our research practices continuously evolve as we reflect on those practices and are not carried out in isolation of the wider context, making assessment of it tricky. Of necessity there are changes in these practices over long periods of time as we constantly try approaches in actual contexts and think hard about them and the impact they have on the research itself.

Participatory research

The projects in this book demonstrate how tools and techniques necessarily changed over time as they are adapted to particular circumstances. Becoming increasingly more participatory over time, both within the lifetime of a project, but also over the course of our academic careers. This reflects the wider move towards more participatory research, but also, as noted previously, the need to apply what is most suitable for what you are doing and who you are researching with.

The benefits of participatory research in general, and using mapping in particular, is that it enables participants to express their views with less interference or input from the researcher. There is a power relationship between researcher and participant and with interviews the researcher generally has more control. With participatory events the participant may have equal, if not more, control over this part of the research process, and certainly more control over the outcomes in the form of the finished diagram (although they often do not get to choose which diagram to use). If done well, it is hoped that a well designed and implemented participatory process can enable more marginalised or excluded people or groups to produce their own 'reality' as they perceive it, as opposed to the 'reality' emanating from the more dominant and mainstream view of the majority. A particular example here is where the scenario mapping in Chapter Three allowed for alternative lines of thought to be mapped, and so recorded, when someone did not agree with what was being mapped by others. Generally we have found that the participatory approach was more satisfying for all involved. However, this kind of relationship building approach is also very time consuming and requires particular skills.

Relationship building is important in participatory research. Both relationships across the duration of the project and during particular events. Project wide relationships can often mean working closely with key actors, through advisory groups or through keeping all participants informed of all plans and developments as the project progresses. Event based relationships can often benefit from the involvement of professional facilitators as we saw in Chapters Three and Four. There can be a downside to all this for certain groups who may be subject to many different types of research projects and be asked to attend many different workshops leading to fatigue or disinterest on the part of some participants. We saw this to some extent in Chapter Six where members of voluntary environmental organisations with limited funds and staff to be able to contribute to all the invitations they receive prioritised their efforts. Equally some stakeholders were reluctant to participate for whatever reason. This can affect notions of representation vs representativeness in the use of mapping in research. This has three aspects: (1) getting adequate representation of all the stakeholders; (2) outputs that properly represent the stakeholders views; and (3) how well the findings support the research conclusions.

Something that can be both a benefit and a drawback, depending on the circumstances, is the size of the groups involved in participatory events. More participants can lead to more perspectives that, if captured, can enrich the final outputs and hopefully represent all views in some way. However, as was noted more than once in the case study chapters, it can be more difficult to effectively and efficiently record aspects of the process (discussions) as well as the products (diagrams) of participatory events.

The downside of such participatory research can be the nature of the relationship between the researcher and the participants. Trust in the process and the researcher is very important, otherwise the participants might not engage at all or in a more limited way. The burgeoning literature on trust and the way that it takes time, resources and dedicated effort to build trust in this type of research, is also noted by Boschetti et al (2016), who call for guidelines for trust building among stakeholders in environmental sustainability projects. However, the complex nature of environmental issues, the many different contexts and variety of potential outcomes mean that any kind of measurement or one size fits all approach is unlikely to work. In this regard, building communities of practice as noted in Chapters Four and Seven can be helpful.

Closely linked to trust are issues around learning. Similarly, there have to be perceived benefits to the participants, either in the learning they get from the process or because the process does help to resolve some if not all of the issues they were faced with. Such learning and resolution is more likely where the involvement and interactions are long term and not just one off. This was clearly seen in both Chapters Five and Eight for the Cobra and Imagine 'projects'. Even with shorter projects it is possible to make participants feel that participation is worthwhile and that they can learn from the process as much as the researchers. This is particularly so where each stage was able to inform the following stage of the research, leading the research in a direction that was relevant to the participants' concerns.

In this book we have seen that, in researching *with* people for solutions to environmental sustainability problems, the research is often small scale and by its nature is focused on the local, is 'grounded' research rather than deeply theoretical, striving to make a difference in some practical way. Much of what occurs is about processes rather than an end product, meaning it is difficult to quantify, results are not instant and impact not necessarily that obvious. However, intervention into environmental sustainability issues does not depend upon research. Indeed, much useful knowledge comes from activity that is not formally recognised as research, particularly if resulting from a systemic investigation.

Methods and methodology

It is important to note that within research there is no right or wrong approach, rather it is about what is most suitable for that particular project and what you wish to find out and who you expect to research with. When undertaking research it is important to consider why you are doing it, whether what you are doing is appropriate or just following a trend, and to consider what the value of doing it is for others. This may appear to be stating the obvious; however, the complexity of research with people and researching options for environmental sustainability means that no aspect of what you do is necessarily straightforward. As the research examples in this book imply, it is important to reflect continuously throughout a project on what you and others are doing and to be sufficiently flexible so as to develop your evolving processes accordingly. Yet this may not sit easily with funding bodies, which require a research proposal that sets out neatly the research process – who you will be researching with and how exactly you will do it. A further challenge for this type of process based user-led research is that current research funding arrangements favour large academic driven programmes solving global problems. Neither does it fit neatly with the academic audit culture with its drive for measures of success in terms of academic papers in highly rated international journals and readily documented, obvious outputs and impacts.

So how your research is funded is likely to be important in determining how you develop your methodology and how you present your results. Additionally, if you have an advisory group (now a common practice in research projects) that includes stakeholders then they can influence the process and outcome of participation. At the same time, participatory events can be done with limited budgets and outside the constraints of a funded project. The examples in Chapter Four of running such events as part of conferences with suitable participants already brought together show that this can be done.

It is also important to reflect on how using visuals methods such as diagramming in participatory approaches challenges and affects the more traditional researcher and researched relationship (as exemplified in Figure 1.1 from Chapter One) including that of power and authority. As previously noted, it is still easy to overlook the powerful role of the researcher in influencing the production and presentation of diagrams. Even where we try to get validation of diagrams by re-presenting them back to participants as photo reports or researcher-generated 'clean' versions, there can be a tendency for participants, outside the original event and on their own, to either not engage or to feel able to subsequently challenge or critique that account. This tendency may, in part, derive from limited experience of revising or reviewing outputs of any kind, written or drawn. Equally, although participants were involved in their generation, the final diagrams may not then be taken forward or used in practice by the participants. We noted in Chapter Five how certain diagrammatic outputs were not used subsequently. While in Chapter Three, we noted the way they can be useful to people in the company participants many years after doing the research, and in Chapter Seven they were used to follow up on the original activities, ensuring that the 'researching' does lead to some action beyond the immediate drive of the mapping events. In some cases intermediaries are needed – people like you as the researcher – to facilitate the translation of less formal knowledge presented in the maps into the formal knowledge required by policymakers and funders as well as participants.

Finally we have not directly addressed another issue relating to ownership of the outputs. This has a number of dimensions which we only touch on here. The first is a legal one of who owns the copyright in any visual artefact. This is an issue for any type of research and it is always important to think this through carefully[1] as it can affect the storage (archiving) and publication of research findings. Ownership of visual products is, therefore, of utmost concern, and negotiating how and where material is stored and access rights is key for ensuring if visual outputs can be made public, or whether they remain within the custody of communities. The second dimension relates to both the moral rights that participants may still have in any works they have co-created and the ethicality behind involving certain people in participatory work and of identifying them as participants within any formal (reports, articles) or informal (blog posts, forum posts) documentation. It is therefore important that all participants give their consent to being involved in the research and to grant the copyright in or rights to freely use their works to the researchers. It is equally important that you, as the researcher, properly inform participants of what you are doing, why and what the implications of participating are.

Final thoughts

There is the common phrase that 'a picture is worth a thousand words' which refers to the idea that a complex idea can be conveyed with just a single image more effectively than a description does. While there is a grain of truth in this view in that certain images can express matters as effectively as many words, it effectively sets up a false duality between words and images, just as we believe there is a false duality between quantitative and qualitative methods and between reductionist and holistic approaches. Words and images complement each other. Indeed, many of the diagrams described in this book involve many words, but not words set out in a linear fashion, as is the case with the text you are currently reading, but in a more diagrammatic form where the relationship between the words is non-linear. So, while we see mapping or diagramming as valued and valuable parts of our research praxis into environmental sustainability (however defined and by whom), and would always encourage others to use them as well, we do not claim that this is the only or better way to do research. Their use depends on context and purpose. But if you have read this far you must be fairly interested in using mapping yourself in complex environmental situations, in which case we hope that the book has sufficiently inspired and informed you to do just that.

Note

¹ Copyright legislation differs from jurisdiction to jurisdiction but in the UK a good guide for researchers is provided at www.data-archive.ac.uk/create-manage/copyright/copyright-ownership

References

Boschetti, F., Cvitanovic, C., Fleming, A. and Fulton, E. (2016) 'A call for empirically based guidelines for building trust among stakeholders in environmental sustainability projects', *Sustainability Science*, published online 23 June.

Bracken, L.J., Bulkeley, H.A. and Whitman, G. (2015) 'Transdisciplinary research: understanding the stakeholder perspective', *Journal of Environmental Planning and Management*, 58 (7): 1291–308.

Costanza, R. and Patten, B.C. (1995) 'Defining and predicting sustainability', *Ecological Economics*, 15: 193–6.

Lane, A. (2013) 'A review of diagramming in systems practice and how technologies have supported the teaching and learning of diagramming for systems thinking in practice', *Systemic Practice and Action Research*, 26: 319–29.

Long, J.W., Ballard, H., Fisher, L.A. and Belsky, J.M. (2016) 'Questions that won't go away in participatory research', *Society and Natural Resources*, 29 (2): 250–63.

Lyall, C., Meagher, L. and Bruce, A. (2015) 'A rose by any other name? Transdisciplinarity in the context of UK research policy', *Futures*, 65: 150–62.

Wals, A and Jickling, B. (2002) '"Sustainability" in higher education: From doublethink and newspeak to critical thinking and meaningful learning', *International Journal of Sustainability in Higher Education*, 3 (3): 221–32.

White, M.A. (2013) 'Sustainability: I know it when I see it', *Ecological Economics*, 86: 213–17.

Index